C.1

B
WADE-
GAYLES

Wade-Gayles, Gloria
    Jean.

Pushed back to
    strength.

(File by Wade-Gayles, Gloria Jean)
B&T
$20.00   11-9-93

DATE		

PUSHED BACK
TO STRENGTH

Gloria Wade-Gayles

BEACON PRESS · BOSTON

Pushed

Back

to

Strength

A BLACK WOMAN'S

JOURNEY HOME

for my family

Beacon Press
25 Beacon Street
Boston, Massachusetts 02108-2892

Beacon Press books
are published under the auspices of
the Unitarian Universalist Association of Congregations.

Excerpts from Gloria Wade-Gayles, *Anointed to Fly*
(Harlem River Press, 1991), used by permission.

99 98 97 96 95 94 93   8 7 6 5 4 3 2 1

Text design by Copenhaver Cumpston

Library of Congress Cataloging-in-Publication Data

Wade-Gayles, Gloria Jean.
Pushed back to strength : a Black woman's journey home /
Gloria Wade-Gayles.
p.   cm.
ISBN 0-8070-0922-9
1. Wade-Gayles, Gloria Jean — Childhood and youth. 2. Afro-
Americans — Tennessee — Memphis — Biography. 3. Afro-American women —
Tennessee — Memphis — Biography. 4. Memphis (Tenn.) — Race relations.
5. Afro-Americans — Tennessee — Memphis — Social conditions.
I.   Title.
F444.M59N48   1993
973'.0496073'0092 — dc20
[B]   93-10380

Contents

Foreword

Gloria Wade-Gayles invites us to come along with her as she remembers growing up in Memphis in a period of intense southern Jim Crowism and then growing up again living in the east. We are her silent companions as she relives moments in the early days of the civil rights movement; and we are with her as she experiences birth anew in the warmth of a black church.

In this engaging set of remembrances, Gloria Wade-Gayles touches those places in our hearts where tears are made and laughter is created. Without assuming the tone of many who occupy the pulpit, stand behind a lectern, or mount a soapbox, she points us toward solutions to the problems that haunt our African American communities. She does so by reminding us how things used to be in our families, in the projects, in our schools, churches, and communities.

And in the pages that follow, you will discover that Gloria Wade-Gayles can tell a story!

You might want to call *Pushed Back to Strength* an autobiography, but it is best described by a term Wade-Gayles uses. Here is a book of *rememberings*. Each of us, of course, engages in this marvelously human process of recalling what has been, and we often do so as a solitary act. The significance of such remembering, made public for all to hear and feel, is that the recollections of one black woman become the mirror into which each of us can see how alike and how different we are. We can encounter the exquisite diversity and amazing similarity in the human condition.

Wade-Gayles's rememberings also give us an opportunity to meet some very special people. An accomplished writer, she fully introduces us to her family, paying particular attention to the characters of her grandmother, mother, father, and uncle. These rememberings of her family help me to see afresh how racism messed with the life of my sister, a gifted musician. It hammered away at the life of Uncle Prince and her mother, Bertha, just as it did my mother, Mary Frances, so that I can imagine them striking up a wonderful friendship in Glory where they both now reside.

Autobiographies are most often presented as complete or at least close to complete renditions of a given life up to the author's writing. Put differently, we are given a sense of the range of roles that one plays in a single life. In *Pushed Back to Strength*, Wade-Gayles shares with us her multiple roles as granddaughter, daughter, sister, niece, neighbor, parishioner, civil rights activist, student, writer, wife, and mother. But there is one enormous part of who she is that is barely hinted at here, and it is a role that she plays with unusual skill and obvious success.

Sister Professor Gloria, as I am fond of calling her, is a master teacher. Ask the women at Spelman College for whom she is an intellectual guide and mentor. The sisters of Spelman, like the sisters and brothers from throughout the Atlanta University Center who fill her classes, will tell you:

Dr. Gayles is a tough and a tender teacher who sets impossible standards for her students to reach and then works with them until they get there.

Wade-Gayles did not choose to write about herself as a professor, but she certainly gives us important clues to her success as a teacher: taking after her mother and the influence of her uncle. She says of the times when their kitchen became a stage for Uncle Prince's recitations of dramatic poems:

> I believe that my love for teaching (which is in a way performance) and my love for poetry were born in those family gatherings.

Perhaps best of all, we come to know Gloria Wade-Gayles as a professor by the manner in which she teaches us throughout this book. Indeed, she does teach us about the power that is lodged within a caring black family; about the enduring strength of black people; about the centrality of education not only for the mobility of an individual but also for the progress of a people; and about the complexity of issues like divorce, abortion, and interracial friendships — issues we too often simplify.

I grew up in an upper-middle-class home, Gloria Wade-Gayles grew up in the projects. And yet each of us, as indeed all African American women, has known and continues to know the bitter sting of the twin evils of racism and sexism. If this book is to be praised for only one accomplishment — although there are many — let it be for portraying how strength to triumph over these twin evils can be passed down from one generation to the next, especially in the maternal line. This happens not by the maneuvers of genetics, but by the power of "talkings to," socialization of, and example setting for our children.

I warmly invite you to enjoy, to learn from, to be inspired and challenged by *Pushed Back to Strength*. It is a very special story of rememberings that is not constrained by the dictates of chronology and completeness which can stunt an autobiography of its natural growth.

Enough of these prefatory remarks. Turn the page and let our Sister Professor Gloria Jean Wade-Gayles tell you her story.

Johnetta B. Cole

Note
to the Reader

My memories would not wait their turn to be called, to be examined and then named in the order in which they had named me. "This is not your incident or your city," I would tell them. "Be patient, wait your turn, and I will get to you when it is time." They would not listen. They entered my remembering when they wanted to, and where, and more than once, they wore on the second entering a face I had not seen before, opened my ears on the third to someone whose voice they said I had muted, and on the fourth returned me to a place I had already revisited but which they said I must visit again because I was seeing now with new eyes. My journey to this present moment in my life might have been linear, but my journey home could not be. Hence the short straight lines that suddenly break away from the center, the sharp curves, the circles, the labyrinthine patterns. Hence my re-remembering in my remembering.

Pushed Back to Strength

GROWING UP BLACK
AND FEMALE IN A
SEGREGATED SOUTH

I remember the city of my birth as a big country town over-looking the muddy Mississippi River and bounded by Arkansas and Mississippi, two of the meanest states in the Union for black people. "Bluff City." "The Cotton Capital of the South." "Home of the Blues." By any name, Memphis, Tennessee, in the late forties, was just a plain ordinary town in Dixie. I will admit, however, that it was a clean city. The "Cleanest in the Nation," billboards advertised. A quiet city. Taxi headlights shone boldly up the back driveway into our kitchens: a city ordinance forbade the blowing of car horns. An up-and-coming city with colleges and universities, medical centers and attractive parks, old money, new money, and a political machine as powerful as the old Tammany Machine of New York. The Crump Machine, it was called.

Black people saw the public relations signs, but did not bother to read them. By law, we were forced to read other signs, the ones that established boundaries and territories on the basis of race, making mockery of the city's claim to progress. "For Whites Only" and "Colored" were more numerous than magnolia trees.

I remember they prevented me from splashing in swimming pools where the water seemed clearer than the finest crystal and from checking out books in the downtown library where overhead lights were as bright as the sun, but softer. They were always there, the signs, locking me out and pushing me back. Even at the zoo where caged animals had no knowledge of race, I saw the signs except on Thursday, which was "colored" day.

Memphis was fanatically bound to Old South ways. Even when there were no holidays, Confederate flags flew over office buildings and private homes; smaller ones flapped from the antennae of cars wearing Dixie license plates. Whites still sang, "I wish I was in the land of cotton" and expected blacks to sing "Carry me back to ole' Virginny." The War had been won, but in their minds it was not yet over. Would never be. Not as long as they could keep "colored" people in their "place."

I remember walking to Main Street—which we called "downtown"—on hot summer days to avoid the humiliation of sitting in the back of buses or enduring the hateful looks of white people who weren't pleased even when we moved to the back, often past empty seats. The law then gave one white woman, man, or child in a bus filled with blacks the right, the power, to determine where we sat. Even when we outnumbered them, we obeyed. Because of the law. Because of their faces. They had a way of lynching us with their eyes which said they were capable of lynching us with their hands. Especially on Main Street.

We went there to shop at the big department stores and at the five-and-dime, and to see movies at the white Malco Theatre. Sometimes we went to "The Old Daisy" and "The New

Daisy," black theatres on Beale Street, but only when we did not mind seeing an old movie or sitting in darkness for as long as fifteen minutes while the projectionist spliced cellophane damaged from many showings, many months ago, at white theatres. Those theatres were accepted only for Saturday matinees with friends. On serious dates, we went downtown.

I can see myself, in an attractive dress and with a fresh hairdo, beside one of my "beaus," as Mama called them, in a starched shirt and tie, walking up fifteen flights of stairs at the Malco. White girls, ushered by white boys, entered through the shiny brass front doors and stepped onto the thick red carpet of the foyer beneath large chandeliers. We entered through a small door on the back side of the theatre near the Mississippi River and the Bluff City Fish Market. The combined odors of dead fish rotting on the muddy river bank and cleaned fish lying on white ice overpowered the inexpensive fragrance I wore. There was no foyer for us. No red carpet. No chandeliers.

We began our climb in a narrow and barren brick hallway. One flight after another of concrete steps. Minutes later, sometimes out of breath and usually angry, we reached the "colored section," called the "pigeon's roost," where the seats were hard, many of them broken, and all of them old. Heat might rise everywhere else in the world, but not in the roost. I always had to take what we called a "wrap," something to keep me warm.

I remember wondering if there were heat and an elevator for the projectionist who worked a few feet behind us in a glass-walled booth. The projector was so close behind us that a colored stream of light rested on our shoulders, and the scratchy sound of turning reels made it difficult for us to follow the dialogue emanating from the silver screen miles below us. Sometimes in defiance, we threw popcorn on white people who sat beneath us in cushioned chairs, secure, they thought, in their power.

In the dark, we vented our rage. But in the bright of day and out in the open, we were often well-behaved and cooperative. "Good colored boys and girls" in the eyes of whites. We were playing it safe, being careful and following our parents' admonitions. "Don't talk back to them. Don't touch them even when you put money into their hands. Don't walk too close to them. Don't look at them hard. Don't do anything to give them a chance to beat you."

Having learned other ways of being safe with dignity, they did not themselves observe these admonitions. We knew that. And, laws be damned, they would fight anybody who mistreated their children. White people knew that. The meekest among black parents would take on the meanest white man, screaming before the charge: "Don't nobody mess with my children. *Nobody.*"

We had no children to defend, our parents told us, and therefore no reason to challenge white people downtown. Until, they would add, we learned how to claim our dignity without losing our lives. We were hot-headed teenagers who had to learn that. *Had to*, they stressed.

We understood the reason for the admonitions. Most of us knew or had heard about someone who had been used as sport in the violent and brutal game whites played with black lives. More than a few of my male friends were stopped and threatened with arrest for violations they did not commit, and one female friend was slapped by a white woman in a downtown department store. "Because she was sassy," the woman had said. Another "don't." I remember hearing at a young age about a black high school student who lost his hearing in a tragic encounter with white policeman. On his way home from working the graveyard shift at Baptist Hospital, he was stopped by a cruising policeman who beat him unmercifully because his stuttering was mistaken for insolence. The story had such an impact on me that I believed for years that black people who were deaf were not born that way. Rather, they had been beaten into eternal silence by white policemen.

As teenagers, many of us were caught between our anger at white people and our respect for our black elders; between a need to vent our rage in the light of day and a desire to remain alive; and between two images of our people: one for downtown and the other for ourselves.

When we complained to adults about our humiliation, they would exhort us to be so strong that nothing white folks did would spin us around too much and tell us stories about their experiences with treacherous white folks who had no conscience. They put our minor humiliations in perspective. My grandmother, Nola Ginger Reese, could do that well.

"Don't tell me about white folks," she would say, barely looking up from whatever she was doing. "You don't know mean." She had deep cuts that had not healed; we had mere scratches that barely broke the skin.

Sometimes my grandmother's stories dulled my anger, making me feel that I was a whining child who could never measure up to her example of courage and toughness. Other times, however, they exacerbated my anger. If only for her, I wanted to fight every white person I saw.

"They haven't changed, Grandmama," I would tell her. "They haven't changed." She didn't say they had.

"They're pushing us back. Always." I would emphasize, "*Always* pushing us back."

"They don't know it," Grandmama would respond. "They don't know it, but they're pushing you back to us, where you can get strong. Get some strength."

Black people of her generation had no illusion about their lack of power, but they believed in their strength. For them, strength was total immersion in a black community grounded in values that translated into a sense of self. Ministers, dentists, doctors, druggists, teachers, seamstresses, bankers, insurance men, morticians, beauticians, barbers, painters, plumbers, and hardworking ordinary and beautiful people were the mirror in which we saw ourselves whole. We learned at an early age to avert our eyes from the mirror white people held before us, the one they had systematically shattered for distorted reflections. White definitions of blackness.

Today, in part because of integration, many black people try in various ways to be validated and legitimized by white standards. But in the forties, when I was growing up in Memphis, black people validated and legitimized themselves. Surviving meant being black, and being black meant believing in our humanity, and retaining it, in a world that denied we had it in the first place. It meant, most of all, surviving *and* achieving in spite of the odds and, in the process, changing the world in which we lived. Understandably, our elders saw our private world, held in disdain (or envy) by Main Street, as a very special place where we were made into leaders because we were born to be leaders. That was the meaning of my grandmother's words about being pushed back to strength.

Strength to our elders was active involvement in black churches where minsters interpreted the gospel from our perspective, preaching in every text that we were God's chosen people. Why else were we suffering? Flinging their arms and bending theatrically, they preached in a style which white televangelists now use, along with our music, to fill their pockets while they build "God's kingdom on earth." Black preachers exhorted their congregations to trust in the Lord God Almighty, "who is able." "He delivered Daniel from the lion's den. *He is able.* He drowned Pharaoh's army. *He is able.* He gave little David a mighty arm with which to slay a giant. *He is able.* He made Jericho's walls tumble down. *He is able.* And his ways don't never change. His ways don't *never* change."

The congregation would chant the refrain: "*He is able. Halleleujah! He is able.*"

The choir would sing a shouting song, and the preacher would continue the refrain, calling new members to the house of the Lord. "He is able. He is able. Able. Able. ABLE to make a way out of no way."

And we were able, the church told us, to dream beyond the narrow confines of our world and to realize our dreams. The churches prepared us to do precisely that. They improved our reading skills in Sunday school and in tutoring programs. They gave us leadership training by requiring us to plan and execute, even to raise money for, children's day activities. Under their tutelage, we became orators delivering speeches in church before large audiences and artists writing plays for Easter and Christmas programs. And angels. The Bible we used depicted angels as white women with blonde hair, but in our eyes angels were black girls and boys. The message of high self-esteem and pride was a daily sermon in our church. The elders would sit in the pews applauding us as we marched down the aisle, black angels wearing wings made of wire and halos formed from coat hangers.

Strength was total immersion in black schools where we were expected to perform! We wanted what white schools

received without asking and what we did not receive in spite
of the begging: new textbooks, modern teaching tools and
facilities, money, and respect. But even without those material things, we were still convinced that we were getting a
very good education.

Back then, the way our parents handled segregated education made such good sense. In the outside world, whites
were in charge. Hence our parent's emphasis on what we
should not do. But inside the world of black schools, we were
in charge. Hence the emphasis on what we *had to do*. Achieve
and excel. As in church, so also in schools, we were Amen-
ed into high self-esteem. We did not feel inferior to white
kids in well-equipped schools on the other side of the city. If
anything, we felt superior to them. Smarter. In our eyes,
they were dull-witted and lazy. When we read about them
in the Memphis daily *Commercial Appeal*, we were not impressed. Contrasted to black students in "inferior" schools
who worked hard to excel, white students "whited" their
way into honors. If white people told jokes about blacks who
were frightened by their own shadows, their eyes large white
disks in dense darkness, we black teenagers told jokes about
white kids who sounded and looked dumb. And *were* dumb.
"Dumber than Dora," the saying went.

━━━━━━━━━

I attribute our arrogance not only to our parents, but also to
black teachers who were tough, challenging, and uncompro-
mising in their insistence on excellent academic performance
and exemplary character. They kept us in after-school deten-
tion for infractions as minor as chewing gum, being tardy,
and speaking barely above a whisper during silent time.
They visited our homes, sometimes unexpectedly, to "tell on
us" or to praise us. If revolutionaries are people who work

to change a system, to bring it down, black teachers were quiet revolutionaries in our communities. Their resistance to miseducation explains why I do not remember February as the month during which we studied Frederick Douglass, Sojourner Truth, Ida B. Wells, and other black leaders, but, rather, as that once-a-year time when small red valentines in white envelopes, always without mucilage, were placed in my desk by secret admirers and in my hands by special friends. We learned black history every day of the week.

Our social studies teachers distributed *Current Events*, the small weekly paper that was required reading for nearly all American school children. But they supplemented it with *our* current events. This list of names, dates, and events, written on the chalkboard and highlighted with colored chalk, was revolutionary information. In 1950, it was the "chalkboard newspaper" that told me Gwendolyn Brooks had been awarded the Pulitzer Prize. And when troops came home from World War II (which ended, we were told, because we were dutiful in collecting cans), I learned from the chalkboard about the discrimination black soldiers, still in uniform, were facing throughout the South. We were proud of the soldiers because we were a patriotic people. We always sang "God Bless America," but we also sang "Lift Every Voice." With passion.

Unlike black students in today's inner-city schools, we never had a reason to chant, "I am somebody! I may be black, but I am SOMEBODY!" That we were special and destined for distinction of some kind was a belief our teachers required us to learn in bold black conspiratorial lesson plans.

———

I grew up believing I was somebody with a special future, in spite of the fact that I lived in a low-income housing project.

In those days, a housing project was a stopping-off place. A decent, but temporary, home you lived in until you were able to buy a real home, and that was often not possible until all of the children were "through school."

My housing project — called the Foote Homes — was a thirty minute walk from Main Street and only fifteen minutes from Beale Street. It was a colorful city within a city composed of attached red-brick apartment buildings, cheap versions of Philadelphia row houses. In the back, units faced one another across a wide driveway that snaked through the entire community. In the front, they faced one another across a dusty courtyard where children played "Stealing the Bacon," "Red Light," and other innocent games. At either end of the units were dark passageways thick with bushes; here, away from the eyes of our parents, we played naughty games of hugging and kissing called "Spin the Bottle" and "Post Office."

If care for one's surrounding is a sign of dignity and pride, residents in the projects had both in abundance. They framed their windows with starched curtains and tailored drapes and planted begonias, roses, and petunias which grew in profusion in the small patches of earth they called their "yards." Papers, bottles, cans, and other throw-aways now associated with poor neighborhoods were rare in the housing project. Women, and men, took seriously the old saying that cleanliness is next to Godliness. We scrubbed porches and steps with lye, washed down screen doors with steaming hot water, and each polished our brass front-door knob to a spitting shine.

We missed nothing in our efforts to make our individual apartments, our homes, as commodious and attractive as houses featured in the Sunday section of the *Commercial Appeal*. We decorated them with plants (usually philodendrons and mother-in-law tongues), quilts (passed down through generations), paintings (bought framed at the five-and-dime), commodious furniture (purchased on time from downtown department stores), and books (many of them by black authors passed down through generations). The project did not shrink in shame from the rest of the city.

Neither did the children who lived there. We, too, were scrubbed clean. Only by our address could our teachers identify many of us as residents of the project. We wore starched hand-me-downs or inexpensive clothes bought on time and in basement sales at stores on Main Street. Shinola polish kept our shoes white or shiny, and shoe repairmen on the corner kept them soled. Boys did not need to leave the community to get their hair cut, and girls did not need to leave home to get their hair "fixed." Though untrained, many fathers and mothers used clippers and straightening combs, respectively, with skill and success. Children in the project were adorned.

And loved. We could go to the lady on the end for pecan pies, to the lady in the middle unit for crochet lessons, and to the man in the upstairs unit for ghost stories on a summer night. Being unheard was never a requirement for us. From blocks away, you could hear us accompanying our play in high soprano renditions of simple rhyme: "Our team is red hot. Your team ain't doodley squat," we would sing to the opposing team from another unit.

We would keep our eyes on the center of the circle while someone skipped behind us to the rhythm of our singing: "A tisket. A tasket. I lost my yellow basket. . . . Don't know where to find it." The white paper would be dropped behind one of us and off that child would go in the chase.

"Aunt Dinah's dead," someone would sing in the middle of the circle.

"Oh how did she die?" we would chant.

"Oh she died like this!" would be the response, followed by movements we were supposed to imitate, saying in a chorus: "Oh she died like this. Oh she died like this."

Our songs were major chords in music that was as distinctive as the blues that made Beale Street famous. They were cacophonous with other major chords: women's voices calling us inside for dinner, for chores, for discipline. Bottle tops banged down on homemade wooden checkerboards. An untrained voice practicing a song for Sunday's service on an untuned piano. Food peddlers announcing their coming with songs. And neighbors singing their bonding any day of the week.

"How's the family, Annie Bee?"

"Fine. Except that Little Clarence has a cold. Bronchitis, I think."

"Bertha, I need just a cup of flour, and ain't nobody home to go to the store for me."

"That's all you need? One cup?"

━━━━━━━━━━━━━━━

I grew up in this warm and embracing community as one of two girls in a small, closely knit family of three women and three men. My father, who was a joyous melody sung at a high pitch, lived in Chicago, and though my sister Faye and I were close to him, given the phone calls, checks, and annual visits to Chicago, he was not a part of our growth and nurturing in Memphis. That was not the case, however, with three lovable uncles, the most complex of whom was Uncle Prince. Although he was absent during my young years, when he returned, he had a profound impact on my life.

I do not remember a day in my life when my Uncle Jack, my mother's baby brother, was not present to bring me laughter and give me advice. As a young man in his early twenties, he was a very able dancer. Dressed in a popular zoot suit and chains, he did a nearly perfect imitation of Cab Calloway, calling "Hi-de-hi-de-ho" and, with agility, mastering a Calloway split. I believe my interest in dancing (second in passion only to teaching) can be attributed to the delight I took in his performances for my sister and me. I know my early interest in motherhood comes from the delight I took in "playing mother" for his two children, a son and a daughter. And my belief in the power of transformation is the result of changes I saw him make in his life. He put aside dancing and waiting tables at a hotel on Main Street for preaching the word of God. Of my grandmother's four children, he is the only one who earned a college degree. By sheer determination, in his later adult years, he studied at what had once been the all-white state university in the city.

My uncle Hosea, related only by marriage, was warm, gentle, and dependable. I loved him because he loved my aunt. I admired him because he pampered her. I remember that he was different from other adult men I knew. He cooked, shopped for groceries, did the laundry, nurtured their daughter, and cleaned the apartment. He chauffered my aunt everywhere. He does so even today. He was the person who taught me how to drive a car when I turned sixteen.

The men in my family were buttresses and protectors, but it was the women who gave meaning to the expression "pushed back to strength." Each one in her own way provided antidotes to the city's racism.

Ola Mae, my pretty and petite aunt of grey eyes, had the genius of song. I think of her when I read Paul Laurence Dunbar's description of Malindy. My aunt, too, had "natchal organs." She used them at home to entertain my sister and me and, at church, to bring new members into the flock. In her early twenties, many years before I was born, she used them in a local nightclub to help the family through hard times. Here is a page from my mother's journal discovered after her death:

> Ola sang at the Brown Derby two nights per week and bought one-half ton of the best coal to help keep the family warm. She was so young to be at the bus stop so late at night, but besides loving so to sing she was helping the family to survive.

For her gift, she was paid enough for one-half ton of coal. The white woman got everything. Mama talked about the white woman and her agent who frequented the Brown Derby to hear my aunt sing. They never talked to my aunt; they simply sat and watched and listened to a pretty black woman who was obviously gifted. Some years after my aunt quit the job, the white woman became a nationally popular singer whose name I want to call, but dare not. She had copied well my aunt's style.

Had the circumstances, and the times, been different and had my aunt continued to sing, I believe she would have been an astounding success in the world of business.

"If you had continued," I tell her now, "It would be Ola rather than Ella."

She delights in my bias which, in my bias, I consider truth. I am not always convinced that she has no regrets. The silence of song would have to be a continuous shrill scream in one's soul, but my aunt says, "It wasn't meant to be, or it would have happened." She believes that. I read again my mother's journal:

> All the fellows in the band took a fatherly attitude toward her. She was so pretty and a perfect lady. She got op-

portunities to travel with bands, but Mama absolutely
nixed it! Mama said she was too young for that and she
could not go along with her because she had the other
children.

I wonder about my grandmother's decision and her wondering about it as well. My aunt says, putting the matter to
rest, "That is history. Mama did what she had to do. I have
no regrets." She speaks out of a magnanimous soul, a generous spirit, that makes her needs, even today, the last to be
considered. For a reason, I call her "my aunt, the angel." She
takes comfort, I believe, in the fact that she sang my sister
and me into achievers. I remember her preoccupation with
correct grammar, enunciation, and etiquette. She turned our
small kitchen into a finishing school where we learned what
fork to use, when, and how. My sister and I could have eaten
an eight course meal at a high state dinner without having to
follow someone else's lead. And we could have "talked with
kings" (my mother's words) without making mistakes. My
aunt taught us to dot all our i's, make our A's broad, and
avoid all contractions. We knew never to use "ain't," the
worst of all errors. Just because we lived where we lived and
just because white folks didn't believe black people could
speak good English was no excuse for mistakes, my aunt
would tell us. I remember smiling to myself and feeling won-
derfully superior when I would hear whites on Main Street
using incorrect grammar and drawling (both of which they
seemed to do all of the time.) How foolish white people were
to believe their own myths about us. And about themselves.
As a teenager, I would sing for my aunt's only child, who
was more like my baby sister than my first cousin. My aunt
named her Chiquita because she loved the commercial popular at that time in which a yellow banana sang.

With some of our peers, though certainly not all, my sister

and I took risks in speaking the way my aunt taught us. In altercations we expected them to taunt: "Trying to talk so proper!" Which was followed by a snide remark about the women in my family: "High yellow women. Uppity. Think their color make them better than anybody else." I remember that tensions around color were often serious in the housing project.

"I can't begin to tell you," my aunt said to me recently, "what a hard time Bertha and I had because of our color." She remembers the ugly name-calling and the accusation that they were the children of a white man who disowned them and, worse, that, like all high-yellow women, they would seek out white men as lovers. "Yellow shit," fair-skinned black women were called.

"Dark-skinned women had a hard time," she told me. "A real hard time. As children other children made jokes about them, and a lot of the teachers mistreated them. They had a hard time, and I felt awful about it." She added, "But we had a hard time too."

Their pain explains, in part, why they were essentially solitary women, attached to our closely knit family. They got along well with everyone, and although they were a part of the gathering of women in the project, they never put themselves in a vulnerable position by becoming too close, by trying to become "one of the girls." They never joined social organizations. "The hostility was too much," my aunt explains, "so we stayed pretty much to ourselves."

My mother was the brains of the family — an avid reader and a passionate polemicist who had a love affair with ideas. She preceded us at the high school we attended where she earned a reputation as a very bright and gifted student. I would walk the corridors of Washington High feeling good that I was her daughter and hoping that, like her, I could graduate at the head of my class. Valedictorian. That's what I wanted to be. I would sit in the classrooms thinking to myself, "Mama might have sat in this seat." I would put my hands on the desk and imagine that I was touching the very spot where she had placed the exam on which she had earned a perfect score. I was proud of my mother's mind.

When my sister and I were students at LeMoyne, the only college in Memphis open to blacks at the time, my mother opened our books and read them. In her own way, she "went to college." Under different circumstances and at a different time, Mama would have won many college scholarships. She would have been an outstanding student, graduating *summa cum laude* and receiving fellowships from leading universities. She would have become an activist, fighting for the rights of children, the elderly, women, and, of course, black people. She speaks about the silence of her songs in words that echo my aunt. "It didn't happen because, then, it could not have happened."

But it *would* happen for us. Mama envisioned my sister Faye and me — "my precious girls," she called us — earning graduate degrees, giving speeches, publishing, traveling abroad, winning medals. Any honor that could be conferred on a human being would be ours, my mother told us. And toward that end, she "scrimped and saved," as she put it, and "went without." She sacrificed for one reason — to send us to college. We had one thing to do with our lives — achieve. Mama had what she called a "single eye"; it focused on our education.

During our high school years, my sister and I worked at a neighborhood theatre — the Georgia Theatre it was called — selling tickets and concessions. We never left home for work without our books, and on slow nights we would open them in full view of our employer. Mama's "single eye" was watching us. And so were the employer's daughter and son. It was not long after we began working at the theatre that they came to us for assistance with their homework, usually to my sister who was far more capable and serious than I. Ashamed that his children were seeking tutoring from "colored girls," our employer informed us after work one night that we were to address them as "Miss Barbara" and "Mr. Herman." Or be fired.

When we reached home that night, our first words to Mama were: "We are going to quit. Tomorrow."

Her "single eye" saw our future, and she began preaching: What other job was as close to home as this one? At what other job could we study? What other job available to black girls was as decent and clean as this one? She didn't want us slinging hash, busing dishes, cleaning other people's houses, or boarding late-night buses for work in the medical center downtown. The theatre was ten minutes away from our apartment; to get there, we passed other apartments and people who knew us by name. Neighbors. Friends. We were safe and fortunate where we were.

"This little job is a stepping stone," she said. "And all these hurts are but a second in your life."

"But you just don't understand," we explained to her. Crying, I remember. "He wants us to give them titles."

"Those people are small and pitiful and sick," she said. "They don't count. Remember that. They don't count." She used her favorite expression for calling someone down: "They're not worth a hill of beans. Don't make them bigger than they are."

The harder we cried, the firmer her position became. "There is no better job for you," she told us, repeating the words that reverberated in our apartment even when she was saying them: "This is a means to an end. A means to an end."

But the means was hurting us!

She understood, but it was a temporary and minor hurt that would prevent us from knowing lasting and more painful hurts in the future.

"You just have to learn to manipulate those people. Play a game with them in order to get through school."

I would read similar words in Ralph Ellison's *Invisible Man* and become absolutely ecstatic that I had heard them first from my mother's lips.

Headstrong and defiant, I demanded the right to quit. For weeks I had set my heart on working at the motel where several of my friends were employed. It was brand new. It was near the Mississippi-Arkansas bridge. It paid well. More than the fifteen dollars I earned at the Georgia Theatre. The higher salary would give me more money for clothes, for books, for helping Mama with family needs. My sister and I worked for necessities, not for luxuries. Mama gave in, but only to make a point.

I was hired to take orders over the phone for room service. When I entered through the rear door, I was sent to a kitchen five times the size of our apartment and given a large white apron and a hair net. I washed pots and pans and dishes until my fingers shriveled from the hot water. I mopped floors, took out trash, and fetched clean tablecloths. I even made lemon meringue pies. To this day, I will not order them in a restaurant because I know how they are made. You walk into a huge refrigerator where hundreds of brown pie shells, large containers of frosting, and even larger containers of yellow meringue are waiting for you. With a large spoon you dip out the yellow meringue and slap it into the pie shell, making certain that it moves into the fluted edges. And with a large rubber spatula, you dip into the white frosting and spread it on top of the meringue, making certain that you remove your thumbprints and, of course, any hair that might have worked itself free from the net.

I made many pies.

I never answered the phone.

I *never* answered the phone.

I was supposed to be off by nine, in time for the last bus home. I was released (from servitude) after midnight. When I walked out of the back entrance of the fancy restaurant that first night, Mama was waiting for me. She had asked a friend to drive her to the river to get her daughter. She did not say,"I told you but you didn't listen."

My employer welcomed me back to the theatre the next night, with relief. He needed my sister and me as much as we needed the small salary, safety, and time for study working there gave us. I say "needed" because people in the community associated the theatre with us, so much so that they nicknamed it "The Wade Theatre."

We continued working there for three additional years, and never once during that time did we use titles when referring to Barbara and Herman. We simply never called their names.

Many years later, after my sister and I had finished graduate school and colored signs had been outlawed, we saw "Mr." Herman when we were shopping in a department store on Main Street. He was fitting shoes on a customer. A black woman.

My grandmother was the fighter in the family. Prissy. Fiercely proud. Independent. If you pushed her too hard or in the wrong direction, you would never push her again. My peers attributed her toughness to her "Indian blood," visible

in the small mountains that rose beneath her cheeks and in
black hair so straight it barely held braiding. She was more
vocal in her racial anger and less willing to accept humiliation than most people in the units. When white insurance
men knocked unexpectedly at apartment G, Grandmother
showed them the disdain and impatience we received on
Main Street. She made them stand outside on the front
porch while she counted her money. They called other women
"Auntie," but they called Grandmother "Miss Reese" or
nothing at all.

It is said that people who have wrestled with adversity and
won are not easy converts to submission of any kind. That
was the case with my grandmother. She learned to defend
herself in the backwoods of Mississippi decades before I was
born. She grew up in a small Mississippi town as the only
stepchild in a family of eight children. She never talked
about her biological father, and the family never pushed her
to do so. We knew only that he was a white man who had
not claimed her or cared for her.

About her stepfather, a poor sharecropper, however, she
talked endlessly. "Mr. P___," she called him, was a "hellion"
who worked his biological children and his stepchild in the
fields without relief. He would beat them for the smallest
infraction. Most especially my grandmother. I remember
how difficult it was for me as a young girl to focus my anger
on the mean man (whom I had never met or even seen in pictures) because my grandmother spoke with such rage about
her mother as well. I remember wondering why Grandmother never visited her mother, never wrote her, or called.

The silence of over thirty years ended when I was in elementary school. My great-grandmother, a widow in her late
eighties, was coming for a visit. I was excited. A great-grandmother whom I had never seen! Who was still alive and well

enough to travel! I was, therefore, confused by the conflict
her imminent visit caused between Mama and Grandmama.
I remember the argument that brought Mama to tears and
Grandmama to the highest octave of her anger.

"Please don't, Mama," I heard my mother pleading. She
said something about "water under the bridge" and something else about age and health. My great-grandmother was
blind. She was counting her days on earth. She was coming
to make amends. My mother was pleading on her behalf.

"Please, Mama," she said. "Let it rest. Forgive her."

My sister and I were not allowed to witness the scene
which, I learned years later from Mama, was painful to
watch because my grandmother unleashed her wrath. My
great-grandmother, who had carried the guilt all of her life,
had expected the wrath, accepted it in silence and, Mama
says, wanted it for her own healing. Her pain, in its own
way, was more profound than my grandmother's. When she
left us, after a visit of two weeks, she went to other children
who lived in other cities where she wanted and might have
received the same treatment.

The most egregious of sins, my family taught my sister and
me, is failure of a mother to protect her children from abuse
of any kind, and perhaps most especially that which comes
from kin. .

I did not like my grandmother's stepfather (though I never
met him or even saw pictures of him), but I was grateful to
him for saving her life. Even *she* gave him that. Had to. She
remembered the day the white man informed her stepfather
that he would be returning the next day for the pretty one,
my grandmother. It was not uncommon for white sharecrop-
pers to ask for, or demand, girls in black families. My grandmother's stepfather did not engage the man in an argument,
but later that night, he had everyone in the family working.

Only this time in the house, not in the fields. They gathered their belongings and by early morning they had left the farm for another small town. My grandmother was only ten.

A new location saved her from the white man, but not from her stepfather's beatings. To avoid them, she married my grandfather, a Methodist minister, an older man whose ego must have been stroked by possession of a child bride as lovely as my grandmother. He sought her out because, like many professional black men in those days (and perhaps now as well), he wanted a pretty fair-skinned woman to decorate his life. She accepted his proposal because, as for many poor black women in those days (regardless of complexion), marriage was about survival on a higher level and not romance. My grandmother wanted security and tenderness and an education. Mama wrote in her journal: "Daddy was a brilliant man and had all kinds of books — we were the only family with a Paul Laurence Dunbar book."

My grandmother was attracted to my grandfather's books which she hoped one day to be able to read. He led her to believe that by marrying him she would gain her education. She expected to finish elementary school and high school and enroll at Wilberforce College, which offered free tuition to the families of A.M.E. ministers. None of us will ever know whether or not my grandfather would have delivered on his promise, but we doubt that he had any intentions of doing so. My grandmother's dreams were not in keeping with assumptions about the place of women in 1913. She became pregnant soon after marrying him and was paralyzed for a year following the delivery of the baby. Soon after she began walking again, she became pregnant again, and again, and . . . She could not stop the babies from coming: "What did we know about birth control then?"

The gods were not kind to her, but Grandmother took

comfort in the fact that her dream for an education would be
realized by her children. All of them. The gods were even
more unkind to my grandfather. Against her advice, he went
to see an ailing parishioner who lived some miles away from
the parsonage. A cold winter's rain was falling heavily when
my grandfather left the parsonage on horseback, my grandmother pleading with him: "Please don't go. You'll catch
your death of cold." I read again from my mother's journal:

> When daddy was given the presiding elder's post, Mama
> begged him not to take it because daddy was not a robust
> man. The men rode horses; they were circuit riders and
> had to make all those little mission churches. Daddy was
> called to some place, but Mama begged him not to go be-
> cause of the weather, but daddy told Mama he had to go
> because that was his mission. They brought daddy home
> very ill; he had developed pneumonia. While daddy was
> so sick, Mama begged him not to leave her [die]. Daddy's
> reply was "my bounds are set and I can't go over them.
> Don't you see those angels and people on the other side of
> the river beckoning me to come on?"

A month after his death, Grandmama, ordered to vacate
the parsonage by people who had once loved her, moved to
Memphis with her small children. "Proud Nola" — our name
of endearment for her — sewed for a living, "making a way
out of no way." She was proud that in her most difficult
years, she never worked in a white woman's kitchen. None
of her children did.

No one could have valued education and dignity more
than she. With only a grade-school education, she tried to
give the appearance that she had gone further in school.

"If you hold your head up and never look down, people
will think you're somebody."

And so, Grandmama strutted, never looking down and

never leaving the house without "fixing herself up." She believed the way she smiled and nodded her head in a conversation gave people the impression that she knew more than she did.

"If you don't open your mouth at the wrong time," she would say, "people won't know what you don't know."

And so, Grandmama had a way of being silent, but nodding and smiling, in conversations to which she could not make a contribution.

At my sister's college graduation, Grandmama carried herself like a grand duchess to whom pomp and circumstance was a routine part of every day. She did not applaud too loudly, did not lean out of her chair too conspicuously to see the colorful procession of graduates, and did not cry out with emotion when my sister turned her tassel. Nobody would know that Grandmama was attending her very first college commencement. No one could have valued dignity and education more than she.

All five of her grandchildren finished high school and continued their education, three earning college degrees and two graduate degrees. All three of her great-grandchildren have earned master's degrees and have plans to continue their education. This is a testimony to my grandmother's belief in the efficacy of education. It makes up for some of the agony and pain she endured as an adult rearing four children alone in a hostile and uncaring world. When she talked metaphorically about racism pushing us back to strength, she meant the example of strength she was for all of us.

Like other southern cities, Memphis has changed significantly since the civil rights movement of the sixties. It no longer wears "colored" signs. Desegregation is working about as well in Memphis as it is in any other city in the nation, north or south of the Mason Dixon line.

The Main Street I once feared and hated is no longer the center of life in the city. It is a ghost town which attracts poor people, 95 percent of them black, who have no way of getting to suburban shopping centers, or tourists who come to see one of two monuments for which Memphis is nationally known: the huge mansion of Elvis Presley (like the white woman who frequented the Brown Derby to hear my aunt sing, he imitated blacks) which sits on sprawling green acres of land well protected by uniformed security guards; and the Lorraine Motel, the site of the assassination of Dr. Martin Luther King, Jr., which, until very recently, had stood unloved and unprotected in a rundown community within walking distance of the old location of "The New Daisy" and "The Old Daisy" theatres of my youth.

I drive past my old housing project and wonder, in disbelief, if I ever lived there and loved living there. There are no patches of earth decorated with flowers, and the courtyards where I once played on hot sticky summer nights, under the careful watch of adults, are empty, desolate, and littered with paper cups and bags from fast food restaurants and broken bottles from corner liquor stores.

Once the windows were open, and through them you could see colorful curtains, the outline of a mother working over the deep, two-basined kitchen sink or of a family, "table ready," eating dinner and fellowshipping. Now the windows are closed, and you can see little through the bars of the rooms that are seldom lighted at night.

I hear car horns honking loudly and regret that children cannot play the games we played with taxi lights shining boldly into our kitchens.

I wonder if they play healthy games like hopscotch, stealing the bacon, and jump, or naughty games in the dark bushes at the end of units.

I wonder into whose apartments they go for pecan pies, Bible stories, piano lessons, and the ghost stories which give them sweating nightmares they boast about the next day.

I hear the loud sounds of tape decks, and I wonder if anyone in the project can sing the jingles of food peddlers.

I see women sitting alone on front porches, and I wonder who gathers with them and what child runs errands for them.

I wonder who tells the children that they are being prepared to be leaders because they were born to be leaders.

I wonder how and why the old mirror was shattered.

It is a world I do not recognize. Children here are old beyond their years; girls become mothers before they outgrow playing paper dolls and jumping rope. They do not entertain themselves with parades in the courtyard because they live in a world of ready entertainment. There are discos and X-rated movies in the outside world, and in their apartments they sit imprisoned by exciting sex and violence on televisions which come from easy-rental stores. They need not talk in whispers among themselves about a deranged lady who carries voodoo dust in a brown paper bag. Real voodoo dust is an accessible commodity in our country, targeted for sale in poor black neighborhoods.

We live in an "integrated nation" which has forgotten how to love children and how to make them into angels with satin wings and wire halos. The children are lost because adults are lost. I am sure that grandmothers today are preaching to their children about the immoral outside world, but antidotes to that world are not easy to find. Black children today are being pushed back into communities ravaged by unemployment, poverty, and despair. The enemies that stalk their lives are far more powerful and vicious than the Main Street of my young years in Memphis.

Before her death in 1974, my grandmother witnessed

changes in the project and in the entire nation. She was
proud of the civil rights activists and exceedingly proud that
her "grandbaby" braved the demons of her old state of Mississippi to help change things. She would sit in her metal
swing chair on her front porch and brag about what "those
young folks and my grandbaby are doing down there." But
she was too saddened by the negative changes in Memphis
and in the nation to be encouraged by positive changes in
race relations. The better things get, she'd say, the worse
they become. And she was troubled.

In the very late sixties, black and white canvassers spread
throughout the Foote Homes like foreigners in an alien land,
knocking on doors and asking residents pointed questions
about life in the project. They were conducting a survey to
determine the needs of poor black people, so that the new
South could address those needs. They meant well, but
they made the mistake of asking about life in the "ghetto."
The ring of the word and perhaps expressions of sympathy
or condescension, or both, on the faces of the canvassers
made Grandmama uncomfortable and vulnerable. They undressed her.

"What's a gotto?" she asked my sister and me when we
went home for a visit that summer.

Choosing our words carefully, we explained what people,
like the canvassers, believe the ghetto to be, what they as-
sume a black housing project to be. A psychological and
spiritual wasteland, without dance and song and laughter,
where broken people have no relief from their burdens and
where the future is envisioned as a longer nightmare of the
present. A nothing world which feeds on its own nothingness
and closes what exits there might be out of the nothingness.

My grandmother narrowed her button eyes, balled her ar-
thritic fingers into a fist, and tightened her lips.

"I never lived in a gotto," she said with anger. "When I was living way back in the fields of Mississippi, I didn't live in no gotto. When I moved with four babies to my friend's two-roomer, I wasn't in no gotto. And all these many years at 596 G right here in this project, I ain't been in a gotto. I ain't never lived in a gotto. Never!"

She never had.

Homecomings

They talked about him, the uncle I had never seen. The gifted son and brother who went wrong. Who disappeared. Without a goodbye note, they said. Without a ritual of farewell. No hugs and kisses and tears. "Just — Whoosh! Left home. Just like that!" they said.

They knew he was alive. Occasionally he called or sent postcards written in near calligraphy, bearing different postmarks and the same message. He was well. He promised to come back. For a visit. They took comfort in his promise. But there were times during Friday night fish dinners when their conversation about him belied their trust. They wanted him home.

In his absence, he was larger than life. An artist who worked magic with charcoal and paints. Who could have become a real artist only if. They had proof. Where Grandmama kept them, I never knew, but I remember her showing them to me. The drawings. The paintings. The proof. I was impressed. This man, this artist, surely couldn't be related to me. I could not draw a straight line or even a curve which, they say, draws itself.

I was impressed, most of all, by the stories that proved my uncle was special, different, gifted. A genius. "That's why he didn't stay in school," Mama would tell my sister and me. "He was bored. Just plain bored." An artist and a genius who loved poetry. Poetry? But men don't like poetry. Surely they were exaggerating. Creating a brother and a son so wonderful they couldn't hate him for leaving home. Without a goodbye note. Without a ritual of farewell. Without hugs and kisses and tears.

I created stories about him which gave me status with my friends. He was my phantom uncle, but when I talked about him, he was real. "I have an uncle who can draw anything and make it look real." I was telling the truth. I had seen the proof. "And he is smarter than anybody." That's what my mother said, and she never lied about anything. "He's been all over the world." More than one place away from the South was all over the world. Sometimes my friends would laugh at his name: "Prince Albert." It was a funny name, but my grandmother said he wore it well.

In my secret fantasies, I saw him returning home dressed like a prince and carrying colorful boxes just for me. Presents from all the places he had been. We would be the best of buddies. He would be the brother I had always wanted, and I would be his princess. We would live in a world all our own of poetry and laughter and secrets bearing our names.

I remember awaking earlier than usual one Saturday morning and going downstairs to open the thick inside door and latch the screen door. It was hot, unseasonably hot even for the South. Our small two-bedroom apartment needed what Mama called "a little breeze of fresh air." I opened the door, but I felt no air. They covered the screen, millions of tiny feet clinging to the small squares and blocking the air.

We had seen them crawling in small numbers, walking aimlessly, leaving no tracks on the earth. Staying on and near the trees in the courtyard. We paid them little or no attention. They often appeared when the trees began to wear green. Spring visitors. Quiet, harmless, even clean. But overnight, it seemed, they had multiplied in number and traveled boldly beyond the trees. I screamed for Mama.

"They're trying to come inside! They're trying to come inside!" I thought they were crawling on me. All of them. I screamed again. "They're coming inside!"

Mama raced down the twelve iron steps that led from the upstairs to the thick inside door of our apartment. She closed the door immediately and pulled me to her.

"Calm down," she said firmly. "Just calm down. They can't can't get through the screen. They don't have teeth."

As I was running upstairs to be with my sister Faye, who was wise enough to remain in our room, I could hear Mama banging on the wall, signaling our neighbor on the left. Within minutes, her hair in foam curlers, Miss Annie Bee was at our back door.

"Girl, Annie Bee," Mama said, leading her to the front window. "You gotta' see this. Caterpillars. They're everywhere."

White fur was everywhere: on screen doors, on porches, and on sidewalks, covering hopscotch patterns we had drawn with white chalk. Mama and Miss Annie Bee alerted other neighbors, and soon women were gathering in the back of the unit where there were no caterpillars because there were no trees. Everyone was talking angrily, loudly, about what they were going to do if management didn't do something. Right away.

No one wanted to try to sweep them off the screens; they might be squashed, and that would be ugly and, for the children, frightening. Besides, there was no guarantee sweeping would work; they were enmeshed in the screen and, in other places, they were inches thick. Inseparable. Like white yarn in a tightly woven rug. The women organized. They placed metal buckets filled with water on top of their small stoves and turned the burners up to the bluest of flames.

Careful not to scald themselves, they threw the boiling water with perfect aim. Silently, the little feet loosed themselves from the screen. The women returned to their apartments, boiled more water, and returned to the front porches, throwing again with perfect aim. Balls of white fur floated to the sidewalk. They refilled their buckets a third time. And a fourth. After sweeping the remains into a pile for the maintenance men to collect, the women filled their buckets again, this time adding adding clorox, or lye, or other liquids good for disinfecting. And they began scrubbing. Scrubbing vigorously as if the porches were to become tables for a communal feast. I enjoyed hearing the rhythm of brooms swooshing on concrete and the feel of soapy water tickling my bare feet. I enjoyed hearing the women laugh when they accidentally spilled water on themselves or almost slipped on wet porches. What had begun as a crisis became in no time at all a ritual of cleansing and, with the removal of the caterpillars, an earned celebration.

By early afternoon, I went outside without fear. I knew caterpillars were crawling in the trees, but I paid no attention to them. Either they would be killed by a pesticide management promised to use in a day or two, or they would disappear on their own as they usually did. I sat on the porch, now dry from the hot southern sun, feeling good that we had conquered the caterpillars and proud that I had participated in the victory. I spread my silver jacks on the porch and threw up the small red ball. It was then that I saw him.

He was a thin man, the color of light caramel. His hair was red and naturally curly. He was unkempt and he swaggered a little when he walked. The kind of stranger I was taught to avoid, run from if necessary. Boldly he approached our immaculate porch. Immediately I ran inside. Seconds later, he was at the door.

"Bertha Lee!" I heard him call. "Bertha Lee!" I thought to myself that he was one of Mama's close friends because only friends and family dared use her middle name.

I will never forget how quickly my mother, who was not thin by anyone's definition, made her way from the kitchen to the front door. Without seeing the stranger, she knew who he was. She ran, screaming, "ThankyouJesus! ThankyouJesus!" Her brother was home.

He had finally arrived, but without the gifts and the majesty I had expected. The man my mother would not release from her embrace was not the man I had heard about for years. I wondered if they, too, had made up stories about him.

In a short time, everyone in my small family was present in our apartment: my uncle, who had become a preacher since Prince's departure; my aunt, her husband, and her daughter; my grandmother; and, of course, Mama and Faye and me. They were thankful to God that he had come home. He hadn't changed, they said. He looked good, they said. They loved him, they said. The questions began.

Where had he been all those years? Traveling. Hoboeing his way across the country. Living here and there, with this one and that one. How did he make it? Working at odd jobs.

Doing this and that. Did he miss us? Always. He wanted to come home, but dreaded returning to the South he hated, the South that suffocated him, took the genius in him and threw it into a junkpile of lost dreams. Was he tired? Of course. He had been traveling for days. Hopping freights and thumbing rides. He needed to rest.

While he slept in the bed my sister and I shared, they went shopping for the celebration — for food, for gifts, for clothes. Mama prepared a feast fit for a prince. A king, really. She cooked collard greens (his favorite), boiled okra (his favorite), cornbread (his favorite), and roast beef with gravy (also his favorite). Everything was for him. The prodigal son returned home. They were excited. I was confused. And disappointed.

My feelings changed when he came downstairs later that day after a long nap. He was clean shaven and dressed in the princely outfit my aunt had purchased for him. He was lovable, colorful, entertaining, and so incredibly warm that I wanted to cuddle up in his arms. They had told the truth. My uncle possessed a magic that made him special and different. A genius.

He regaled us with stories about his travels, describing places and people so vividly I felt as if I had been with him in all of the experiences he shared. Our kitchen (which is where we gathered) became a theatre that echoed with my applauding laughter. It was quiet only when he was quiet, and that was only when he drew. My sister and I stood on either side, looking over his shoulders, and watched the pencil move in his thin fingers. Lines and circles became people, places, objects, even feelings. For me, a young girl of eight who had never known an artist, the pictures were miracles.

His magic continued when he recited poems from a repertoire which, I would learn over the coming months, was large. My mother and my aunt requested two of their favorites, "My Last Duchess" and "Face on a Barroom Floor." As if on stage, with the proper scenery and a large audience leaning forward to hear every syllable, my uncle changed his voice, he moved his hands, he walked around, he cried, and he fell lifeless on the kitchen floor. I had not yet been introduced to dramatic poems, adult poems that required you to think and to feel, but I sat in rapt attention as my uncle made the poems come alive. He was brilliant. I believe that my love for teaching (which is, in a way, performance) and my love for poetry were born in those family gatherings.

For weeks after that night, we gathered in the kitchen to savor the joy of his homecoming, and after each gathering, he became more special to me. I spread the word among my friends that my uncle was home, and they came in small groups to watch him perform as I requested. "Draw her, Uncle Prince," I would say, and he would comply, missing nothing in his representation of the face that, like mine, smiled in awe of his masterful hand. "Tell them about the time you hoboed from Illinois to Indiana," I would request, and he would comply, adding hyperbole, I am now certain, for our enjoyment. He recited poems and sang the latest songs comically. I was proud of him. He was my poet-uncle. My artist-uncle. My friend. My prince.

The family lost no time helping my uncle put his life back together. They bought him a full wardrobe: suits, colorful ties, dress shoes, and a Stetson hat. They made a home for him in all of the places where each one stayed. He could have stayed with my aunt and her husband, or my grandmother and his brother, but he chose to stay with Mama, Faye, and me. That is where he was supposed to stay, I believed. We were supposed to share the same space because my dreams about him were what had brought him home.

Over the coming weeks his colorful stories captivated my imagination and made me hunger for a hard life. For adversity I would miraculously overcome so that I could deserve accolades like the ones we gave my uncle. I wanted to be the heroine of something other than a battle over a plague of caterpillars. I wanted adventure, excitement, and danger. I wanted to go far away for a long time and return for a homecoming. Like his.

To this day, my family does not realize what my uncle meant to me, how he rounded out my life and made me feel special. We had something in common, he and I. He was an old renegade who had done the ultimate — turned his back on all the rules, risking everything. I was an upstart renegade. That means I was a tomboy. I had no interest in girly things. Shooting marbles and climbing trees (and even cussing a bit among my peers) were like second nature to me. I was the spitting image of my uncle in spirit and in spunk.

The celebrations, of course, became less frequent and, in time, ceased altogether. We became a "normal" family that went about the "normal" business of trying to remain sane and make it in a segregated world. My uncle talked frequently about that world, often with sarcasm or wit that camouflaged his anger. He had a hundred stories to tell about white folks in the South. "Mean as hell," he would say. "Worst than rattlesnakes." No one disagreed with him. In fact, everyone in the family had something to say about "mean white folks." But no one seemed as worked up about them as my uncle. It wasn't that his stories were any more grim than theirs. I doubt that they were. But the past in Uncle Prince's stories seemed to be in the present. Or in his gut where it grew into a cancer of rage.

My family had not lied about my uncle. Nor had they told the whole truth: my uncle was an alcoholic. For four years,

I saw and heard, but I chose denial. I was still young and, besides, his drinking did not alter my world one bit. If anything, it made him more charming and magical. When he drank, he recited poetry with a slur that made him absolutely fascinating to me. When he drank, he danced around the women in the family, calling them "Pretty Mama." When he knew Mama or Aunt Mae was angry with him, he sang, tipping an imaginary hat, ""Hey, pretty mama. How come you treat me so bad?" I thought he was most beautiful then and wished my friends could see him. He was my funny uncle, and I loved him.

Mama and Aunt Mae could not stay angry with my uncle for long. He was gentle. Humble. Loving. Easily forgiven. "He has a heart of gold," Aunt Mae would say. Sober or intoxicated, he couldn't hurt anyone. When he fell asleep on the living room sofa, fully dressed because he had had one drink too many, I would cover him with a blanket and sometimes, when no one was looking, kiss him on his forehead. When he came home very late at night and yelled for us to open the door, I would rush downstairs to let him in. As young as I was, I knew that his drinking was related to the stories I had heard him tell and to the world I was slowly beginning to see with new eyes.

It might have been the collective consciousness of the race that gave me understanding of racial pain, but I think it was the message I read in Uncle Prince's eyes when he recalled the difficult times my mother's family had had growing up. During the first two decades of the twentieth century, they had lived in Clarksdale, Mississippi. Later they moved to Memphis, "as bad as any Mississippi town," my uncle would often say. Theirs was a reality of racial violence. My uncle just didn't "have the stomach" for it, Mama often said. It was devastating for someone as sensitive as he.

"And, then too," Aunt Mae would add, "Prince was so bright, the schools didn't know what to do with him." The teachers would tell my grandmother that he learned everything so fast they couldn't keep him busy. The truant officer who returned my uncle to school many times was determined to save him. My aunt remembers the words passed down by my grandmother: "Prince Reese," he would say, "you too smart not to be in school." Many years later, I would read Toni Morrison's *Sula* and think about my uncle. Sula had no outlets for her creativity. A frustrated artist without clay or paint, she became destructive and self-destructive as well. My uncle, an artist, had only the pencils available to him in my grandmother's kitchen and nowhere to display his art. In addition to the harsh reality of racial violence in the South, my uncle, hungry for knowledge, attended schools that had no programs for gifted children. And so he grew bored, pained, angry, was suffocated and destroyed. When my grandmother "pinched and scrimped," as she said, to buy him a bicycle to encourage him to return to the classroom where he handed out papers and ran errands for the teacher, he took a hammer and bent the bicycle into metal even a scrap yard would not want. That was his rage. I understood him and told myself, "He has a right to drink!"

He usually had what Mama called "spending change" or, when she was angry with him, "drinking money." He earned it by working with the Italian market man who had a monopoly in the black community on the south side of Memphis. Sometimes my uncle would announce the market man's coming with a song, but his job was to bag the vegetables people selected from the wagon and carry them to their doorsteps. When the weather was warm, he earned additional money — "light change" — by "shaking the red card" on Beale Street. Mama called it gambling; I called it magic. My uncle would lay three playing cards, two black clubs and one red ace, face up on the sidewalk and then turn them face down as he demonstrated for onlookers what he was going to do. He would move the cards fast, but not too fast because, in the trial run, they were supposed to win. Once they were hooked and bet money on being able to find the only red card in the trio, my uncle's magic began. He would "shake" the cards faster than before, sliding them fast to the right and fast to the left, very fast over and under one another. The betters would watch every move, closely, but my uncle's slim hands were too fast for their eyes. So fast that none of the card hustlers could beat him "shaking the red card." So fast that he was nicknamed "Beale Street Red."

I understood why Mama wanted him to make a decent living for himself. After all, he was an adult. A man. But I had mixed feelings about his holding down a job. Steady employment would cut into his time with me and, worse, demean him. He was too special, too different, too gifted to work at menial jobs, and those were the only ones available to a black male without an education and without skills. I remember feeling sad and angry when, at my family's insistence, he took a job as an orderly at John Gaston Hospital.

In retrospect, I realize that the job wasn't the problem. Rather, it was the place itself. If you were black, you didn't need to be an adult or a researcher to know about racism at John Gaston. Regardless of the medical emergency, if you were black, you were not seen until all white patients had been treated, and dismissed with a smile and the promise of recovery. Horror stories about racism at John Gaston were rife in the black community. "I knew a man who went there with a simple wound in his foot," went one story, "and he had to go home and come back so many days, waiting 'til all the white folks 'been seen, that he got gangrene. They cut off his foot, but he still died. The waiting, that's what killed him." I just didn't want my uncle to work at John Gaston.

Two days after being hired, he came home well past midnight wearing old clothes instead of the good ones the family had purchased for him and loafers that slipped easily off his thin heels. He had sold his clothes in order to buy cheap wine. He was very intoxicated, and yet very clear about what he had done, and why.

"They think I'm some kind of fool," he said to my mother. "I might be a drunk, but I'm no fool. I'm not a damned fool."

At other times when he had disappointed the family, my uncle would say he was sorry and promise to do better. But this time, he had no apologies.

"Not me, Bertha," he told my mother. "You won't find me pouring out other people's piss with a white man looking over my shoulder. Not me!"

It might not make sense to say that an alcoholic has dignity, but in my uncle's case it makes all the sense in the world. I was convinced that it was his dignity that made him drink, and his dignity that made him remain unemployed. "I ain't working for white folks," he would say with conviction. Unfortunately, they were the only people for whom he could have worked.

His unemployment was somewhat of a benefit to my sister and me, and perhaps to Mama as well: he became the housemother of the family. Mama worked, and Uncle Prince stayed home cleaning and washing and cooking. When my sister and I came home from school, he would be waiting for us, smiling "like a chess cat" over the work we showed him. He pushed us to be serious about the very experience he had rejected. There was little we were studying that he did not know something about. History. He knew the names of all the presidents, knew the Preamble, the Bill of Rights, and the Emancipation Proclamation, knew about wars this country had been engaged in, and knew something about the lives of so-called leaders. He had read the books. Geography. He had traveled all over the States and could draw a map better than any in our books. Math. He knew that, too. Literature. He was our talking, performing anthology. And politics. That he knew in a painful way. I was not embarrassed by his drinking because he was so smart, so artistic, so supportive, so very maternal.

As the years passed, my uncle remained the same, but I changed. I grew into a young lady who worried Mama about "fixing" my hair in different styles, knowing that her Woolworth tin curling irons could do only so much. I wanted to wear makeup and, in spite of my skinny legs, stockings and high heel shoes. In relationships with boys, I wanted to trade kisses rather than marbles. I entered puberty and a world of romantic fantasies. My uncle became a problem for me. He seemed to choose the worst times to become intoxicated. When I was walking home from high school with a boy I hoped would like me, he was there. When I came home from a date, he was there. He was never ugly, never obtrusive, never profane — just intoxicated. That was enough to open a chasm between us. My sister, who was always saner than I about everything, was tolerant, if not also understanding. She accepted him; I attacked him.

"Why don't you do something with your life?" I would ask, looking at him in disgust. "All you do is hang around and get drunk."

He buffered my harsh words by dancing and singing. When he was intoxicated, that is. He would sing, "Hey, pretty mama," or sometimes the refrain from a popular song about a stubborn black woman named Caldonia. "Caldonia!

Caldonia!" he sang. "What makes your big head so hard. Bam. But I love you. . . ."

"Don't try that on me. It won't work anymore," I would say, interrupting him before he began his dance. "I'm not blind anymore. I see you for what you are."

"Glory Jean. Glory Jean." He would chant. "Glory Jean. Glo*ree* Jean." Affectionately.

"That's *not* my name," I would say, rejecting what had once been a term of endearment for me. "My name is Gloria. Glo Ree Ah. Gloria Jean. Not Glory Jean."

"I know you, but *you* don't know you."

"And what is that supposed to mean?"

"Just keeping on living," he would say. "Just keeping on living."

Years earlier when he would say those very words, offering them as words of wisdom about the uncertainty of life, I accepted them as profound, even prophetic. But now they began to sound like nonsense. And I would mimick him.

"Just keeping on living. Just keep on living," I would say, poking out my tongue. "That's not saying anything. Everybody is going to keep on living until they die."

"That's the point," he would answer, his mood changing, becoming serious. "Just keeping on living and you'll see. You know where you've been, but you don't know where you're going."

He could have said ugly things to me; he knew my vulnerabilities. He knew that I had a complex about my size; the children said I was so skinny they could whisper in my direction and I would be gone with the winds. But he never responded to me in kind. He took my harsh words and swallowed them the way he swallowed cheap wine. Like wine, they burned inside. But they did not lift him to temporary

euphoria. They wounded him. I could see the pain in his eyes
when I ended our arguments with the same phrase: "I wish
you would leave. Go back where you were. I wish you had
never come back." I wounded him.

The family was in conflict over what to do about my uncle's drinking. Depending on the day of the week or the incident under discussion, someone was always reprimanded
for indulging him. Enabling him. My mother reprimanded
my grandmother for babying him, for not turning him away
when he came by drunk. Grandmama would respond: "I
can't do that, Bertha. He's your brother, but he's my son." I
would hear a similar response from Mama when I reprimanded her for letting him destroy our lives. "He's your
uncle," she would say, "but he's my brother. I taught him
how to walk. I can't throw him away."

We tried what today would be called "tough love." We
took away his key and refused to open the door when he
came home intoxicated. Inebriated. Drunk. We would let
him sleep outside. But if there were rain, just a light drizzle,
or if the temperature dropped, just slightly, Mama would
open the door and lay out linen for the living room sofa.

After a major binge, he would promise not to drink again.
To get a job and stay sober. I remember one time in particular that we deluded ourselves into believing he could cure
himself. He placed his hands on the family Bible and swore
that he had heard God speaking to him. He wept. He lay
prostrate on the floor, praying and thanking God for the
revelation. He would become a new man. A miracle was what
we always knew would be needed to change him. We were
exuberant. Grateful. Expectant. He left home, a new man
in search of a job. He returned later that night unchanged.

In the face of a problem one cannot solve, anything that is
not a problem becomes a blessing. Something to celebrate.

That is how it was with my family's reading of Uncle Prince. "All he does is drink," the family would say. And they were correct. He was impeccably clean about his person and about our small apartment. He was compassionate. I remember how he felt for my sister and me when we would get monthly cramps. I remember, too, that it was my uncle who volunteered to go to the drugstore for sanitary napkins. In fact, I remember his efforts to meet needs before they were anticipated. And he was honest. For alcoholics, we were told, honesty is rare. Many are known to steal from their loved ones in order to feed their habit. We kept an open jar of coins and small bills in the kitchen cabinet. My uncle never touched it. He was generous. Out of the little he had, he was willing to give much. Had I not been angry with him, he would have been what we called in the project "a dollar uncle." Not a "nickel uncle" or a "quarter uncle." When he had money, he shared. The only liquids in our small refrigerator were milk, juices, and soft drinks. My uncle never drank at home.

I remember the routine of his life. He worked with the market man from dawn to two in the afternoon. He was with his drinking buddies by four and by midnight he was inebriated. At least twice a month, sometimes more frequently, he was in a cell in a downtown precinct. My mother or my grandmother would take a bus downtown, pay the eleven-dollar fine, and return home with my uncle.

Stories about his incarceration afforded us laughter when we would agree to give him an audience. And sometimes pain. Although his offense was drunkenness — nothing else — he was sometimes beaten at the precinct. Not enough to bruise him badly, but enough for him to experience real pain. His mouth, he would tell us, not his drinking was the problem. He never went easily into the police car or into the cell.

It all depended on who was on duty, he would explain. Two white policemen who had arrested him many times took a liking to him (perhaps he shook the red card for them), called him "Red," and protected him from abuse. Even in jail, my uncle had the audacity to be charming and defiant.

The frequent arrests and beatings did not change him. He continued to drink, and I began to see him as a visitor who had stayed too long. Who had filled my life with his pain. That was the source of my anger. His pain, which was always with me. I could feel it and smell it. Hear it pleading for my understanding. Angered by my own helplessness, I refused to acknowledge his existence. When he spoke to me, always with affection, I would not answer. When he entered a room, I would leave. Once, in a fit of rage, and pain, I pounded on his chest with my fists. I wanted him to leave. Become my phantom uncle. Larger than life. Perfect. I wanted him to leave. I wanted to love him again.

It was a Friday night my junior year in high school. I know it was Friday because the family was at our house on Fridays and at my grandmother's on Saturdays. I know that it was my junior year because when my uncle and I only a week earlier had argued, he had said to me, "You know where you've been, but you don't know where you're going. Glory Jean. Miss Smart Ass Junior."

We were sitting in the kitchen talking. My uncle was in the living room, or so we thought. Suddenly, he walked into the kitchen and in a clear voice said something about our not having to bother with him anymore. Trying "tuff love," we ignored him. This time, he said, he meant it. We wouldn't have to be bothered with him anymore. We ignored him. He put a bottle to his mouth and began drinking. Another one of his performances, we said to one another with our eyes. Someone said that he had emptied whatever was in the bottle and filled it with water. We ignored him. He finished drinking and walked out of the kitchen. Minutes passed. How many I don't know. He returned to the kitchen. We ignored him. Suddenly, he collapsed.

I remember the sound of the ambulance siren as it searched for our apartment and the countless hours my sister and I stayed at home alone waiting for some word from the hospital. I remember praying, "Please don't let him die. Lord, please don't let him die. Please. Please. Please. I'll love him when he comes back. Just please let him come back. Please let him come home."

The phone rang early in the morning. We picked it up before there was a full ring. Mama was on the other end. My sister and I were screaming. "Stop crying," Mama said. "Stop crying. He's going to be okay. They pumped his stomach. We got him here in time. He's going to be alright."

There was no big feast for this homecoming; my uncle could eat very little. But there was a celebration, more special than the first one. We sat around in the living room, not the kitchen, the entire family, entertaining him, performing for him. He knew he was loved. When he became tired, we helped him up the iron steps that led to the room my sister and I shared. He would sleep there until he was strong again. I pulled the covers around his thin body and kissed him on the forehead as I had done when I was younger. "I love you, Uncle Prince," I said softly. He squeezed my hand gently and said, "Glory Jean."

Even if he had not attempted suicide, my uncle would have returned to his special place in my life. As I matured, I would have learned how to handle the difficult combination of helplessness and love. I would have become woman enough to do what counselors call "reality therapy," which makes it possible for us to accept what we cannot change without anger, without guilt. That change in me began when I entered college. There I learned from books much of what my uncle had learned from his painful life. Growing racial awareness brought us closer than we had been in earlier years. He was no longer my toy. My performer. He became my confidant and my teacher.

I began college in the early fifties, when all across the South black people were becoming intolerant of Jim Crowism. I was my uncle's "child." I was angry and impatient. I wanted to organize a boycott of Memphis buses like the one that was taking place in Montgomery, Alabama. My mother was concerned about my safety because I had begun "talking back" to white people and refusing to sit on the back of the bus. "Just walk everywhere, Gloria," she told me. "Walk everywhere." I remember a new surge of anger when Nat King Cole, whom my mother loved, was attacked by a white mob in Birmingham. I remember that a group of us at LeMoyne, among them Marion Barry, who would later become mayor of Washington, D.C., challenged the racial position of the board of trustees of the college, creating somewhat of a uproar in Memphis. I wore my racial anger like a badge. My uncle understood. In his own way, he had nurtured the anger, but, in a strange way, his presence in my life prevented me from letting the anger become consuming rage. When we were pushed back to strength, we were also pushed into his pain, his defeat, his regret. He never spoke of regret, but I saw it in his eyes, and I felt it in the hugs he gave me when I did well in school. I heard it when he encouraged Faye and me to be "smart girls in school," offering his own life as an example of the failure we should avoid. I understood what could happen to any black person who re-

sponded to racism with consuming rage. Mama said rage
was a corrosive emotion: "If you give in to it, you never
win." I wanted to win — for my uncle. For all of them.

Understandably, I was pleased when, in my senior year, I
was named a finalist for a Woodrow Wilson Fellowship.
Such an honor called for family singing at high octaves; our
singing was muted because I had to travel to Birmingham for
an interview. Everyone was concerned about my safety, most
especially my uncle. "Somebody oughta' drive her there,"
he said. "White folks in Birmingham are mean. Real mean."

On the day I left for Birmingham by train, my uncle told
me what not to say, what not to do, how not to look — how
not to breathe, it seemed to me. He talked constantly about
my being alone in a city that, in his racial memory, was one
of the most vicious. He had reason to be afraid for my safety.
I came close to losing my life in Birmingham.

The many stops of the milk train made the trip seem inter-
minable. I needed to get to Birmingham quickly and get it
over with. It wasn't the interview I feared, but the violence
that had begun to seem inevitable. Each time the train pulled
into a small town, I would become angry again, rageful that
racism was marring this beautiful moment in my life.

When the train arrived in Birmingham, I went immediately to the brightest area in the terminal. Light was no small
consideration because I had planned to study for a philosophy exam during my six-hour wait before the interview. The
terminal, I remember, was empty, and I did not see — or did
not make an effort to see — "Colored" signs. I sat down and
opened my book. Within minutes, a tall, big-boned white
man was standing in front of me, shaking a fist the size of a
grizzly bear's paw. "You better move your nigger ass," he
snarled. "Colored supposed to sit over there." He pointed to
an area that was too dark for reading. I did not move, but

only because I couldn't. I was frozen in fear. He continued shouting, and just as suddenly as he had appeared, he left. I do not know how many minutes passed before a middle-aged black man rushed toward me and pulled me from the bench. "You gotta run, Miss," he said. "You gotta run." As we ran out of the terminal, I looked behind me. The bear-clawed man, now carrying a stick and joined by several other angry-looking white men, was headed in my direction. I followed the courageous black man, running for my life. We ended up in a small "colored" cafe, dimly lighted, but safe. "They would have beaten you half to death," the man said. I spent six hours in the cafe, but I never once opened my book. I wept uncontrollably, out of shame, out of fear, out of rage. There were only a few people in the cafe, but all of them understood my pain and the danger I had faced. The cook, a short and thin black woman, fed me. All of them counseled me, and when it was time for me to go to Birmingham Southern University, the site of the interview, they called the bravest taxi driver in town. He was as kind as my rescuer; not only would he take me to the university, he said, but he would also wait for me because on "that side" of town, there was no telling what would happen to a "colored" girl.

The panel of white men who interviewed me, sitting like judges around a grand oak table, did not know that for every question they asked me about literature and history, I had a hundred to ask them about racism. They could not have known that I was suppressing my rage only because they had something I wanted and needed, something my experience in the terminal had given me the right to receive.

My Birmingham experience, combined with my uncle's stories and my penchant for defiance, a gift from my grandmother, prepared me for involvement in the civil rights movement. Everyone in the family understood that and, therefore, no one was surprised when I wrote a year later from Boston, where I was enrolled in graduate school at Boston University as a Woodrow Wilson Fellow, that I had joined an organization that was "picketing places," as my mother put it. They had no fear of tame experiences in the East. The *real* movement, the southern movement, which I joined when I returned South from Boston was something different. My family *did* fear my involvement with it. They wanted a new South, but they did not want me to sacrifice my life to bring it into existence. In time, however, they substituted pride for fear and began to give accounts to neighbors about what I was doing and, after each release, would report exactly how long I'd been jailed *this* time.

My uncle's racial memory became mine, and my struggles in the movement his. I am convinced that had there been a movement when he was growing up in a vicious and cruel South, he would have been involved as a leader giving moving speeches, an artist drawing compelling posters, a thinker shaping strategy. But it was the tragedy of time that there was no channel for his rage and no channel for his genius. During all of my experiences in the movement, many of them more frightening than any my uncle could have imagined, I thought about him. He was in my mind and in my heart in every demonstration and in every cell block. In my own way, I was seeking revenge, a nonviolent one, but revenge nevertheless against the system that had stolen his life.

Uncle Prince lived to see the beginning of a new South. Signs designating places where only whites could drink or eat were removed reluctantly, but they were removed even in Birmingham. We thought the opportunities and security and freedom to live in dignity that he had never experienced were imminent for blacks in Memphis. My uncle was happy about the changes that were taking place in the city, but he saw them as minor alterations. They were mere cosmetics concealing a deadly backlash against the movement, one which would long victimize blacks in the city, among them my uncle.

I did not know about the tragic incident that crippled my uncle for the remainder of his life until my husband Joe and I went to Memphis three days after Christmas in 1969, following a holiday celebration with his parents and two brothers in Birmingham. Christmas at home was always wonderful. It would be especially so this year because we were bearing special gifts for the family: our son Jonathan, whom they had seen as an infant the previous year, and daughter Monica, an infant of two months. Mama had not yet told me about what had happened to Uncle Prince because I had been in my ninth month with Monica when it occurred. With a composure that did not succeed in concealing her rage and her pain, she now told us the heart-breaking story.

When he did not return home and the family did not receive a call from the downtown precinct, no one was overly concerned. Sometimes he spent the night incarcerated, sleeping off the alcohol. They were concerned the second night, but not in a state of panic. By the third night, though, they knew something was wrong. My mother called every precinct in the city and in outlying areas. There was no record of his arrest. She called John Gaston, the only hospital in the city that admitted poor people, blacks and whites, and hospitals in West Memphis, Arkansas, across the bridge, where he sometimes went with drinking buddies. There was no admissions record for a Prince Albert Reese. The family never thought he had left home again. In their souls, they knew something was wrong. Terribly wrong. "It is that way with love," my mother would say when she talked about that night. They feared for his life.

On the fourth night, my family made the calls again, and this time John Gaston had a record of his admission. He had been in the hospital for three days, transferred there from the workhouse where he had been taken after his arrest for drunkenness and vagrancy. The police had not informed us of his arrest. They had concealed his whereabouts. En route to the hospital, my family feared the worst because the authorities — white people — had kept him from us for three days.

He lay unconscious, hooked up to wires, in the black section of the hospital. My mother said she became a mad woman wanting answers. Insisting on them at the risk of being arrested for disorderly conduct. A police sergeant came. He was careful with his words. My uncle was arrested. Taken to the workhouse. He became sick there. Very sick with seizures. So they transferred him to the hospital. No one explained why my uncle was unable to talk coherently.

I heard the tragic story that Christmas with disbelief. Extreme sadness. Grief. Wrenching pain. Rage. Guilt. I wished I had been home when he needed me most. Rationally, I knew I could have done nothing to protect him, but I had never been rational about my uncle.

Once the family's best performer, my uncle became a spectator to our performances of love. A man of silence, speaking only with his eyes. He moved slowly, with effort, fearful of losing his footing and falling as he had done so many times on Beale Street sidewalks. He would sit in one place for hours, looking straight ahead and responding to questions in half sentences. Sometimes struggling for words that never came. Even our names he could not pronounce. "Who am I?" we would ask him, hoping that some miracle had occurred since the last time we asked the question. He would point to us, smile, and say only, "You know." He had made progress. For me, "You know," meant "Glory Jean." I was twice-over a woman, but still his "Glory Jean."

He could not hold my toddler son and my infant daughter in his arms, but he studied them with eyes that were remarkable because they smiled. Mama pointed to Monica. "Who

is this, Prince?" My uncle said, "You know," meaning that
she was, as everyone in the family agreed, the spitting image
of my grandmother. As an infant, my son was a mixture of
his father and his paternal grandfather, but he was not a
child anyone in either family had "spat" out. When asked
who Jonathan was, my uncle only smiled.

In spring of the following year, my uncle was admitted
once again to John Gaston Hospital and, while there, he
suffered first-degree burns. He was smoking in bed when the
sheets caught on fire. A nurse was called only when another
patient saw the flames. My uncle, unable to speak, could not
call for help.

When we went home for Christmas in 1972, he was moving more slowly and with stiffness because of the skin graft-
ing. Genius. Artist. A gentle man who didn't hurt anyone.
My uncle deserved more from life. "How are you, Uncle
Prince?" I asked. He would answer "You know."

With each year, the children's faces changed. In 1973, at
the age of three, Monica was beginning to look more like me
and like her paternal grandmother. Jonathan, at the age of
five, had become a number of faces — his father's most definitely, mine somewhat, and increasingly my uncle's. When
we were home for Christmas that year, my uncle could not
keep his eyes off of our son.

"Who is this, Prince?" Mama asked. "Who is this? Do you
know who this is?"

My uncle smiled. He pointed to himself.

That was the last time I saw him. My Uncle Prince died
June 4, 1974.

━━━━━━━━━━

Through the years, I have preached, literally preached, to
my children about the dangers of alcohol. My sermon is not
unlike my mother's sermon: "You got it in your family. Don't

ever drink." The sermon worked for my sister and me; it also worked for my children. Both of them are very conscious about what they eat (making efforts to be vegetarians), and neither one touches alcohol. Their good habits, I tell them, are gifts from my Uncle Prince. They remember him only vaguely, but they know who he was and what he meant to me. Because of the stories — his and the real ones I share about my life with him.

My daughter, at twenty-two, still resembles my grandmother, but each day she becomes more the spitting image of her father and me. My son, at twenty-three, wears my uncle's face. Like my uncle, he has a winning personality. He performs for the family — singing, dancing, delivering speeches, telling jokes, reciting poems. He loves and even writes poetry. He draws and paints. He talks race and change. My uncle was a renegade; my son is a young revolutionary. I think that my Uncle Prince has had his final homecoming in my son. I see each man in photographs of the other. The only difference is in the hat. My uncle wears a Stetson; my son, an African kufu.

Train Departed

REMEMBERING MY FATHER

AS DADDY

Once upon a time not so very long ago, in the late forties in my memories, America had a love affair with trains. Back then there were no bustling airports where huge jets hit tarmacs hard and rolled heavily toward accordion gates. Instead, there were large concrete railway terminals, unadorned with carpet or chandeliers, and barren except for the masses of people rushing to trains that stood still, waiting for them to board. There were few aspects of life at that time that did not, in some way, conjure up images of trains. Adventure, romance, comedy, mystery, intrigue, war, and even fantasy.

I remember trains in movies, trains in children's stories, trains in coloring books, trains in department stores (especially during Christmas shopping days), trains in songs ("John Henry" was my favorite), and even trains in sermons: "Gamblers and whoremongers can't ride the train to glory."

I remember most especially real trains in the Memphis terminal. Explaining the excitement of that terminal to my children, who have known only airports, is almost as difficult as explaining the richness of jazz to someone who has never heard Coltrane or Sarah or Ella or my father's favorites, Dizzy and Louie. It can't be done. Airports remind me of magazines with high-gloss covers and touched-up photos. They are too modern, too radar- and computer-controlled, too much like Star Wars, and too white to have soul. Hundreds of thousands of frequent travel points have not erased the soul-ful image of train terminals from my memory.

I can see the train belching white smoke. I can hear it exhaling every few seconds. And I can taste the aroma of the heavy oil that greased the rails. The conductor—always white, usually old and often wrinkled—walks up and down the platform in a black uniform which is shiny in places where it should not be. He wears glasses ringed with wire and a silver badge shaped like a star. I remember his eyes. Not the color of them, but the absence of a smile.

He walks authoritatively, giving orders to porters—always black—who shorten their tall structures by bending at the waist, ever so slightly. He takes the large-faced watch from his right pocket, unsnaps its cover, and reads the arrowed hands. He signals to porters. They remove small stepping stools and close the doors to all coaches except one. All is clear now.

The conductor climbs the steps and, leaning half in and half out of the open coach, sings, "All aboard. All aboard." Slowly, the train departs from the station, its metal wheels screeching against metal, its engines breathing a choo-choo sound.

I cannot remember trains and terminals without thinking about my father. Like the trains, he was dependable and strong. Like the trains, he stood still waiting for my sister and me at the same place, capable of taking us safely to a destination he had chosen and we desired. And like the trains, he was physically in and out of our lives. Returning and then departing. He lived in Chicago. We lived in Memphis.

As much as I missed my father and wanted him physically present in my life, I never thought my family was supposed to be structured differently. It was stable and secure, stronger than many, including some with two parents present, and more loving than most. As a young girl of seven, I actually thought I was blessed. I had a mother, a grandmother, an aunt, and three uncles adoring me in one city; and a father, an aunt, and three uncles adoring me no less in another city. I have since learned that such a positive attitude toward the separation of one's parents is rare for young children, but no other attitude was possible for my sister and me. We were nurtured on annual trips to Chicago, frequent long-distance calls, occasional letters, generous checks, and most especially by my mother's kind words about our father. Over the years we would love him for what he meant to us, but in the beginning we loved him because Mama did.

I was two when they separated and six when my sister Faye and I made our first trip to Chicago. I had seen my father many times before that trip. He would visit Memphis to see us, of course, and Mama of course, and many old friends. He was, therefore, not a stranger to me.

But neither was he a father in the traditional sense of the word which includes limitations, discipline, and the humdrum of routine which comes with sharing space. He was "Daddy." In the fairy-tale sense of the word. A kind and gentle man who loved us more than he loved anyone else on the face of the earth. Who took us to fun places and bought us almost everything we wanted. Who was never tired. Never impatient. And never angry. Who always smiled love. Every summer, my father lived up to those expectations.

With money Daddy had sent for the trip, Mama would

shop wisely for items we *had* to have in Chicago: fancy night-gowns, cutesy houseshoes, and pretty robes that buttoned down the front and touched the floor. On the night before our trip, my sister and I would lay our clothes on the bed and respond to Mama's reading of a checklist we had prepared together. "Socks?" Mama would ask. "Check," we would answer. "How many?" We would count them and respond. "Slips?" "Check." "How many?" Again, we would count. "Panties?" We had plenty of underwear, plenty of socks, plenty of playwear, and, of course, enough dresses for special occasions, many of which my grandmother had made from hand. As we grew older, the list would include bras and even sanitary napkins. We would be prepared for everything. And we would be well-dressed and well-mannered.

"Don't worry your father to death," Mama would tell us. "And don't nag him to buy you everything in sight."

My sister and I listened with respect.

"Be on your best behavior." We heard that when we went anywhere, next door in fact. "Act like you have good home training. Because you do."

My sister and I listened with respect.

Mama would remind us how proud our father was of us — our intelligence, our character, our demeanor.

"Don't disappoint him," she would say, and then add, "but I know you won't. You never disappoint any of us."

I remember there were special words for me. Rightfully so because I was so very different from my sister Faye. Two years older than I, she was disciplined, well-behaved, and neat. She kept her clothes on hangers and folded neatly in her drawer. She left the bathroom cleaner than she found it, especially if I had preceded her. She would play for hours in the dusty park down the hill from our unit and return home unsoiled and unwrinkled. She was the lady; I was the tomboy. I had no interest in the order of things on my side of the closet nor in the whiteness of the socks I wore. I was mannerable, especially to adults, but exceedingly and consistently mischievous. Mama had to speak to me in a pointed way.

"Gloria, clean up after yourself in the bathroom, and help with the dishes."

"Yes m'am."

"Try to keep up with your things," she would stress, remembering the time I went to the library with a brand new coat and returned home only with books.

"And don't be running through your father's apartment." They said I had ants in my pants, which is why I could never sit still. "Try to behave yourself." She knew I had forgotten her words the moment she had spoken them.

I agreed to be neat and orderly and careful not to break anything.

Everyone in the family went to the terminal to see us off, as if we were en route to a faraway place at the invitation of dignitaries who knew how special we were. Only the ticker tape, the band, and helium balloons were missing from our farewell. We would board the train, find a seat in a colored section near the platform side of the terminal, and immediately begin meeting their kisses with our own. As the train departed the terminal, I felt that it was for my sister and me that this iron coach had been waiting all the time.

A short distance down the tracks from Memphis, I would want to open the shoe boxes of food Mama had prepared for us, but my sister Faye would remind me that the trip was long and, since food in the dining car was too expensive for our budget (Daddy said it was highway robbery!), we shouldn't eat unless we were really hungry. We entertained ourselves in several ways: We would slap our hands together in "Merry Mack" and other lap games. We would color and work crossword puzzles. And we would read, sometimes out loud to each other.

Bored by those tame activities, I would go hunting for mischief. I knew my sister would "tell" on me, but I didn't care. I would go repeatedly to the small rest room located at the end of the coach to give myself an experience only a child can truly appreciate. Inside I would make balls of toilet paper and arrange them on the tiny ledge beneath the tiny mirror. "Bombs away," I would say, throwing the balls, one by one, into the hole in the middle of the toilet which opened directly onto the moving rails. I could see metal and gravel moving beneath my feet. I was thrilled when the paper disappeared before my eyes, never hitting the rails, so fast did the train move. I wondered where the real stuff went when we pulled down our panties and used the toilet. I was glad I did not live near train tracks. Because of my game, or my vivid imagination, I always wanted Faye to go with me when I had a real need to enter the small room. I was afraid of being pulled through the hole and disappearing, like my paper balls, into the winds that pushed the train speeding fast over the rails.

I would also skip from coach to coach, feeling good when my small hands commanded the huge metal doors to open. In the space between coaches, I could see the rails moving beneath my feet. I would jump over the dangerous spot to another door that opened to another coach. Several times, by accident, I entered a white coach. I knew to turn around immediately and return home. In my quick glance, I could see that they were riding a different train. Their coaches were carpeted, the seats were cushioned and farther apart, and the windows through which they watched the world pass by seemed larger. I would turn around quickly and re-trace my steps over the danger zones back to the colored coach.

I would fall asleep only when passing barns and houses disappeared into the darkness of night. Back then, Pullman sections were reserved for whites only, so my sister and I slept sitting up, waking periodically when the white conductor came through the coach to announce the next stop. I loved his stentorian call: "Next stop Cairo. Next stop Cairo." I would become most antsy and excited when I heard, "Next stop Kan — ee — kee. Next stop Kan — ee — kee." We had crossed the Mason Dixon line. Being colored would no longer be a problem. I was happy, but also afraid because, after Kan — ee — kee, the train would slowly cross over a wide river, its wheels hesitating at each half-turn. The bridge over which we traveled seemed too fragile for the locomotive, but every summer it held its own against the weight of metal riding on metal. When the train turned, coming off the bridge, I could see cars in the distance, inching into the turn, becoming smaller, and smaller, like the thin tail of a snake.

We always arrived on a Saturday, and my father was always there with a broad smile that made the gap between his teeth more noticeable. I remember that he always strutted out of the terminal with my sister holding one hand and me holding the other. I remember, too, that he always asked, "How's Bertha?" calling my mother by name.

In the early years, he would take us to a two-bedroom apartment on Calumet Avenue and in the later years to a nicer two-bedroom on South Cottage Grove. In both places, we knew to expect Daddy's sister and three brothers to gather as soon as we arrived in celebration of our summer homecoming.

Aunt Mae, my father's only sister, would be at the apartment waiting for us. A thin woman with skin as dark and smooth as rich fudge and slanted eyes, which explains her nickname "China Mae," she was my adult twin in mischief.

Every summer, Daddy would open the door and call to her that we were home. She would pretend to be too busy cooking to welcome us.

"Bob," she would say, "can't you see I'm busy."

My father's throat would vibrate with laughter. "Come on, Mae," he would say, participating reluctantly in the game. "Someone is here to see you."

"Who?" my aunt would ask, still not looking at us. "Who is it? Can they speak?"

"Me, Aunt Mae," I would answer, enjoying the game.

"And who is me?"

"Me. Gloria Jean."

"And who else?"

"Faye," my sister would answer.

"Faye and Gloria Jean," I would say. "That's who."

"Well, if that's who it is!" My aunt would take us into her arms and hold us tightly. "Where you been for so long? Where you been?"

She would turn us around, measuring with her eyes the number of inches we had grown since she had last seen us. She had sad eyes, but I remember that, like my father, she punctuated her sentences with laughter. And like my father, she asked, "How's Bertha?"

If my father had lived in the deepest regions of Alaska, reachable only by a sled drawn by a rare breed of dogs difficult to find and twice as difficult to train, his three brothers would have located him and moved near by. Like my aunt, they worshipped my father and had never lived for any length of time away from him. They would arrive later in the afternoon with kisses, hugs, and the greeting we knew to expect: "How's Bertha?"

I remember that they were nothing alike, my father and his three brothers. My uncle Edmund, who had only one eye, was a relatively quiet man who chain-smoked and walked almost with a limp because of bad feet. Sickly and fragile from years of heavy drinking, he was the brother my father took most closely under his care. He rarely talked, but he listened with an intensity that spoke more loudly than words.

My uncle Johnny, whose eyes were slightly crossed, made me think of sunshine and picnics and water spraying from a fire hydrant on a hot summer's day. Jovial, free-spirited, and forever young.

My uncle Chuck was a lady's man who was dapper in all colors, textures, and styles. He was fiercely independent and invariably stubborn. He laughed, but with caution. Had he not been my uncle, I would have feared his short sentences, his suspicious eyes, his unmistakable maleness, and his easy anger. Only with him were my sister and I unable to escape the racial anger that permeated life in the South. He had a consummate hatred of white people.

I remember the summer he took us to Wrigley Field as his contribution to our entertainment; each uncle had to do something special for my sister and me. On the first leg of the long trip to the baseball stadium, we rode the elevated Chicago train, called the "L," and on the second, a city bus full beyond its capacity. Everyone, it seemed, was going to see the Chicago Cubs play. An elderly white woman stood in the aisle trying to keep her balance. I gave her my seat. At the very next stop, my uncle pulled the cord. As punishment for the unpardonable sin I had committed against my people, we had to walk the remainder of the distance to the ballpark.

I remember the hot sun, the long city blocks, and my uncle's terrifying rage. I prayed that no white people would attend the game that day. I was convinced Uncle Chuck was capable of murdering all of them.

In the safe warmth of Daddy's apartment, Uncle Chuck participated in the celebration. It was always the same for our arrival day. The women would sit on the sofa while the men entertained us. The "Four Wade Brothers," their name in Southside Chicago, were talented in a number of ways. Uncle Chuck could dance. Uncle Johnnie thought he could sing, and Daddy thought he could imitate Ole Satchmo. I can see him standing in the small Calumet Avenue parlor with a handkerchief in one hand and a dented trumpet in the other. He is blowing imperfect notes, wiping his forehead, and singing like Satchmo in a scratchy voice. My mother would tell Faye and me years later about the time my father took trumpet lessons. She knew he did not have a chance to make it big in the world of entertainment, but she encouraged him in his dream.

Their individual performances, especially Daddy's, delighted me, but it was their collective singing of old songs that kept me from being the antsy child I was. I sat still, as Mama had instructed me, enthralled by their singing of the blues.

"I went down to St. James Infirmary," one of them sang.

"And saw my baby there," the other came in.

"She was stretched out on a long white table . . . so fine.

"So cool."

"So fair."

Their entertainment would end and ours, as Daddy instructed, would begin. When we were in elementary school, we would sing children's songs and recite simple poems, most of them learned for Easter and Christmas pageants at

church. When we became older, we would recite the preamble to the Constitution, the Gettysburg Address, poems,
sonnets — anything that demonstrated we were educated.

I remember the summer I recited James Weldon Johnson's poem, "Creation." I did so with skill because I had been
tutored by Mrs. Roberts, a truly gifted and demanding English teacher in my high school. Daddy's eyes filled with
tears. His baby girl memorizing all those words.

"And God stepped out on space," I said, hitting the d's and
the t's with my tongue positioned as Mrs. Roberts had
taught. "He walked around and looked around on all that he
had made."

I moved slowly, as she had taught me, looking to the right
and then to the left. I clapped my hands loudly to indicate
God's thunder and I rubbed them together to indicate the
making of man from clay.

In the midst of my recitation, the silence which Daddy
demanded whenever my sister and I were in performance
was broken by laughter. My aunt had written a note and
passed it to Uncle Edmond, who passed it to Uncle Johnny,
who . . . By the time it reached Faye, my aunt lost her composure. Everyone was laughing except Daddy and me. We
had not read the note which said: "You know God didn't act
like *that*."

We relished our humor! Sometimes it was the result of
practical jokes and other times the result of something my
sister and I did innocently.

I remember: A large man wearing dark glasses rang the
doorbell. "Tell Bob I came for my eye opener," he told my
sister when she answered the door. Faye conjured up terrifying images of how Daddy would actually open the man's
eyes. She awoke him with her screams: "Daddy! Daddy!
There's a man who wants you to open his eyes." We laughed

about that for several summers. An "eye opener" meant a drink of alcohol.

I remember: Her apartment was the largest and most beautiful of any I saw during all of our visits to Chicago. She was a prominent woman in the South Cottage Grove community, and she honored us by inviting us to a formal dinner. She set the table with linen and crystal and silver and candles. Lighted. We showed off the table etiquette my aunt in Memphis had taught us. Daddy was proud of us during dinner, but devastated by shame because, on departure, I said to the woman, "Thank you for the little snack."

I remember: I was twelve, and I lied. "I can cook real good," I said, wanting to impress Daddy with my maturity. I prepared a pot of fresh turnip greens, his favorite. He praised me when he saw the greens looking the way they were supposed to look back when no one cared about high cholesterol. I had put extra pieces of fat back in the pot, and they made the circles of grease iridescent. Daddy piled the greens on his plate, took a big forkful, and began spitting. He rushed to the bathroom to rinse his mouth. I had forgotten to wash the greens clean of dirt and sand.

Daddy provided humor with stories about white passengers on the Illinois Central, where he worked most of his life as a pullman porter. He had seen every kind of white person on the face of the earth, he told us. His stories were not unlike those told by women at home who worked as domestics in white homes or by Uncle Prince, who had also known trains, but only as a hobo.

He was the kind of trickster who would tip his hat for white people and say "yes sir," flexing his marvelous muscles as he carried their bags. They always "greased his palm," which made it possible for him to care for his two daughters and his brothers, especially Edmund.

"White people," he would say, laughing. "You can make fools out of them any day of the week. As long as they think you think they the big shot, you got'em where you want'em. In the pocket."

He would talk about white men getting so drunk on the train that they wet their pants or threw up their food or cried like babies, often exclaiming their love for black people. "I luvvvv colored people," Daddy would imitate a drunk white man, crying.

I would learn later that in the section of the train we never saw — where there were berths and sitting rooms — black porters earned their biggest tips from serving liquor after hours to white passengers.

White women were the forbidden fruit, but Daddy said you could pluck some of them easily. In fact, you had to be careful that they didn't fall into your arms. They would rub seductively up against black porters or ring for service in their berths after dressing in frilly nightwear. "Ain't nothing a white woman can do for me," he would say and add that none of them could be half the woman Mama was.

I do not believe it was an accident that I never saw Daddy in his porter's uniform. He chose the image he wanted us to see. Only in terminals and on trains was he a hat-tipping black man. Downtown on State Street, where he took us shopping for school clothes, he gave no hint of his occupation. Salespeople treated him with deference as he counted out the bills with ease, and regarded my sister and me with deference as we tried on outfits, and hats as well. I would skip through the stores drinking from every fountain I saw because I could and because a cold stream arched itself willingly to my mouth.

Each summer, Daddy's calendar of activities for us remained unchanged. We would go shopping, usually at Montgomery Ward, his favorite store for some reason. We would eat in one somewhat fancy restaurant in downtown Chicago and at egg foo yung cafeterias on the Southside, where moo goo gai pan was as greasy as a bowl of chitterlings made in the deep South. Chinese food, blacks in Chicago believed, could make a drunk man sober in a matter of minutes. I suppose that is why the neon signs I remember flickering at eye level, minus letters, in Southside Chicago, advertised "Fried Rice," and then "Liquor."

In addition to these fun places, Daddy, without fail, would take us on a car tour of the University of Chicago. "This is where the smart white boys go to school," he would say, pointing to white men walking to and from buildings that we never entered and carrying the books that Daddy said made them so smart. He could not foresee that many years later his first grandson, Loren, would be a student at the Lab School in one of those buildings. He never talked about the university opening its doors wide to black students. That was beyond the realm of possibility in his thinking, but there was a reason for the centrality of this place to his tours. He wanted us, in spite of racial restrictions, to think education.

In the black community, Daddy was an ebony prince, a god whose garment everyone wanted to touch. I have vivid memories of walking with him down South Cottage Grove and hearing people call his name from windows and even from passing cars. "Bob Wade. Bob Wade. How long you in town?" He was not a flirt — at least, not in our presence — and yet he drew women to him wherever he went. My mother said Daddy had sex appeal.

"Strong and natural sex appeal." That explains the women.

"And he had charisma. He was a dazzler." That explains the men, the children, and the older people. Everyone loved my daddy.

And Daddy loved *his* Chicago because it was black. I would return home and brag to my friends about having lived for months without answering the door to a white salesman or opening our apartment to white inspectors who, once a year, rated us on cleanliness, checking even our dresser drawers and closets. Daddy's Chicago belonged to us, I would tell my friends. Decades later, I would see the other Chicago, the one Daddy kept hidden from us and perhaps from himself. It was a world in which black people moved faster and more freely than they did in the South, but with a strange kind of silence that drew my attention to faces that rarely smiled and to the absence of children playing in parks or walking to libraries. It was the world I would read about in Richard Wright's *Native Son* and Horace Cayton's sociological studies of blacks in southside Chicago. But in those idyllic summers with Daddy, I saw a world of black concentration that had no "whites only" signs. It was a world in which my sister and I lived like princesses because we belonged to Bob Wade.

Mama knew that the fairy tale would end when we became young women. For though presented in fairy tales as mindless beings, women in real life, Mama taught us, ask questions and examine the answers they receive. We did that when I was fourteen and my sister Faye, sixteen.

I believe my sister deserved the answers more than I because, even as a young girl, she understood the difference between a father and a "Daddy." I loved "Daddy." I think she worshipped him as "Daddy," but she wanted him as father. Even as a young girl, she studied reality with a mind more capable than mine of seeing all the pieces, even those scattered, or hidden. I was too busy playing at mischief to know that I had been playing at having a father. The questions, and Mama's answers, moved me from the bliss of innocence to the pain of knowledge. I was no longer a child.

Why did he leave us? Leave Mama?

The story of their marriage and their divorce unfolded like a large and special quilt kept for years in the top drawer, removed, shaken, and used only when nothing else will end the numbing cold.

Without apology, she shared her memories. They were in their late teens when they married. Mama had graduated from high school and was working at her first job putting together wooden straight-backed kitchen chairs at the Wabash Screen Company in Memphis. Daddy, who went no further than the eighth grade, was working as a delivery boy at a corner drugstore. They met. They fell madly in love. They married. They moved into the two bedroom house on McLemore where Mama lived with my grandmother, my aunt, and my two uncles.

"Robert Junior," Mama's name for Daddy, "was a good man, but a weak man."

Unfolding. My father loved friends. "Too much," Mama felt. Being an orphan, perhaps he needed their attention and adoration.

Unfolding. Daddy's mother, "a beautiful woman," died when she was in her early thirties, and his father followed her in death two years later. The five children moved from Lexington, Mississippi, to Memphis, where they were cared for by their father's brother, Uncle Luke, whom I remember as a man tall enough to be a pine tree.

"Uncle Luke was a remarkable man," Mama says. "He vowed that his brother's children wouldn't be separated. Wouldn't be put into foster homes. He didn't have much himself, but what he had was theirs."

They lived in near poverty.

My father, the oldest child, assumed responsibility for his brothers and his sister.

"He never had a childhood," Mama says.

Shortly after their marriage, Daddy's brothers and sister moved in with them. Somehow Grandmama found space for everyone.

"Didn't that bother you?" we ask.

We knew how she would answer. It was common in those days. A way to get ahead. To make ends meet. To be connected as a family. Besides, they were such "loving boys" and "so very talented." Johnny was a leather craftsman, capable not only of repairing shoes, but also of making them. Edmund was a tailor. With his one good eye, he could turn fabric into a good-looking man's suit.

And there was, of course, Daddy, who, in my mother's opinion, was the best barber in the South, or in the nation. Word of his ability spread so quickly throughout Southside Memphis that my grandmother's small house became a thriving barbershop. Daddy was generous with his money, sharing it with Grandmama, his brothers and his sister, and, Mama adds, "friends."

My mother's family never closed the door to my paternal aunt and uncles. I understood why all of them, shortly after receiving us home each summer, asked, "How's Bertha?" and often, "How's Miss Reese," my grandmother.

But why didn't the marriage work?

They were simply too young to be married and too young to start a family. Their first child, a son born a little better than a year after they married, died when he was less than two months old while sleeping, peacefully they thought, in his crib. Then little was known about Sudden Infant Death Syndrome. The death, so mysterious and so unexpected, was

shattering for both of them. I wonder would they have remained together if Daddy's son had lived.

I ask Mama, masking my seriousness. "What if my baby
brother had lived? Would you and Daddy have stayed
married?"

She answers an uncategorical and emphatic "No." There
were other causes.

Unfolding. Though the marriage was weak in Memphis, it
might have survived if they had remained in the South.
Flowers grow in the cold North only with special tending.
The same is true, Mama says, of families.

If that is the case, my sister and I want to know why they
ever left the South. Left "home."

Enter racism.

Daddy was working at an optical store in downtown
Memphis. If my research is correct, it was the same store at
which Richard Wright worked and about which he writes
with bitterness in his autobiography, *Black Boy.* Like Wright,
like all black men in the early forties, Daddy was a "boy" in
the eyes of white men although he was already twice over a
man, caring for not one family, but two. In order to survive,
he endured the humiliation, but a charge of theft made continued endurance an act of emotional and spiritual suicide.

Mama remembers the night the police came to their apartment, bursting in without a search warrant and asking con-
temptuously for "the nigger Robert Wade." They pulled everything out of the closets and dumped the contents of
dresser drawers on the bed. One drawer was locked. This,
they were certain, contained the stolen goods. They broke
the lock with a sharp knife and cussed openly when they
found birth certificates and death certificates. Only papers,
valuable only to Daddy and Mama. She remembers shaking
uncontrollably when they left. Out of fear because they

might return, next time to beat her, and out of anger because she was powerless against their rage.

"Why didn't you stay in Chicago?" we ask.

Confession. She missed the South. She missed home. She was lonely. She hated the city that stole Daddy from her. All his life he had known cramped places, confinements and limitations, burdens and responsibilities. He was finally free in Chicago. A good-paying job, a decent place he would call his own, a family, and friends familiar with the fast life in Chicago. Daddy lost all sense of direction. He found the childhood, the freedom, and the open places he had been denied.

I felt for him, but I wondered. Faye wondered.

"Was he ever unkind to you?" We wanted to know. Had to know.

"Loneliness is always unkind," she answers.

"Did he?" We can barely frame the words. "Did he ever hit you?"

Reluctantly, she says, "Yes. Once." But once is too many times, she taught us. There are no circumstances that justify a man striking a woman. "Once," she repeats, "Once, and never again."

She remembers imploring him not to go out, to stay home with her and the children. She pulled on him. She blocked the door with her body. He slapped her. And then he begged her forgiveness. Profusely, she remembers. That night he stayed home. The damage had been done, however.

She pressured him to move with the family back to Memphis. In a moment of weakness, or sanity, he agreed. He sent us back South on a train with wet kisses and promises that he would get things in order in Chicago and join us.

Over the coming weeks, he became a voice on the phone making promises Mama knew he would not keep, perhaps was incapable of keeping. Just a little more time. That's what he needed. A little more time, and he would be coming home, he told her.

He never did.

"Why didn't you go back to Chicago? Why did you stay home?" We were searching for answers, not for blame.

There was nothing for her in Chicago except Daddy, whom the city had stolen and would not return. Going back would have brought misery to both of them. Perhaps instead of one slap, there would have been more, and more, and Mama would have found herself a battered wife. The thought crosses my mind, but I reject it. There was only one slap. One too many. But only one. That is what I must remember. There was only one slap.

I am angry with Daddy not for abandoning my sister and me, but rather for breaking my mother's heart.

Mama does not judge him harshly.

"Your daddy knew what was best for us. Chicago was not a place to raise a family." He was confident that, in the South, Faye and I would become ladies, good students, successful women.

"You'd never be the girls you are today if we had stayed in Chicago," Mama says.

We believe her. But we want to know why he didn't come home. Back to the South?

""He would have lost his mind in Memphis," she explains. "It was a mean city. It would have destroyed him."

Mama does not judge him harshly.

"We were just too young. Too young to be married. Too young to start a family. And the world was too mean."

Together, they decided what was best for all of us, especially for the girls. A divorce. Financial support. Nurturing from a distance. And their close friendship. *They* decided, she tells us, saying nothing about her consummate grief. Nothing about pain so acute it almost became, like Chicago, a thief taking another parent from us. Only from my Aunt Mae in Memphis did we learn that Mama had to fight her way back to life after the divorce. My aunt remembers the night Mama began to heal.

"Bertha got down on her knees and begged God not to let her ever love a man the way she loved your father. She prayed so hard, do you hear me. That's how much she loved Robert Junior."

The seesaw of emotions began. I forgave Daddy because Mama did, but hearing her sing one of her favorite songs would pull from me feelings of resentment I could not always dismiss.

> She may get weary. Women do get weary.
> Wearing the same shabby dress.
> But when she's weary, try a little tenderness.

He remarried. Her name was Rose. Like Mama, she could not keep Daddy from departing. She bore his third child, a girl who, like Faye, had Daddy's round face, flawless skin, and gorgeous legs. Roberta, she was named. For Daddy. He talked to Mama about the marriage, about the new daughter, about his life. Always, they were the best of friends.

Mama also remarried. Initially, I blamed Daddy because I knew that she married my stepfather for the same reason that my grandmother had married my grandfather: security, economic survival. She grew to love him, but not in the way she had loved Daddy. She had prayed for that.

I adored Dan, my stepfather, and Mama loved him because he loved us, because he provided for us and, most importantly, because we were sexually safe, and even protected, around him. That, Mama said, is the most important test a stepfather, or any other man, must pass. Dan passed it with flying colors. He was a hard-working man who managed his money so well that he opened a small convenience store in North Memphis. Daddy, too, was hard-working, but he would have felt imprisoned in one place. His job and his personality were one. He loved working on trains that rode the rails at high speed, slowing down only at switching points, going in and out of terminals, entering and departing.

Mama believed it was a psychological thing with Daddy. "It kept him from becoming an alcoholic like Edmund and Johnnie," she said, and "a bitter man like Chuck." It was the rhythm he had always known in life: entering and departing. His mother departed, and then his father, and though Uncle Luke was good, the orphaned children moved from one relative to another. And because we know very little about Daddy's past, except that he worshipped his mother and was traumatized by her death (that much he shared with Faye and me), as Mama said, "we just don't know what all Robert Junior didn't experience in his life." His obsession with "friends," which I learned did not mean womanizing, was Daddy's attempt, Mama believed, to fill a void in his life.

Unlike Daddy, my stepfather did not have a coterie of friends touching him, calling his name, and taking him away from Mama. He worshipped her and, in his jealousy, he believed everyone else wanted a chance to worship her. With Daddy, Mama knew freedom because he insisted on having his. With my stepfather, she knew confinement. She was his world. He wanted to be hers.

In the second year of their marriage, he died from a cerebral hemorrhage brought on by high blood pressure he did not know he had. Mama, who was in her late thirties, almost lost her mind. For a year, she was a woman I barely recognized. Morose. Depressed. Sleepy. Not very communicative.

Given to frequent and uncontrollable fits of crying. Not given to giving affection, even upon request. She was traveling my grandmother's path. When everything was going well in their lives, the men on whom they had depended were taken away forever.

As fate would have it, and it always seems to be unkind to good souls like Mama, at the same time that my stepfather died, Daddy lost his job with the railroad. Since he was "bumped" rather than fired (meaning that someone had beat him out on a long trip), he would be able to return to Illinois Central, and that is why he could not work at a job that owned his time. He had to be ready at a moment's notice to rush to the terminal and ride the trains again. Driving a Yellow Checker Cab gave him money and kept him on standby. He continued to be connected to us. In fact, there was never a time during his life that Daddy was not in our lives. He continued to call on a regular basis, talking at length to Mama after talking briefly to us; to send clothes, especially the heavy winter clothes available only in a cold place like Chicago; and to write our names on special delivery envelopes containing money just for us. I felt privileged when the mailman knocked on the door and asked us to sign for cash and for money orders. But the amount was never enough. Mama needed more.

We had a difficult time.

Mama worked miracles with what she had. Bacon was strick-o-lean she fried crisp after boiling it long enough to remove the heavy-grained salt. Margarine began as a soft white substance in a cellophane package, in the center of which was a ring of red liquid the size of a penny. We would massage the liquid until it turned the white substance to yellow, becoming our margarine. For special dinners, Mama bought cheap cuts of meat and beat them repeatedly, and hard, with a metal mallet in order to make them tender enough for eating. Only when Mama was pained by not being able to give us something we had requested, but could do without, did I feel deprived, and then only of her smile.

In my remembering, I am in a clothing store (Lerner's, I believe), and Mama is begging the white saleslady to let her add to her balance. I am angry with her because I think she is ingratiating herself. I pull on her and say something about our not having to beg white folks for anything. She turns to me, narrows her eyes, and says firmly, "Hush up. Just hush up." We left the store with the dress I had needed for an activity at church.

In her remembering, my sister is in her freshman year in high school. All of the tickets for the big football game have been passed out in homeroom. The dismissal bell rings. My sister begins walking the fifteen blocks from school to home, choking on tears because she had thought Mama could afford to buy a ticket. When she is in halfway home, she sees Mama walking toward her, rushing. Mama says, "I was trying to get there before school closed. Is it too late for you to buy the ticket?"

Both my sister and I remember the day Mama made herself beautiful for the man who was coming to our apartment to interview her for a job. All of us were excited because if Mama got the job, life would be easier. "Cross your fingers, girls," she told us. "And pray. Your mama needs this job."

Three days later, she learned that someone else had been given the job. My sister remembers Mama's pain. "I couldn't stand it, Gloria," she tells me. "Mama was so hurt. So very hurt. She got on her knees and pounded the floor with her fists."

Three days later after being told that the job for which she had interviewed had been filled, Mama received a call about another job, at the same place. She wept. She danced. And she prayed in gratitude.

Like Grandmama, Mama made a way out of no way. She supplemented the criminally low salary she earned at a black insurance company with small change earned from typing for different people and preparing Sunday's programs at the church we attended. And Faye and I contributed from the pennies we earned at the Georgia Theatre. We did not want for any necessities, and because Mama denied herself every-thing — especially clothes, I remember — we had more than our share of luxuries.

She had a habit in those difficult years of counting on her fingers at the beginning of every month. "Let's see now," she would say, touching the thumb of her right hand. "I owe Goldsmith's twenty dollars and Sears, twenty, and . . ." She would move from her thumb to all the fingers on her right hand and then to the other hand, naming her debts.

I do not ever remembering my mother complaining about debts or whining about problems. She was upbeat, optimis-tic, stoic, and spiritual. Only once do I remember her being none of these. That was the night she came home, later than usual, in a state of murderous rage.

She had stayed after work, at his request, to finish some-thing he said he needed the next morning. By then, she had been promoted from clerk in the insurance company to chief bookkeeper, a move up that made only a minor difference in her salary. He buzzed for her to come into his office. When she entered, he rushed to the door and locked it. He un-zipped his pants and told her what he wanted her to do. "I got on my knees," Mama told us, "and begged him. 'Please. Please don't do this to me'." She cried and pleaded. Calmly, he told her that it didn't make sense for her to say no. He could fire her. Without cause if he wanted to and she could do nothing.

She continued to say no. The physical battle began. "I fought him the way a man fights another man," Mama said. Words. Threats. Physical force. She fought him. After an hour, he gave up. His parting words: "Don't tell anybody about this and you'll keep your job."

"Depend on yourself. Always depend on yourself." How often did my sister and I hear those words when we were growing up. If our husbands abandoned us or died, we had to be able to take care of ourselves. Hence her emphasis on education.

"Feed your mind. Feed your mind." Those words, too, we heard on a daily basis. Ideas, she taught us, were more important than things.

"Never envy anybody," because it takes you away from caring for yourself.

We had to live our lives in such a way that if anybody defamed our character, they would be lying, and the whole world would know they were lying: "All you'll ever have in this life is your own integrity. Don't ever give it up for anything or anybody."

All of these lessons in daily living we could understand, birthed, as they were, by her difficult life. But the other, until recently, confused me: "Be generous." From her little pennies, she contributed on a regular basis to programs that took care of those less fortunate than she. Mama's hard life had given her a magnanimous soul and a generous spirit. I wished that I could do something special for her with my life. Always I wished that. And always I wished that Daddy would return home. To Mama.

Three important events took place between May and June

in 1959. I graduated from college with a Woodrow Wilson Fellowship for graduate study at Boston University. I married Jimmy, my college sweetheart; professors and administrators saw us as "twins" in academic achievement and integrity, students "most likely to succeed." *And Daddy said he wanted to return home.* This time, I was praying he would keep his promise. Faye, married a year earlier, was living in Chicago; I was preparing to move to Boston. I was concerned about the imminent void in Mama's life, and I hoped Daddy would fill it. I thought he could do this because, at forty-two, Daddy was a changed man. At a different time and under different circumstances, he and Mama would have remained together and grown old together. Gracefully. There was still a chance. Though their branches did not touch, their roots were intertwined. I believed they had never loved another person as they loved each other.

Which is why, I thought, they should try again. Begin a second life together. Which is why I was delighted when they slept together in the same bed. I asked Mama the next day if they had made love; she smiled and answered no.

I remember that they were like two old friends sharing stories from a long trip they had taken together. They talked endlessly over coffee, touching each other with their laughter. If a counselor could have observed them, thinking that they were married, she or he would have said that Mama and Daddy had reached the plateau that all couples hunger for, but few rarely experience. It is that space in which each, though separate, is enmeshed with the other and feels comfortable sharing their essential selves. Without fear of disapproval or rejection. Without the need for explanation. It is that space where intimacy holds them spiritually when they are not holding each other physically. I remember their conversation. Daddy praised her for being a good woman. A good mother. He was brittle with regret. Faye and I had done well because of her. We were the ladies he knew she would raise. He had been such a fool. Nothing out there is more important than family. He wanted to come home. This time, really come home. He wanted to come home, back to her, never to depart again. He would make it up to her. Could he?

They were sitting at the kitchen table, the family gathering place. Mama leaned over and kissed him on the cheek. She touched his hand and said, "Robert Junior, I will never see you again."

"I'm going to surprise you," he said. "This time, it's for real."

The words were familiar, only this time they were spoken in Memphis, not in Chicago. He would go back North, get things in order, and return. He would live with her in our apartment in the project that would be empty with my departure and my sister's.

"I believe you mean it, Robert, but I don't think I'll ever see you again."

I left Memphis headed for graduate school in Boston, praying that Daddy would keep his promise this time.

He left Memphis headed for Chicago with a mental checklist of things to do.

A week later, on a Saturday afternoon, the phone rang. Mama says that she had a strange feeling when she answered. A friend was calling. At a civic club meeting, Daddy had complained of a maddening headache. Two hours later, his blood pressure was dangerously high. Three hours later he died.

Sexual Beatitudes

PASSION IN YOUR
OWN UNWORRIED TIME

It was not uncommon for white men to cruise through our neighborhood in Memphis in search of black women who, they assumed, were naturally sensuous, sexually superior, and easy. For obvious reasons, they rarely came by foot into the community. They were not that bold. No doubt they realized that the only white men who could be safe in the community were those known by face and by name. All others were "up to no good" and, therefore, would risk their lives if they invaded our space. And so, they cruised in their cars, up and down Mississippi Boulevard, Lauderdale Street, and Vance Avenue. We were taught at an early age how to spot them and avoid them. If they drove slowly, if they circled the block, if they stopped to ask for directions, and if they smiled (especially if they smiled), we knew to run fast. Screaming.

"Dogs," the women called them. "Dirty white dogs trying to pick up innocent girls."

"And how come?" they would ask. "Any day of the week, white men can go down on Gayoso and get all the black women they can pay for."

Gayoso (near Ponotoc and Beale) was the heart of the red light district where gambling, whiskey, and prostitutes were as plentiful and visible as cotton at the height of the picking season. Protected by a city ordinance which made every conceivable vice legitimate and profitable, and protected as well by the color of their skin, white men were not ashamed to be seen on Gayoso. There they acted out fantasies bequeathed to them by their fathers and grand-fathers about the blacker berry giving sweeter juice.

Professional white men, however, did not frequent the brothels on Gayoso. They had keys to apartments in black communities. My friends and I would point to those apartments, one of which faced the hockey box in the community park, and say, "That woman goes with white men." I can't remember ever seeing the women themselves, but I vividly remember seeing white men entering and leaving the apartments, sometimes in the light of day. We knew to avert our eyes. The women were not pariahs, but neither were they members of the community family. They lived comfortably — for obvious reasons — but like strangers among their own. We were taught to frown upon such alliances. "All a white man wants from a colored woman," I heard many times, "is what he can get in bed."

I heard the same comment about black men from other black men and, of course, from black women. Men want one thing from a woman, and they will try every trick in the book to get it. And after they get it, they're gone. Because they are *men.*

"Just born that way," a man in the community would say, helping us with our sexual socialization and adding an Amen to the women's litany about sexual politics.

"That way" included committing any number of grievances against women, perhaps the least of which was pretending that they loved you in order to get what they wanted and then leaving, never having loved you in the first place. It included battering.

I have positive memories of the men in my immediate community. They were visible as protectors, guardians, and entertainers. The man in the upstairs end unit that faced Mississippi Boulevard invited us to his apartment for ghost stories which we considered authentic since they came from his work in a nearby funeral home. A man in the middle unit, who contracted tuberculosis when I was in grammar school, was mild mannered and sparing in words. I remember him as the gentle father of twin boys fifteen years my senior whom I secretly loved. Mr. Hurst, who lived across the court, shopped for groceries, cooked meals, cleaned his unit, and frequently combed his daughters' hair into attractive styles. He could not have nurtured his four daughters more if he had been a woman. He was the type of father I imagined Daddy would have been had he lived with us. But Miss Annie Bee's husband — "Mr. Clarence," we called him — was considered by most people in the neighborhood to be the ideal husband and father. His wife and four sons had only to ask and, out of his good salary at Firestone, he gave. Mama called him "a good man, a *real* good man" because he welcomed his mother-in-law into his home and treated her like blood kin. No one was surprised when, in 1953, a large moving van appeared in the neighborhood. We knew "Mr. Clarence" had delivered on his promise to move his family into a "nice brick house."

Only one man I remember as an exception to these positive images. He beat his wife occasionally (which was, of course, too frequent). She retaliated with hard blows and volatile words. I would think of the two of them when I would read about the fights between Pauline and Pecola in Toni Morrison's *The Bluest Eye*.

Although I knew personally of only one relationship in which battering took place, the women's discussions evidenced that it was far more widespread than I could have imagined. That is how they explained the strange woman who walked through the project, always with her head down, carrying a brown paper bag which, rumor had it, contained voodoo dust. She was a victim of constant battering. Her husband, after years of abusing her, left with a younger woman.

"That way" also included control of money. Even though most black women worked, and thereby contributed to family income, men, by and large, decided how money was spent. Men in the community would say, "It's just the way we been taught. A man is supposed to be the head of the family."

Women would advise us: "Always have money put aside which your husband doesn't know about." No matter how good a husband is, a woman must be prepared to take care of herself.

These caveats were central lessons about gender which were as important as lessons about race. Both furrowed our path toward wholeness.

We learned early about biological differences between girls and boys, but the women rarely explained the differences in explicit terms. In fact, their language danced around biology. I remember hearing "kitty cat" for vagina, "worm" for penis, and "number one" and "number two" for bodily functions. Some mothers would tell their daughters at bath time, "Wash as far up as possible, and don't forget to wash 'possible' real good."

Their coded language did not in any way curb our curi-

osity about sex which was hidden, for the most part, in bed-
rooms with locked doors. Today, teenagers don't have to
look long or go far to know about sex, which might explain
why they become sexually active at such an early age. We
sell it to them in movies that should be R-rated and aren't.
In porno magazines visible behind store counters. And in
songs that give the whole nation ownership of a woman's
body. Sexual explicitness is so "okay" — "correct," if you
will — that in the late eighties leading scholars came to the
defense of 2-Live Crew, a popular black singing group,
taken to court in Florida for obscene and abusive lyrics.

When I was growing up, we sneaked into the world of
sex. I remember someone handing me a Dick Tracy porno-
graphic book a little larger than my hand. The drawings
were more comical than obscene.

I remember mannish boys grabbing my right hand and
scratching my palm which meant "Give me some." I remember mannish boys writing love notes about "doing it" and a
girl and a boy who were caught "doing it" on the hill in the
community park.

I remember seeing the "dirty" words scrawled in huge letters in public toilets, though never in those at school.

I remember, too, the night a circus-sized fat man died of a
heart attack while having sex with a woman in my unit. At
least, that's what was said. We wondered how he managed
not to crush her small frame.

Adults were contradictory in their treatment of sex. On
the one hand, they used coded words; on the other, they
talked very openly about pregnancy. White women might
have told their children about a white stork with long stick
legs flying among cumulus clouds with a bundle of joy hanging from his beak. Black women in the project told the
graphic truth: "A woman can get a baby when she opens her

legs to a man." We were told to open our legs only on our wedding night. "Keep your pocketbook closed" and "Heads Up, Dresses Down" were common sayings in the project.

The onset of menses catapulted girls into a world of old wives' tales ("when you're on your period, wash your hair with coal oil, not with water"), preoccupation with cleanliness ("change your pad frequently, even when you think you don't need to), and stories about the time when some unsuspecting girl got pregnant "the very first time." We were taught to be "good girls" which meant being virgins.

I would think about my gender upbringing years later when I studied nineteenth-century black women's history and read about women activists championing black women's virtue. "Lifting As We Climb," though not used by all black women's organizations, was an appropriate motto for nineteenth-century efforts to challenge myths about the sexual licentiousness of black women which was in direct contrast to the piety and virtue the Cult of True Womanhood prescribed for white women.

The women in my community were not unlike their ancestors. Their insistence that we remain virgins until we married was in large part a response to myths about our sexuality which made Gayoso profitable and black mistresses possible. These myths motivated white men of means in the South to hire high-class black prostitutes for their sons' first sexual experience because they believed the saying, "A boy can't become a man until he's had tan."

The women of my youth did not see white women as paragons of purity. Far from it. In their eyes, white women possessed neither modesty nor virtue and knew nothing about cleanliness. Black women who worked as domestics in white homes had more than a few stories to tell about white employers.

"You can't find a woman more nasty than a white woman. They put their dirty drawers anywhere."

"They'll do anything, and try anything."

"They don't think nothing about letting me see 'em buck naked."

After such a pronouncement, the woman would often rub her right index finger against her lips and, with it, make the sign of the cross on her chest. "I ain't lying," she would say. "I swear 'fore God, I ain't lying."

As much as I reject stereotypes of any kind, I am sometimes tempted to believe that the permissiveness with which white mothers rear their children — a sharp contrast, as documented by scholars, to the tight hold of black mothers — represents lack of modesty and virtue. The temptation is understandable given the extent to which I grew up believing that I had to have both.

If we had to be virtuous and modest because we were black, we had to be all the more so because we lived in a housing project. Race, gender, and class were the axes on which our socialization turned. There was always something we had to prove because of who we were racially and sexually and because of where we lived. "Just because you're a girl." "Just because you're colored." "Just because you live in a housing project." Just because people thought we couldn't achieve and couldn't be virtuous meant, in the minds of our parents, that we had to be. We had to be the exception to all assumptions, all rumors, all myths, all predictions about failure.

Mama was very clear about the sexual beatitudes she wanted us to remember.

> Blessed are the shy girls,
> for they shall be adored.

> Blessed are the smart girls,
> for they shall be admired.
> Blessed are the pure girls,
> for theirs is the kingdom of respectability
> and control
> and success.

These teachings did not keep her from being, in my eyes, a rose among thorns in the gathering of women which was a ritual in my community. Let me explain.

As soon as the weather turned warm, we would play outside in the evenings in the light that spread from the lamppost into a circle in the courtyard, and the women would congregate on concrete porches, some of them sitting like self-appointed judges in straight-backed kitchen chairs. Mama was with them but not of them when it came to young girls' sexuality.

The woman in the downstairs unit that faced Mississippi Boulevard, whom we called Miss Gotta-Know-and-Then-Tell-Everything, was the elder spy in the community. She stood only five feet tall, but she towered like a giraffe over other women in her self-righteousness. Between the ages of eight and twelve, I was one of a group of girls she would call into her beautifully decorated and immaculate apartment on the pretext of serving homemade cake and ice cream. We knew what she really wanted to do, but we liked her baking well enough to play her game. We would eat, and she would talk. About sex.

"Don't be messing around with these mannish boys," she would tell us. "All they want to do is get you pregnant."

We would, of course, agree with her, biting into a slice of rich chocolate cake.

"And don't be doing no smooching because that's how you get into trouble."

We would agree with her, eating ice cream made with fresh peaches.

"And don't think we can't tell when you've had sex." There was a saying in the project that your hips grew notice- ably wide the day after your first experience. "One day, you're skinny, and the next day you have hips like a grown woman."

And that wasn't all, she told us. The moment we became pregnant, we would develop a small Adam's apple which would bob up and down when we talked. Our "sin," then, would be visible before we began showing. And the more pregnant we got, the sicker we would become. We knew she was trying hard to frighten us when she said, "And then you'll look like death riding a soda cracker." An expression among teenagers.

"And when you get pregnant," she continued, "folks will talk about you from amazing grace to floating opportunity." An expression among adults. She didn't believe in any of us. I can recall thinking to myself that, in her eyes, we had to fail because we came out of our mothers' wombs as girls, not boys.

Several women in the project were major nuisances who deserved the names we called them behind their backs. Miss Saditty who, it was said, was kept by a white man, com- plained when we played too late in the courtyard. Only then did she acknowledge our existence. Too "refined" to come to her door and say directly to us, "Keep the noise down," she called our parents and in an official-sounding voice made her complaint. Miss Meanie, the oldest woman in our unit, spoke directly to us. Shouted, I should have said, and threatened us with spankings if we got the better of her grandsons in a fight. We were heathens; her grandsons were angels. Miss Think-She's-White never raised her voice, but she was nonetheless a nuisance. She would interrupt our fun and order us to pick up paper in places where we had not played. "Acting like she owns the whole project," we would say while obeying her orders, "because she thinks she's white." These women were irritants; Miss Gotta-Know-and-Then-Tell-Everything was a demon. My dislike for her became more intense after her altercation with Mama.

They were sitting outside on the front porch, and the conversation turned, of course, to girls and sex. The woman made a snide comment about women who acted as if their daughters were angels and couldn't have sex. She was referring, of course, to Mama. "They go upstairs while boys are in their house *with* their daughters," the woman said, "and I think it's a disgrace."

Mama, who was, by nature, nonconfrontational, tried to avoid an argument by saying that women had to trust young girls. "Besides," she said, "if the mother is still in the house, that's all that matters."

In her seventies, Mama still remembered the woman's response: "I knew a girl who got pregnant in the kitchen while her mama was sitting in the living room."

That was it! "I gave her a piece of my mind," Mama told us. "I said 'I can't stand old women who have nothing better to do than sit around and tell lies on young girls. You're worse than a peeping tom. You think they're going to get pregnant because you did. That's the problem. You did all the things you accuse them of doing. And worse!'"

Mama used this experience, and others, to reinforce what we already knew: women were easy targets of rumors perpetrated by other women and also by men. Perhaps that was another reason neighborhood women stressed virtue. "Men can get away with murder because they're men" was a common saying in the project. They can walk as hard as they want wherever they want, but women have to watch their step. And even when we tiptoe, the women would say, "folks lie on us." Mama said, "Lies hurt, but they won't kill when your conscience is clear. Your own truth. That's all that matters." In the late sixties, my "own truth" kept me from collapsing in the presence of a big lie about my character.

The year was 1965. I was living in Washington, D.C., in a one-bedroom apartment that overlooked a neatly kept courtyard in a complex that my presence "integrated," and I was immersed in my graduate studies. Six months after moving, I began to have a frequent male visitor in the person of Howard Moore, a civil rights attorney who would gain national attention in the seventies for his defense of Angela Davis. He was the husband of my close friend Jane and also the attorney for those of us who had demonstrated in Atlanta in 1963. When I learned that Howard would be making frequent trips to D.C. on behalf of the struggle that was continuing in the South, I did not hesitate to offer my apartment as his D.C. hotel. Free housing and, when my schedule permitted, free meals would be a major financial contribution to the struggle. Howard accepted the offer with gratitude. Because he would sometimes take early-bird flights in order to save money and work late into the night with other attorneys, I gave him a key — for my convenience and his.

My neighbors, all of them white, reported that *men* were seen entering and leaving my apartment late at night and early in the morning. With their own keys, no less! I had turned my apartment into a brothel. The landlady, whom I had threatened to take to court when she tried to deny me the apartment because I was black, finally had proof that I was an unfit resident. She evicted me on moral grounds. I had neither time nor money to fight her legally. I am certain I would not have been able to recover from this humiliating experience without the grounding in self Mama and other community women gave me. That was what the spy-woman, the demon, Miss Gotta-Know-and-Then-Tell-Everything did not understand. Girls had to believe in themselves and be strong enough to fight off traducers of any kind. "In the worst kind of winds," Mama would say, "you have to stand up tall."

She *was* a rose among thorns. Atypical in many ways. She loved privacy, books, and polemics. She was not a "churchy-fied" woman. And she had what, in the forties, was considered a dangerous parenting style, especially for black girls, and more especially those living in a housing project. She did not whip us with thin switches pulled from overgrown bushes. In fact, I do not remember Mama *ever* whipping us, though Grandmama did a few times. She did not arrange our days around a list of household chores, the completion of which took hours. And she gave us too much freedom. Too much latitude. When we had dates, she would greet them, engage them in conversation (sometimes longer than I wanted) and retire for the night. Miss Gotta-Know-and-Then-Tell-Everything was right: we could have gotten pregnant with Mama in the apartment. While she slept upstairs, my sister and I entertained our dates downstairs. Mama's explanation for her atypical behavior: "I trust my girls."

It was, in part, her trust that encouraged my sister and me to follow her sexual beatitudes, and more than once we were convinced that doing so had its rewards, especially when we would walk through rough sections of the neighborhood on our way to work. On hot summer days, men gathered outside a pool hall three doors down from the theater, stripped down to their waists, their biceps glistening in the sun. Judging from their gestures and their raucous laughter, we knew they were telling obscene jokes. When we were within earshot, we would hear, "Man, watch your mouth. Those girls right there? They the Wade Sisters."

With men who did not know us, however, the story was quite different. They would undress us with their eyes and violate us with their words. "Hey, sweet thang," they would call, sometimes touching their genitals suggestively, "I got something for you." Mama and other women advised us against acting offended. If we did, they said, the men would "shonuff talk" about us. One day a friend, who lived in a middle-class community on the other side of town, made the mistake of giving a group of whistling men a disdainful look. The obscenities were like Chinese firecrackers. Bam! Bam! Bam! Staccato explosions! "Who you think wanted you," they began, "with your ugly ass. I'd have to put a bag over your face first, and I still might not want you." Had I been alone, I would have ignored them or smiled and said, as project women advised, "How are you, sir?" It always worked. I swear it always worked. Men would often become so unnerved they would tip an imaginary hat.

The women had different names for men based on their behavior, especially toward women. "Scum" was the category in which they placed men who screamed obscenities at women in public. There were only three categories for young men who dated girls in the project: "lazy," "up to no good," and "decent." More than once I heard the women (but not Miss Gotta-Know-and-Then-Tell-Everything) say to Mama, "Bertha, your girls take up with some decent boys." Our dates *were* "decent boys" who would observe any mother's rules for behavior in her house, but, like the women, they, too, were amazed that Mama was lenient on curfew and did not give them the third degree before we left the apartment. They did not read the smile which said to us, not to them, "I trust you."

I remember the night my date tried to make it down an unpaved road which heavy rains the night before had turned into quicksand. We were pulled into mud that had the hold of a heavy glue. It took a tow truck hours to pull us out. On the way home, my date, wearing the evidence of our experience up to his knees, was afraid that my mother would be angry with him. I was afraid that she was walking the floor in worry.

Before I could turn the key in the lock, the door opened. My mother pulled me toward her in a tight embrace. She had been crying.

"Thank God," she said. "Thank God, you're safe." Not waiting to hear my explanation, she asked, "Are you hungry?"

My mother had walked through the refiner's fire and come out remarkably beautiful in soul. She was a peacemaker. As are most Libras, those who believe in signs would say. To avoid conflict, she made an effort to see the other person's point of view. She was willing to compromise, but not at the sacrifice of her conscience. "That kind of peace is hell," she would say.

She was generous with her money, her love, and her advice.

She was compassionate and especially toward underdogs. She had seen enough in her life to believe that many women suffered because they were women.

"Women can be such pitiful creatures," she would often say. "So dependent. So out of touch with themselves."

It was this philosophy that prevented her from castigating young girls in the community. The only thing girls did not need, in Mama's opinion, was a prediction that they wouldn't amount to any good because females don't. Shore them up. Bolster them. Inject them with pride. "Tell them how wonderful they are."

That was Mama's philosophy, and it translated into her unconditional trust in my sister and me. She believed a mother had to be her daughter's friend and that she should hold back nothing, especially in matters of sex. Which is why in one breath she advised us against premarital sex and in another she discussed sex in a way that could have easily tempted us to do the very thing she said we should not do. She tried to teach us about sexual exploitation, but not at the expense of our sexuality. Mama actually wanted us to *enjoy* sex. But at the right time.

"It's a wonderful experience," she would tell us. "It feels good. And it's beautiful."

If it's all that, I remember saying to myself, why should we deny ourselves?

Mama's explanation made sense. "It's beautiful but not in the back of a car and not in a motel room. It feels good but not when you have to worry about someone finding out."

You can't experience the "real thing," she would tell us, when you have all those worries interfering with your pleasure. "You have to be able to take your time. Take your own good unworried time."

What young boys in heat could take their time, she wondered.

She talked openly about biological differences between women and men and about emotional differences as well. Men could have pleasure in a second, and with anyone. A perfect stranger, in fact. A woman's pleasure, on the other hand, she said, required time, intimacy, and commitment.

"All three are hard to find in a young relationship."

She was not, however, always academic in her sexual teachings. Frequently. Correction. Often, she was pure emotion. Like the other women.

"Just keep this in mind," she would tell us. "That's what a man wants if he can get it."

She taught us how to distinguish between the boys who wanted only that and the others who were genuinely involved with us but would, of course, get it if they could.

She would recite, "If they tell you after the third date that they are madly in love with you. If they can't keep their hands off you. If they rarely want to take you where there are other people. If they say you would do it if you loved them. If they say they don't want to go all the way in. If they threaten to quit you when you continue to say no. If they tell you they are getting sick because they're not getting it. *Leave them alone* because all they want is your body and since that's all they want, once they get it, they're gone.

"And, just think about this," she would add. "If you're having sex with him, how do you know it's you he loves and not the sex."

In other plain and simple words, sex altered a relationship, and teenagers were far from ready for the alteration.

Another caveat was: "Do not ever touch alcohol. First of all, it's in your family. And second, it robs you of self-control. Don't ever *ever* drink from a cup someone gives you. Only from a bottle, and only from one that *you* opened."

Mama was serious.

And more. "A man does not like a woman who is not a challenge. If you're too easy, he'll lose interest." Was she suggesting that we use denial of our bodies to entrap men? That was *not* what she said. She *said*, don't let men trap us with a lot of jive talk into giving them our bodies before we were ready, before we should. In other words, remain virgins until we married.

Did she say we should save our bodies for a special man?

That was *not* what she said because that suggests a man has a deed to a woman's body and a right to her purity. It calls for sexual genuflecting. What she *said* was virginity had nothing at all to do with men and everything to do with women. It gave us protection, self-esteem, and even control.

Was she saying that the desire was in our head and not in our bodies. That was *not* what she said. What a ridiculous idea. What she *said* was, "Of course you are going to want to have sex. That's natural. It's what you're supposed to feel. And if you don't feel it, then something is wrong."

We're supposed to feel something we are not supposed to express? Hmmph. It was easy for her to talk. She was no longer young and in love. She was not smooching in a car at a drive-in restaurant and dancing a dangerous slow drag on a song that curled your toes the way she said sex can. "Oh, my love, my darling," the voice crooned at a high school dance. "I've hungered for your kiss a long lonely time."

But Mama trusted me, I would tell myself, fighting the urge to give in. The struggle was more difficult in college where many girls, including those who made the Dean's list (which proved that they were not derailed) were sexually active and didn't hide it. Even flaunted it. My knees would buckle when I danced to my favorite song. "Each night before I go to sleep, my baby. I whisper a little prayer for you, my baby." The words were hypnotic, the struggle unbearable. "And tell all the stars above that this is dedicated to the one I love."

She was expecting too much of me. What about the hormones? They had centrifugal power pulling me toward a sexual center.

But Mama trusted us.

What should I do about the centrifugal pull?

She had no easy answers.

She trusted us.

"I want you to have it all," she would tell us. "Education. Education. Economic sufficiency. And sexual passion. Pleasure."

Confusion. Struggle. Hormones. Conflict.

But Mama trusted us.

"You'll be glad you waited," she said with certainty that we would wait. "Trust me. You'll be *so* ready. You'll be glad."

Mama was right.

A Second Baptism

The minister reaches toward the congregation as if he were scooping us up with his own two hands the way Mama scoops up dried beans in the barrels in Ramsey's store. Some fall back into the barrel, but most drop into the bag that is taken to the counter, weighed, paid for, and taken home for our nourishment. I look around me trying to predict who will remain in his hands and be taken to the front of the church where they will be weighed for Jesus. I choose women who shouted or cried softly throughout the sermon. I do not know whom among the men I should choose. In comparison to women, they have been quiet worshippers.

The minister reaches again as a woman no taller than four feet plays a shouting song on the piano that sits to the left of the choir loft.

"The doors of the church are open," he says. "The doors of the church are open. Come unto Jesus and be saved."

Those who have already been saved testify with hand clapping and shouts. "Yes, Lord! Thank you, Jesus. Thank you, Jesus."

"I am the way, the truth and the light, he told us," the minister says, scooping deeper, "and unless you go by me, you cannot enter the kingdom of heaven."

"Yes, Lord," someone in the congregation shouts.

"Unless we choose the Lord God Almighty, we will not be saved."

Witnessing sounds echo in the small sanctuary. I hear them coming from the balcony, from the mourners' bench in the front, from somewhere to the right of me and to the left, meeting over my head and calling my name.

One by one, people walk from their pews to the front of the sanctuary toward the scooping hands. They have accepted Christ as their saviour, and from this moment on, they will be different.

The preacher pushes sitting sinners to join those who have come forth for Jesus.

"You'll look at your hands, and they'll be new. You'll look at your feet and they will too. Because the Lord Jesus will put clapping in your hands." He claps rhythmically and loud.

"He will put running in your feet." He runs across the pulpit, from the right to the left.

"He will give you a new heart. A new life. He'll save you from hell's fire and open the gates to heaven if you believe. If you accept him as your personal savior."

He says again, scooping toward us. "The doors of the church are open."

No one comes forth. He "closes" the doors, and the ritual of receiving the newly saved into the community of God begins. I hear the names, their personal testimonies, and the date of their baptism.

"Let the church stand," the minister says, "and give the right hand of fellowship."

The rows begin moving in the order directed by ushers, I

bounce from my pew in anticipation of the strut down the aisle to the front of the church where I can show off my Sunday clothes and meet the eyes of a boy I hope will wait for me after church.

I return to my pew to sing the closing song.

> Blest be-a the tie that binds
> Our hearts in Christian love.
> The Fell-lo-shi-ip
> of kin -en -dred minds
> Alike to those above.
> Aaaaaaaaaaa.
> Men.

After each worship, I would rush home where Mama would be waiting for my sister and me. She chose to worship in her own sanctuary where she could pray, sing, and meditate while wearing her brown smock and cooking dinners that were always more special than any she prepared during the week. The church, Mt. Vernon Baptist, sat back from the street at the corner of Mississippi Boulevard and Lauderdale Street, overlooking the housing project. In five minutes my sister and I would be home.

Faye would engage Mama in a discussion of the service, replaying the sermon almost in its entirety. I would rush upstairs and take off the confining clothes in preparation for play. On sunny and clear days, I would go to the park in the middle of the project. On cold or rainy days, I would skip down the back driveway to Vera Lee's house where paper dolls would be waiting for me to speak for them or to make them new clothes out of newspaper Vera's mother had saved for us. I forgot church very quickly.

I went because I was required to. Even infidels and atheists (if there were any in the black community) believed children should go to church. Mama would say, "it was the yea-sayer in a world of nays." We designed it, controlled it, and made it work for us. It was the only institution in the community in which we never saw white supervisors, white inspectors — white people in charge. It was an empowering institution.

When I make that statement to today's Africentered students, they laugh. Scoff even.

"What about the white Jesus?" they ask. "And white angels?"

I answer, "What about them?"

They also belonged to us. They were in *our* world, saying what we wanted them to say to us, speaking in cadences and metaphors we had taught them. Instead of feeling inferior, we felt special, empowered, chosen. We were as assured of liberation and empowerment on earth as we were of salvation in heaven.

Like secret religious gatherings of slaves, the black church during my growing up years in the South was never exclusively about the salvation of our souls. It was a finishing school, a reading program, a leadership institute, and a counseling center, and in all of these services, the focus was on developing the children into articulate, respectful, well-mannered, responsible, disciplined, and self-affirmed individuals wearing a green light for success.

"Thou shalt not steal," we would chant. "Thou shalt not lie. Thou shalt not covet thy neighbor's wife. . . . Thou shalt have no other gods before thee. . . ."

Salvation required that we keep the commandments Moses brought from the mountain top. Self-esteem and survival of our people required that we keep other commandments not printed in King James. I can remember reciting them with my inside voice when I heard the cues in the

preacher's sermon or in the choir's songs, the coded messages
of self-affirmation:

"You must love yourself and your people."

"You must believe that you can do anything you set your
mind to."

"You should let no circumstance remove you from the center of your dreams."

"You must never forget from whence you came."

"You must reach back to others."

"You must serve."

These black commandments, and others, made hatred of
white people foolish and self-destructive. Without apology,
we talked about whites, anger and rage rushing from us the
way water rushes from fire hydrants on hot summer streets.
With the force of ten cannons. We were never silent about
our injuries and their iniquities. But we stopped a good distance from hating them. Let *them* do the hating, and let them
lose. That's what they were doing. Losing. We were winning
because we loved ourselves, served our people, and did good
to others. Hatred was a corrosive emotion. It rusted the soul.

We took stories from the Bible and contextualized them
black.

The Hebrew children were doing well, in spite of their
struggles, until they denied their own people and chose
wealth over sacrifice, pleasure over struggle. We must not
deny our own. We must stay with the struggle. We must
shun things and serve the spirit.

When Jesus was on the cross, they taunted him. "Show us
your power now," they said. He answered: "Father, forgive them for they know not what they do." On the cross
of our suffering as a people, we must believe in our power,
and we must pray for white people who will either repent
of their sins or burn in the fires of hell on earth.

The race of the people in the stories, where and when they lived, were never relevant to us. We took what we wanted from their lives and created an epic about our salvation, our liberation, and our superiority, and we passed it on to each generation. We took pride in taking the moral high ground on suffering.

I accepted the racial teachings of the church long before I decided to accept the religious teachings. But there was no pressure on sister and me to walk toward the scooping hands of the minister. Not from Grandmama, who every Sunday would leave her home early enough to walk ten blocks to the church and arrive on time, looking pretty in an outfit she had made and wearing the dignity of her practiced smile. Not from Aunt Mae, who was a featured soloist in the choir in spite of the fact that she did not sing gospel. And certainly not from Mama, whose critical mind rejected literal interpretations of the Bible and the "whooping and hollering" resonant in some churches.

We took church seriously (which is why Faye and I never missed a Sunday), but, as a family, we were not known to be church people, or "churchy-fied" people, as the saying went. They were the people who gave generously from their meager earnings to every activity in the church. We gave, too. I remember Mama wrapping coins and sometimes a dollar bill tightly in a handkerchief, telling me not to lose it (a necessary reminder for me) and instructing us to give only to certain collections: church maintenance, the missionary board, and the sick-and-shut-in. She was adamantly opposed to love offerings for the preacher and, no less so, to those for new buildings.

"Now just tell me," I can hear her saying to neighbors when they talked about church. "Just tell me. Why should I, a poor struggling mother, give a *love* offering, an appreci-

ation offering, to the preacher. We already pay him a good
salary, plus rent for the parsonage, and gas for his car. I'd
look like a fool stretching my pennies to give him more."

To this day, I keep my purse snapped tight when envelopes are distributed in church bearing the words: "A Love
Offering for the Minister."

Churchy-fied people made the institution of the church the
center of their lives. For them, service was confined within
the structure. For Mama, it was outside the structure. She
took seriously the scriptural admonition against worshipping
mammon and believed profoundly in the Beatitudes. The
"blessed" among us were indeed the "pure in heart," the
"peacemakers," and those that mourned, and those that were
unselfish in their giving and in their love.

Churchy-fied people invested both time and money into
looking good when they went to worship. Mama had little
interest in clothes. I remember as a teenager wanting her to
look like the other women in the project. It wasn't that I was
ashamed of her. Rather, it was that I knew she could be
prettier if she got a new hairdo, bought some attractive
clothes, and fixed up her face. She didn't even bother to wear
makeup. When we complained, Mama would tell us the only
thing that mattered was that *we* looked pretty. She couldn't
afford three different wardrobes. But more was involved
than her limited funds. Mama simply didn't care about things:
furniture, clothes, cars, jewelry. She loved her girls, her
family, and nature.

In my memories of fun times with Mama away from our
apartment and the Georgia Theatre, where we went to see
old movies at a cheap price, I see the three of us studying
animals in a cage at the Memphis zoo. Several times during
the summer, Mama would pack a big lunch for our all-day
stay on "colored" day. She felt sorry for the caged animals,

but she loved to study them because they were a part of nature and, therefore, important to Mama, who believed everything was in nature: answers to all of our questions, cures for all of our illnesses, and evidence of God, the Spirit. Mama was too spiritual a woman to be churchy-fied.

Her distance from the church as an institution might have had its beginning in Mississippi, when Grandmama was forced by church people to leave the parsonage and, without church support, care for her children as a single parent widowed at eighteen. Grandmama would tell us about the church people who would see her coming and cross to the other side of the street, fearful that she would ask for their assistance. Mama probably never forgot that.

She also probably never forgot Grandmama's annual trips to the church conference where ministers were given new assignments and mothers with small children were given their "widow's mite," or the eventful one at which a bishop propositioned Grandmama, promising a larger check in exchange for favors. She probably never forgot that money became more scarce after Grandmama, a proud woman, rebuffed the bishop with vitriolic words and decided never to go with stretched-out hands to anyone, not even church people passing out what was rightfully hers.

Regardless of her attitude toward the church as institution, Mama was a deeply religious woman who believed in prayer and meditation and in the Bible as a book of eternal truths. Metaphors in the Bible were lessons about life that she passed on to my sister and me, and to her grandchildren. "Read this often, but with comprehension," she wrote on an inspirational poem about the parable of the mustard seed she sent to her grandson Loren during a difficult period in his life. It began with the question she put to all of us in her own words: "Would you like to undertake some mountain moving?" We could be mustard seeds, she taught us, and we could move mountains, she told us. Her texts for parenting came, we knew, from the Bible.

Mama might not go to church with us, but we *had* to go. *Every* Sunday. She prayed that we would come to believe, as she did, in the doctrines of love, service, and salvation that were fundamental to her religion, her spirituality. Of course, Faye would be the first of her girls to join the church.

I remember the Sunday when Faye chose to sit on the front pew located to the right of the pulpit. The "mourners' bench," it was called then for those who would mourn themselves into salvation. I watched her as she wept when the preacher waved his hands exhorting all of us to "come to Jesus." I watched her rise from the bench when he said, "The doors of the church are open," and as she walked to the front of the church, I was afraid she was walking away from me. Unwilling to let that happen, I quickly joined her.

In retrospect, I realize that this was the wrong reason to join church. Sacrilege, in fact. Unadulterated and inexcusable. I didn't care. My sister and I were inseparable. Wherever she went, there I would go also. Even into the scooping hands of the minister.

The church taught us that the Lord protects us from "thine enemies," even prepares a table for us in their presence. That was what my sister had done all of my life. She protected me from "mine enemies." Some of them I made with my mischievous ways, Mama said, and others with my joyous personality. I was always happy. "A jumping bean of joy," Mama said, who never walked anywhere. I always skipped or danced my way to school, to the store, and when I was young, to church, scuffing my patent leather shoes. Still other "enemies" I made because the boys liked me. Mama said I had sex appeal. Whatever the reason, I was always getting into fights that I could never win because I knew I could depend on Faye to protect me. Sometimes I pulled her into impossible situations.

Like the time at Porter Elementary School, across the street on the north side of the projects, when the girl who sat behind me told me she was going to "beat my butt" after school. I hadn't done anything to her, I would tell Mama later. She was angry because I had made the highest grade on the math test and my essay had been put on the class bulletin board. I didn't deserve to get my butt whipped for that. In my vanity, I also thought she was angry because her hair needed to be fixed, and mine was very neat and pretty. And, too, she had short hair, which was then the kiss of death for black girls.

I met her threat with my own. If she tried to bother me after school, I would tell my big sister to beat her up. And then I added something about my sister being on the school patrol, which made matters worse because only A students were allowed to wear the yellow belts and direct traffic in the corridors.

"Well, I got a big sister, too," she said, brandishing fists I knew would have struck me if the teacher had not been in the room.

The mischief in me took over. I lied about how tough my sister was and how many girls she had beaten up just for looking at me the wrong way. I wasn't afraid of her. She was shorter than I was and her sister would be shorter than Faye. We wouldn't even have to fight, I was thinking to myself. We could just give them a hard stare and that would be that.

I saw Faye in the hallway when classes changed the next hour and told her about the impending fight. Of course, I made the girl into a monster who had been bothering me for a long time. She who always protected me from "mine enemies" told me not to worry. She would talk to the girl and to her sister. And if talking didn't work? Well, she'd just have to fight. To protect me, her baby sister.

At the end of the day, Faye and I met outside school. When the girls were not visible right away, I wanted to leave. But my sister, whose integrity sometimes made me sick, wanted to wait for them. Because I had said I would. Because we needed to get this behind us. "She'll keep bothering you, Gloria," I heard her say, "until you stand up to her."

At that moment, I saw the girl and her sister coming from behind the building. She was still short, but her sister was a giant of a girl. Much taller than Faye. I pretended that I did not see them and began pulling on my sister's hand. "Let's go, Faye," I said nervously. "Let's go home."

"No, we are going to take care of this today. I am not running away from anyone who has hurt you."

Faye must have sensed that they were approaching because she looked in their direction. At that moment, I said, "There they are, Faye."

My sister took one look and jerked me by the hand, shouting, "Run! Gloria, run!" I remember that we did not stop running until we reached the front door of our unit and took protection inside, behind Uncle Prince.

All other times, my sister stood her ground and fought for me. She fought the Walk boys who lived next door and Geraldine, who lived five units away, and the tough kids who lived in the section below us which was not as pretty with flowers as ours. She even interceded on my behalf with teachers who said I talked too much in class or came back too late using the hall pass to the girl's lavatory. What else was I expected to do when she walked to the front of the church?

As the preacher continued to wave his scooping hands, I prayed very hard to feel what my sister's tears said she was feeling. I heard the words, "And the Lord said, 'Repent ye of your sins and prepare to enter into the kingdom of heaven.'" I thought of my many sins and asked for forgiveness in silence.

I had not always done on time the few chores Mama gave us. I asked for forgiveness.

One night, while we were playing in the courtyard, Grandmama asked me to go to the corner store to get her two scoops of vanilla ice cream. In my skipping/running rush to get back to play, I held the cone precariously and the top scoop fell to the ground. I picked it up and wiped it clean with my tongue. I never told Grandmama what had happened. I asked for forgiveness.

I told my teacher that I left my homework at home by accident. I lied. I had never completed the assignment. I asked for forgiveness.

I told Mama I had returned my library books. But there was a fine because I had left the books at Vera Mae's house. I asked for forgiveness.

I had used profanity (but only one time!) in an argument with Little George, the boy next door, and Mama had said I should not use language like that. I asked for forgiveness.

I had laughed at the fat man who sang a solo last Sunday because with each high note he hit, his extended abdomen became a larger balloon. I asked for forgiveness.

I had gone with my friends to the sanctified church across the street from the Georgia Theatre, and I had laughed when the women began dancing in the aisle. I asked for forgiveness.

When the church gave me the "right hand of fellowship," I felt better about what I was doing. God said repent of your sins. I had done that. The minister said accept Christ as your personal savior. I did that every day I entered the church. I had a right to stand next to my sister.

When we told Mama that we had joined church, she wept and began wringing her hands, which always meant deep emotion she was having difficulty controlling. Faye cried the Christian's cry. She could feel her hands looking new and her feet, too. She was going to be a different girl, a better human being. That wouldn't take much for her since she obeyed all the rules. I remember going upstairs and getting on my knees at the bed I shared with my sister. I prayed that the Lord would make my joining the church as real for me as it was for Faye.

The test would come at baptism. If you choked when you were dipped into the water, we believed, you had not been saved. I remember when I was very young going to baptism just to see who was "for real" and who was "phoney." Who would be watching me like that at my baptism, I wondered. I had nightmares about choking and, in the days leading up to baptism, I practiced holding my breath. "Oh God," I prayed, "please do not let me choke. Please do not let me choke."

I remember going to the church on the Saturday before our baptism to watch the janitor fill up the baptismal pool, whose location beneath the choir loft, made evenings, after all church activities, the only time possible for baptisms. The pool was a square metal tub large enough for twelve people to stand in without crowding at the same time. The water was dripping slowly into the pool. Perhaps it would not be full in time for Sunday, I thought. Oh God, please do not let me choke.

Baptismal Sunday was the most spirited of days in my church. Increasing the fold brought to the worship a joy, a passion, an intensity that only the most hard-hearted person would not feel. The choir marched down the aisle in bright green robes, swinging from side to side, in step, their voices richer than usual.

> Pass me not O gentle saviour.
> Hear my mournful cry.
> While on others thou art calling.
> Do not pass me by.

The words had special meaning for me, and so did the song they sang once they had reached the choir loft.

> I know the Lord. I know the Lord.
> I know the Lord has laid his hands on me.

I don't remember the minister's sermon, but, like the songs, it must have spoken to me in a special way. I remember wanting to join the church again when the doors were open, this time with a pure heart and a clean spirit.

Mama went with us into the dressing room where we changed from our clothes into white robes. The basement was ringing with the voices of the choir singing song after song as people gathered in large numbers to witness the baptism. Once dressed, we were lined up to the right of the pool. The choir stopped singing. In the hushed silence, I could hear the minister wading into the water. The ritual of baptism began.

One by one, we walked into the cold water to the middle of the pool where he was waiting to receive us. He placed one arm around our waist and the other on top of our head. "In the name of the Father, the Son, and the Holy Ghost." He dipped us backwards into the water, held us under for a second, and brought us up to the sounds of the congregation's praises to the Lord. I did not choke.

My life *did* change. Perhaps because my baptismal and puberty happened simultaneously, but it changed. I changed. I was less mischievous and more mature. I was not fanatical. I never said, "Praise the Lord." I did not become "saintly." I dressed the same. I continued to go to parties and to dance and to joke. To have fun. But I made an effort to be different. To be kind. To be thoughtful. To be caring of others. To be grateful for all of my blessings, the most important of which was my family. And to be mindful of my smallness in the universe.

Although church had always been important to me, it now became the center to which everything in my life was in some way attached. Even secular activities took place in or through the church: picnics, outings, dates, piano lessons, singing lessons, ballet lessons, reading clubs, Girl Scouts, tutoring, black history celebrations . . . Segregation proscribed narrow places for us, but the black family, black schools, and the black church together showed us the world. It was ours, they said in unison, to claim and to change.

I held on to my religious convictions and to the church through college and graduate school, two experiences black people back home considered a threat to one's faith. Lectures by learned professors, they feared, would challenge sermons on which we had been nurtured. Hence, the text for commencement Sunday: "Goodbye, God. I've Gone to College." I held on until reason and rage convinced me to let go. Christianity, I decided, had crippled my people. Made us too forgiving. Too submissive. Too resigned to suffering on earth as a prerequisite to eternal life. Too incapable of organizing and executing the revolution we needed. I would march with ministers, assemble in churches for rallies, and bow in prayer before demonstrations, but I was not a member of the community of believers.

While I was marching in the sixties with ministers, assem-

bling in churches for rallies, and bowing in prayer before
demonstrations, I was fighting to hold on to my faith. After
four young girls lost their lives in the Birmingham church
bombing, I decided never again to believe in my people's
religion. And with the advent of Black Power in the seventies, I made what I thought would be a permanent discon-
nection from the black church. In my new so-called revolutionary thinking, I saw it as the white man's weapon against
my people. During the sixties I listened to Martin. During
the seventies I meditated politically to the sound of Malcolm's voice on tapes that were selling on every street corner
in black neighborhoods. I wished that I had followed him
when he was alive. Christianity, he said, is a slave religion. I
agreed with him.

Once I had lost my faith, nothing I saw in reality made
sense of anything I had once believed. Every tragedy was
proof that the church had lied. Why do people suffer? The
reality I read about in the newspaper and knew about personally could not be explained away — not anymore — by the
dogma I had once accepted. If God is merciful, kind and all-
loving, how could we explain violent and brutal racism? The
senselessness and barbarity of the Vietnam War, which was
raging at the time? In what song, in what prayer, in what
scripture, in what sermon — where in my religious beliefs
could I find an explanation of slavery?

I would wonder during those years of faithlessness whether
or not I had ever believed. Perhaps I had choked during my
baptism without realizing it. That would explain why my sister had remained faithful to the religion both of us claimed
as teenagers in a black southern church. Without apology, I
embraced my unbelief.

They say you can't stay away for long. They say that age
and marriage and motherhood pull you back from the other

shore. They say that the loss of your mother will cause you
to sing the old songs and to bow in prayer again to the God
in whom you once believed. They say you do indeed go
home again.

━━━━━━━━━━

I went home for all of those reasons, and for another that is
not as easy to explain. I call the reason change. Change in
the terrain of black life following integration which, along
with other factors, has made us spiritually desolate. In communities that lay like wastelands in America, the black church
is the only place where elders feel wanted and needed.
There, they can sit erect and, in security and pride, share
what they feel and what they know. In a nation where much
of the music blasted into the psyche of the young is an intro-
duction to sex and violence, the black church is the only
place where the young can hear elders sing the old songs that
once sustained us as a people.

"I love the Lord, he heard my cry," a single voice sings. It
is a call for response from a chorus. Lining, as it was called,
stretched a line from one person's soul into a song that could
last for half an hour. Each word in the line, each single word,
became a melody. Not only in jazz did black people impro-
vise. No one could write the notes of lining songs on five
lines marked by a G clef because, with each singing, the
songs were different. Improvised for the Lord.

And where else except in the black church will the young
hear "sorrow songs." Created by slaves, spirituals are among
the most musically brilliant and moving of songs. To sing
them is to be in touch with the spirit of our ancestors. To
hear them is to be reminded of the resilience of their spirit
and, therefore, to be renewed. "Jordan's River is chilly and

cold; it chills my body but not my soul" has relevance for us today for, ultimately, it is our soul that we must save.

The church to which I am returning is not a perfect institution. It cannot be in this, our imperfect, world. Like other institutions in this nation, the black church has high levels of sexist toxicity. Men make policy decisions and women fan fainting worshippers. And cook meals, serve meals, make choir uniforms, type church programs, raise funds. Work. Though dominated by men, the church gets its strength and power from the spirit of the women. Call it nurturing, call it maternal, call it humanistic, call it healing — that spirit is what we so desperately need today.

Like other institutions in this nation, the black church is undergoing change. Serious and fundamental change that removes gender as a criterion for preaching, officiating, trusteeing, and nurturing. In some churches, worshippers move from the mourners' bench to the scooping hands of a woman. As a gender-reformed church, the black church to which I am returning will do even better its work of transforming black lives.

I remember how movingly women in the old church sang my favorite song: "I'm gonna do what the Spirit say do." I am convinced that the Spirit is directing me to the church. And so, I am returning because that is where our elders are. Because that is where we sing the songs. Because that is where we can lay strong and loving hands on our young. Because that is where we can be renewed in spirit and in will. Because that is where we can, in unison, recite the epic of salvation and liberation, and pass it on to future generations. I no longer believe in God the father-he, or in Jesus as the son of God, or in an actual place called heaven. But that doesn't matter. And, in truth, it never mattered in our definition of salvation. What mattered then and matters now is that we recognize our smallness in the universe and see kindness as the only avenue toward a larger self.

With new hands and new feet, I am returning to the black church as an elder who believes that, in its combination of the religious and the political, the black church remains a vital and compelling institution. Emulating the elders of my day, I want to teach the young the Beatitudes, the Ten Commandments, and the commandments of empowerment:

"You must love yourself and your people."

"You must believe that you can do anything you set your mind to."

"You should let no circumstance remove you from the center of your dreams."

"You must never forget from whence you came."

"You must reach back to others."

"You must serve."

In a long black robe, I will wade into the waters of my new baptism.

In the East,
Headed South to Home

Boston in 1959 was a strange city. Unattractive, cold, and spiritually desolate. Disappointing. At least for me, a black woman from the South. A daughter of the sun. I was accustomed to people talking with animation on street corners, in grocery stores, and across dusty courtyards. People sitting on front porches watching children, all of whom "belonged" to them. People approaching me with smiles followed by warm hellos. Nothing seemed right about this city. Even its music was wrong. Monotone. Without soul.

I tried to take comfort in the fact that the city had a river, but the name left me unmoved. "Charles" made me think of a young boy bored with life. Privileged and pampered. An appropriate name, I thought to myself, for a frivolous body of water called a river. That's how I saw "the Charles" then. Frivolous. A playground for small boats that moved only when the wind was strong enough to puff their sails. Up and down. Down and up. Or in circles for the pleasure of those who could afford the pleasure. In contrast, the Mississippi (now that's a name for a river!) was serious. Its wide bosom attracted big boats. Boats big enough for a large crew. Big enough to require engines that sometimes puffed smoke. Barges big enough to carry cargo to a hundred different cities along the Mississippi. Real destinations.

I was forced to admit that, even without a serious river, this was a significant city. Historic. The birthplace of America as a free nation. On any day of the week tourists of every hue and ethnicity, every political and religious persuasion, boarded double-decker buses near Copley Square and headed for the Old North Church, Bunker Hill, and other historic places bearing the names of patriots — most of them men, all of them white. And some of the buses toured the many prestigious colleges and universities that faced one another across the Charles River. One of those universities that had brought me to this northern city.

And I was supposed to be grateful for being there. A black girl from a housing project in the deep South attending graduate school in the East. A Woodrow Wilson Fellow at that. I couldn't remember in what circle Dante placed ingratitude, but I remembered where it belonged in my mother's cosmology of hell. For her, violence against self and violence against others were the only sins closer to the inferno than ingratitude. Being ungrateful in my new home — academic and temporary only — placed me in the hottest region of hell. In 1959 Boston was a venomously racist city.

In the South we knew what to expect. We saw the signs which were brighter than neons, flashing "Colored." Which meant, "Black folks need not apply, enter or even approach." Boston needed no signs. The city's behavior said it all: "We, too, hate Blacks." Whites moved away from us on the train. They took their "blessed time" serving us in restaurants. They made us wait forever in department stores. And those who were not "refined" enough — or phoney enough — to pretend, hurled racist epithets that won a close first with lynching language associated only with the South.

Boston failed every test on racial sensitivity and racial justice. With its rigidly drawn lines, it failed miserably in employment. I wondered who employed blacks in Boston since even waiters, busboys, and cleaning women were white. For me, it failed most miserably in housing. Black students at universities in Boston and Cambridge had identical stories to tell about realtors who sent us searching for apartments in communities that hid custom-made racial signs behind sugar-sweet politeness that soured quickly when we heard, "If only you had come here yesterday." Many of us succeeded in finding affordable and decent housing close enough for a not-so-long walk or a safe bicycle ride to the universities only with the aid of civil rights organizations. If we suspected discrimination, white volunteers would attempt to rent an apartment we had been denied. Only rarely were they told, "I'm sorry. Someone is moving in tomorrow." Together, we would confront the landlord who would either rent to us or find himself, or herself, in a lawsuit, which we would publicize in a demonstration. Picket signs and all. How humiliating it was to find a decent "home" only through confrontation and entrapment.

Universities could have made a difference had they been different. They were not. They were a microcosm of the world outside their gates. Alien places for a student who graduated from a historically black college where professors knew us by name and pushed us, confident of our performance, into rigorous academic challenges. At big universities students are often faces without names, and many professors are scholars without dedication to the faces without names. I had grown up in a learning environment where mentoring outside the classroom was every bit as important as lecturing inside the classroom, and creative teaching was as valued as a significant essay in a scholarly journal. Scholarship was not narrowly defined as publication. It included serious preparation for lectures that would inspire students to pursue excellence and the highest of goals. I was at this university in the city without a serious river because of that definition. Because of scholars who taught with passion, and who inspired by example. They reminded me when I left home why I was leaving in the first place.

"Remember what you're there for."

"Don't get behind in your studies."

"Don't let them make you doubt yourself."

"Remember you're every bit as smart as white students, and smarter."

"You're doing this for black students who will come after you."

"Remember what we've taught you."

"Make us proud."

"Excel!"

I missed them. I missed the small campus in Memphis which was resonant with the history of my people. I missed the lectures and convocations and conversations about mission which meant giving back to the place from whence you have come. I missed the humanistic approach to education that made historically black colleges so very distinctive and so capable, in spite of small endowments and small libraries, of producing leaders. The cold whiteness of universities in Boston made me dislike the city even more.

I wondered if my father had ever been to Boston on one of his many railroad trips. I thought often about our car tour of the University of Chicago, where we saw "smart white boys." I knew that he wanted desperately for my sister and me to go further and further . . . to get all the education we could. I wondered if he knew how much I loved him.

Grief. Racism. In the beginning I did not believe I would ever adjust to living in Boston. I am sure I would have remained detached and angry if Jimmy had not been with me. He was my friend and my soulmate, holding my hand through each new Boston experience. Having spent a year at M.I.T. as a Danforth Fellow the year before I began my studies at Boston University, he had grown to know well the Boston touted in brochures and in feature stories on culture printed in magazines and award-winning newspapers. He loved the white city. That is not to say, however, he was blind to Boston's racism. Far from it, he was a fighter, bold and unrelenting in his struggles with racist whites. In fact, it was in part his refusal to let them control his life, along with his love of adventure, that made him a connoisseur of every delectable the city had to offer.

He was my tour guide. I followed willingly and with pleasure. With him, I skated in the Boston Commons when a hard New England winter froze the water that belonged to wooden swans. I listened from the balcony of Symphony Hall to encore performances of classical music while occasionally watching picture-book performances of white people walking to their seats wearing money and privilege. I laughed and cried during productions at the Shubert Theatre and at university playhouses. I frequented museums, galleries, bookstores, the aquarium, and other places of culture. I immersed myself in the charm of Boston, and the city became a rare and vintage wine. Chilled. I sipped slowly in order to savor its rich taste, becoming intoxicated. Addicted.

I allowed my eyes to see a rainbow of ethnicity that never arced over Memphis. At home, whites were white. Southern and white. Period. In Boston, whites were divided into distinctively different groups who claimed different sections of the city as home: the Irish in South Boston, the Italians in North Boston, the Jews in Brookline. There was Chinatown and Greektown. Whites expressed their distinctiveness in cuisines, music, ways of worship, and sometimes in dress. At that time there was no talk of multiculturalism, and no one referred to non-European groups as third world, or first world people. And that explains, in part, why blacks could not seek asylum in those ethnic neighborhoods. If anything, we found more outward hostility. I resented the way these groups looked down on and treated blacks, but I went to their neighborhoods as one goes to a fair or to a carnival. With excitement. In anticipation of experiences only they could offer.

In time, I began to tell myself that the Mississippi River was neither a pretty river nor a kind river. Not to blacks during slavery, or since. It represented much of what was wrong about the South. Why was I romanticizing *that* river with its bulky barges? Sailboats are more graceful, and they move on water that has no odor and is sometimes clear, as the Mississippi never is. I began to see the Charles as a picturesque river. Graceful. Colorful. Clean. With all its faults and in spite of my anger, I began to love Boston and to claim it as my nonsouthern home. Academic and temporary, but "home."

I knew about Roxbury, the black community to the east, but I went there only when it was time to get my hair "fixed." Looking back on those years with very different eyes, I realize that I could have easily been accused of disconnecting from my people. Becoming white, the verdict goes. But my associates could not have made that accusation. Most of them were white and those who were black like me studied, lived, and "played" in the white city.

Then, I would have defended myself ably, and passionately, by explaining my racial politics which necessitated alliances with enlightened whites who, like me, wanted the invisible racist signs removed. Instead of disconnecting from blacks in Roxbury, I would have said, I was, in fact and with determination, working on their behalf. I was an integrationist of the first order.

That explains why Jimmy and I, along with a few other blacks, joined the Unitarian Church. It's been so long since I worshipped there that I don't remember where it was located. Somewhere near the Commons, I think, or in that general neighborhood. I was convinced this church offered what I needed at the time: open dialogue about religion; respect for all denominations and even for non-Western religions; a nonliteral reading of the Bible; and, most important, an integrated congregation that dared be different, that dared challenge the status quo.

In those days the heightened racial turmoil in the South, the struggle for freedom had to be central to all of my experiences, including religious worship. If any church were to make a difference in the Boston area, I was convinced it would be this one.

I confess, however, wishing many Sundays for the sound of a black choir singing gospel or a woman shouting unashamedly as the holy ghost touched her. I wanted to see black mothers hushing crying babies or walking proudly down the aisle in their ushers' uniform. I even wanted at times to see a black preacher strutting across the pulpit, singing and dancing. And although I had long since stopped taking the Bible literally, I sometimes wanted to hear sermons about a real Daniel who fought off real lions and a real Jonah who stayed in the belly of a real whale — until a real God released him.

But I was comfortable, even happy, in my new church

home primarily because the people were real, and sincere.
Unlike whites in other settings in Boston, they were neither
curious about my blackness nor guilty about their whiteness.
Both are sure signs that all is not right. Racially. I never saw
those signs in the Unitarian Church. It was the one place in
Boston where whites seemed committed to change, with or
without the help of blacks.

I believe the church directed me to Boston Committee on
Racial Equality (CORE) or perhaps, with Jimmy, I happened by Trailways one day and saw the pickets. I can't remember. I know only that my life changed when I became
an activist with CORE in 1961. The South which I had left
was changing. In 1960, black students challenged segregation at lunch counters. I saw the beatings on television, and
I wept. In 1961, the Freedom Rides began. I saw the beatings, the bloodied faces, and the eyes of hatred. And I wept.
I began to remember horror scenes from my past. There
were flashbacks of the lynching of Emmett Till and the picture of his bloated body in *Jet Magazine.* Flashbacks of the
lynching of Mack Johnson. Flashbacks of white policemen
in Memphis beating a black man near my community. Flashbacks of my grandmother's stories and my uncle's stories and
my father's stories. My people's stories. My guilt was profound. My people were struggling and dying; I was walking
safely into large libraries and reading books about white
people which I wrote about in papers only white professors
would read. I needed to be involved in the movement. Ac-
tively involved.

I could have joined the Boston chapter of the NAACP, but
CORE appealed to me more. It attracted a different type of
activist. Instead of working in the courts, it worked in the
streets. I needed visible and public proof of my commitment,
especially since I was living in a white world.

Later, in the sixties, CORE would temporarily erase lines of division among Boston University, Harvard, Northeastern, M.I.T., and other colleges in the Boston area, bringing students and some faculty together as one force fighting racism in hiring, the focus initially being on Woolworth's. However, from 1959 to 1963, my years in Boston, the CORE with which I worked was small and not very well known, and it had no impact on the senseless division among the area's institutions of higher learning.

It was called Boston CORE, but many of our meetings took place in Cambridge in a small, three-bedroom apartment not far from Harvard Square — symbolically in a mixed (not to be confused with integrated) community. What I remember most vividly about the long hours Jimmy and I spent in that neighborhood, planning demonstrations, painting picket signs, and preparing leaflets in the small, modestly furnished apartment, was our sense of ourselves as a family, as brothers and sisters fighting a common foe. I don't remember any of the whites in CORE apologizing for what other whites were doing to black people in the South or in Boston. Nor do I remember feeling that I was the "beneficiary" of white paternalism, ingratiating sweetness, or authoritarianism. Perhaps my own racial pride made such postures unthinkable, or perhaps the whites with whom I developed a close friendship were not the kind who later would be called "white liberals" and held under close scrutiny and suspicion in the wake of the Black Power Movement.

I remember developing a close relationship with a couple because their children, ages four and five, filled a void in my life I had not known in the South where the laughter of children playing freely in open fields was as distinctively southern as the white man's drawl. These two children, understandably, became important to me.

On the Saturday I am vividly remembering, some forty years later, I am sitting at the table addressing envelopes and the children are crawling on the floor beneath the table. A small voice interrupts chatter among CORE workers.

"Mommie," the voice says. "Mommie. Gloria has brown legs."

The tone is one of surprise, not disappointment. Even one of pleasant and delightful discovery. The child had spent months with me, often sitting in my lap, but she had never seen me racially.

I would have occasion many years later to look at that experience and others associated with my life as an integrationist in a white city and in a predominantly white organization. As the saying goes, "Time changes things," but not all things. I still see beauty in that experience because it affirms my belief that children have to be taught to hate. What I see now, and could not and did not see then, however, is the extent to which, in spite of genuine bonding between blacks and whites in CORE, the cultural exchange taking place was essentially a one-way street. I was eating their cuisine, studying their literature, listening to their music, admiring their art, worshipping in their church—immersing myself in their culture. I taught them very little about African-American culture. And there was so much I could have taught them. So much they should have learned. Ironically, if they had asked me to educate them about my culture, I would have taken offense and accused them of seeing me only in racial terms.

We were missing essential parts of the whole society we thought we were creating. In retrospect, I know that we were doing the best we could during a time when integration meant assimilation of blacks into white American culture. In other words, we believed the more like white Americans blacks became, the better the chances for racial harmony in the nation. For our myopia, we would reap the bitter fruit of racial bitterness and increased racial polarization.

In retrospect, I know that as genuine as my white friends were in the late fifties and early sixties and as committed as they were to change, they did not understand white privilege which is different from white racism, but feeds it and feeds on it.

In my subconscious, I knew that all was not as right with us as we wanted it to be. There were times when I felt a big part of me was missing or invisible — or visible, but silent. Not *silenced*, however, because I never attributed this awful feeling to my friends or even to myself. It was simply there, telling me on a regular basis that I was not doing all I needed to do in a movement whose demand for justice was beginning to thunder in places far from the South and would one day be heard in Boston.

I wanted to be inspired by the charismatic black preacher who was larger than life on my small television screen. I wanted to link my arms with the demonstrators, blacks and whites, who were singing victory songs in Tennessee, Alabama, and Georgia, and dancing into vans that carried them to southern jails. All of that, and more, was missing in my Boston experience.

If I could walk back into history as the person I am now, I would change the Boston chapter in my life. My Saturdays with my white CORE friends would be dramatically different. Either we would be the closest of friends from mutual sharing, or we would not be friends at all. I would share my racial essence with them, and it would enrich their lives. I would take them to a section of Roxbury similar to my old community in Memphis and to a black church where they could hear songs of spirit that are fundamental to the humanity and soul of my people. We would be intimate friends, or antagonists.

But most of all, I would go alone to Roxbury to connect with people who could interrupt my sentences and complete them with words I was prepared to speak. I would look for the children and, after them, for the older people who, even when I was in Boston, knew the art of sitting outside on concrete steps because they understood that only by going outside can you see, know, and bond with your neighbors. I would not give up my life in Boston. I could not and continue with my graduate studies. But I would expand it. Roxbury would be as much a part of my schedule as all-day study sessions for literature classes that ignored the existence of black writers. I would work in both worlds, for both worlds, hoping for one world.

Sometimes the shortest chapter in a book moves the story forward and adds dimensions to characters that make their future actions plausible, and perhaps compelling. That is how I see my stay in Boston. Though brief, it was an important chapter in my life, the beginning of my metamorphosis into a different woman. A different self. It began with my feeling that it would be the worst of times, because of my father's death and my experiences with racism, but it ended with my feeling that it was the best of times. That is what Jimmy and I felt when we decided, with regret but without pain, to separate in 1963 and, a year later, to divorce. We never had an argument or conflict of any kind. We had had the best of times as friends who were close enough to be blood kin. As the best of friends and as co-activists, we moved to Atlanta in 1963. At the end of the year, Jimmy returned to Boston and, some years later, received a cabinet position in the state government. I remained in the South. I was home.

The Making of a Permanent Afro

I have not always worn an Afro. My mother reminds me of that fact when she turns the pages of our family scrapbook or my high school and college yearbooks with pride. "You see how you used look," she says, stopping short of telling me she prefers the way I "used to look." I claim the face in the pictures, and the smile. "You always did smile," she says. But I am reluctant to claim the hair. It is greasy, unnaturally straight, shiny, and, I think, very unbecoming. I try to imagine how I would have looked on Easter Sunday in a white eyelet dress, a pink bonnet, black patent baby dolls, and an Afro. Christmas pictures are easier for my imagining: the coat-hanger halo wrapped in foil would have adorned an Afro, but an Afro would have made me unacceptable as an angel bearing the "good news."

Twice a month (either on Friday night or late Saturday afternoon) and sometimes more frequently if we had been caught in a hard rain or if we were participating in a special activity, my sister and I prepared for the ritual that would change our hair. We would brush our hair vigorously in order to stimulate the scalp. In order to make the hair grow. Then, black girls did not want short hair. When the brushing was finished, we would place our heads under the faucet in the deep kitchen sink and feel fingers dancing on our scalp. Mama scrubbed our hair with ivory soap. Rinsed out the suds. Scrubbed again. The ritual had its own rhythm. Water off. Water On. Scrub. Rinse. Off. On. Scrub. Rinse. Off. On. Scrub. Rinse. Only when our hair was squeaky clean, did the rhythm end.

I don't know whether or not hair dryers were in use in those days. If they were, we didn't use them in our ritual. We couldn't afford them, and we didn't need them. Mama would turn up the oven (even on hot summer days), and in less than an hour our hair dried naturally. Only Mama, however, would decide when it was "good and dry." She would run her hands, never roughly, through our hair, checking for wet areas and combing with a large-toothed rubber comb bought at the five-and-dime.

When it was dry to her satisfaction, Mama would sit in a straight-backed kitchen chair dangerously close to the stove. On a blue flame, she placed a metal fine-toothed comb also bought at the five-and-dime. In the middle of the stove, where there were no flames, she placed a wet heavy towel. Sitting on the floor between her legs — one at a time, of course — my sister and I could not see Mama at work, but we knew exactly what she was doing. When the comb was hot, she removed it from the flame, rubbed it several times on the wet towel, and began to straighten our hair.

"Hold your ear," she would tell us. And we would bend our ear toward our face to protect it from the hot metal. If she accidentally burned us (Mama was not a professional beautician), we would scream out in pain. Mama would say: "Beauty suffers."

I welcomed the suffering because I wanted to be "beauti-ful" and that required straightened hair. I was proud that my hair was not too kinky and even bragged about its shoulder length. Even had the nerve to sling it around and, in the presence of would-be boyfriends, twirl it around my fingers. And yes, I thought I was rather cute in the greasy hair that looked good in pigtails in elementary school, in a ponytail in high school, and in stylish curls in college. I have not always worn an Afro.

Interestingly, my preoccupation with straightened hair did not include a preoccupation with the color, features, and eyes that were supposed to come with it. I did not want to look like white women, and I certainly did not want to emu-late their behavior and their speech. They were "Miss Ann" or "Miss Scarlet," and we considered them immodest, pam-pered, and weak women who could not cast their own shadow on the earth. They were appendages to white men. Dependent and shallow. Without courage. Without ideas. But their straight hair, that we wanted and needed in order to be beautiful.

When I look back on the experiences and the people who were responsible for my giving up the metal straightening comb and, later, scalp-burning chemicals, for a pick — a simple, inexpensive and easy-to-clean pick — I think imme-diately of the civil rights movement and the women and men, blacks and whites, who risked their lives for change. But they only made possible that which was started long before I met them. I would never have joined the movement and, therefore, never have changed my hair had it not been for my family. Let me explain.

I attribute my involvement in the movement to a family ritual that had nothing to do with hair. It was a ritual of sharing, of discussing anything and everything (even sex)

with passion, of debating anything and everything (even religion) with conviction, and of dramatizing the most routine
experiences as if they were extraordinary. They were gifted
storytellers, my family, and all of them enjoyed center stage
in the ritual of "holding forth." But my grandmother Nola
was the most gifted of them all.

She claimed Washington, D.C., as her place of birth, but
she was actually born in Shaw, Mississippi, in 1900. The first
thirteen years of her life were eventful ones in black American history. When my grandmother was three, Du Bois published *The Souls of Black Folk*. When she was nine, the
NAACP was founded. When she was eleven, W. C. Handy
wrote "Memphis Blues," which made him famous in the city
she called home. And when she was thirteen, Harriet Tubman died. I saw my grandmother as the Tubman in my
family.

I was in awe of her formidable memory. She could recall
details of events in her life like the time of day, the temperature, who wasn't there, exactly where she was standing, who
was wearing what, and even aromas. The details fascinated
me, and the passion riveted me to my chair as I listened to
stories I had heard more than once and wanted to hear again.
And again. Grandmama was doing more than telling stories;
she was reliving a painful past, bleeding herself for healing.

Many of her stories began, "Don't tell me about mean
white folks." The story I remember her retelling most frequently was about her train ride from Chicago back to Memphis. I think this one stayed at the front of her psyche because it was associated with a major event in her life. She
was returning home after spending a week with a brother
she had not seen since he had left home as a young teenager.

She was riding the Illinois Central. Seated comfortably in

the Jim Crow car. Everything was fine, she said, until the train crossed the Mason Dixon line.

"That train stopped. Just stopped. All of a sudden. And these two ugly white men got on the train and pulled a colored man off. Nobody said nothing. The train started up all a sudden and that poor colored man was just laying on the grass. Dying in his own blood."

She always ended each telling of that story with the way she began it: "Don't tell me about white folks."

Grandmother had seen so much racial violence in her younger days that she became one of those "bad colored women," the kind so angry that they are crazy enough to be crazy around white folks. That was my grandmother. A formidable opponent when she chose to be. I was with her the day a white clerk called her nigger in the downtown Woolworth's, an identity visible only because I was with her. She reached for a hammer that was lying on the counter and brandished it. "I'll bash your head in, *woman*," she said. "Do you hear me. I'll bash your head in." God but she was beautifully tough.

On the day that stands out most vividly in my memory, she was with me downtown at Goldsmith's shopping in preparation for Easter. I was perhaps seven. Then black people could not drink from water fountains except those in the basement (where the water was never cool), nor use restrooms except those in the basement (where there were no doors to the stalls). And we could not try on hats. The grease used to straighten our hair would soil the merchandise, they claimed.

On this day, Grandmama and I were on the third floor. She was busy studying dresses. I use "studying" for a reason: she would look closely at how the dresses were put together, fingering every seam and looking, with gifted eyes, at every stitch. Then she would return home to recreate that which she had studied. She would place newspaper on the kitchen table and cut pattern pieces from memory, free hand. She would pin the pieces to fabric, also placed on the kitchen table, and cut them with perfection. I remember her sitting for hours working the treadle on the old machine that sat to the right of the kitchen door. She would not move until she had finished, all except for the hem, an enviable copy of the original.

Whenever I shopped with her, I would have time to be mischievous because she was busy "studying." That is what happened on the day of the incident. She was busy, and I was mischievous. I put on a pretty pink bonnet. Immediately, the white saleslady jerked it off my head and called to my grandmother: "You know better'n let this nigger put on a hat in this store." Within seconds, my grandmother went into action. She ordered me to put the bonnet on again. With tightened lips, she told the saleslady, "Now touch it. Just you touch it."

Perhaps it was my grandmother's near-white complexion (she often passed when doing so benefited her family) or the intensity of her rage that froze the saleslady in an expression of, first, surprise, and then fear. My grandmother said again, with tighter lips, "Just touch it." The saleslady did not move. I modeled the hat as my grandmother instructed. "Turn around, Gloria Jean," she told me. "Let's see." I twirled a bit. After we had tasted victory for a few minutes, my grandmother said, "Take it off. It's not pretty enough for you."

Other incidents, though not as dramatic as the bonnet experience, taught me about my family's refusal to be head-dropping, side-stepping, yassiring, submissive colored folks. I can't say that they were militants who took on the establishment. Like most black people, they observed the rules just enough to stay alive. But in small, often brave ways, they walked outside the narrow circle of humiliation for blacks expertly drawn by whites. My aunt made a point of talking loudly about the white water fountains on the upper floors of the department stores: "Who would want that water? It's poison. See those people (pointing to whites). They are gonna die from drinking that water."

My mother would not answer if white people called her by her first name, and to prevent them from knowing her name, like most black people, she signed only her initials on anything that would fall into white hands. She was, by nature, a very peaceful woman, but she once came close to striking a white man in the basement of Goldsmith's. I skipped too close to him and, in anger, he shouted to Mama: "Get that pickaninny out of my way." A black woman nearby restrained Mama, saving her from a beating which she would not have been able to protest in court.

In their own way, my family taught me racial pride that would eventually find expression in an Afro. That explains why no one in my family ever doubted that I would become one of those militants they were reading about in the newspaper. And why I was at home in the movement before it ever began. Having listened to their stories and having seen my family's example of quiet and steady resistance, I knew how to walk when I hit the pavement for freedom, and though I could not carry a tune (but I had learned from my Uncle Jack how to dance!), I knew I would sing the freedom songs passionately. They were resonant with my grandmother's spirit of defiance.

When I moved from Boston to Atlanta in 1963, I immediately joined the hundreds of thousands of blacks and whites who called themselves civil rights workers or activists. My involvement began when I participated in a demonstration at the largest white Baptist church in Atlanta located on Peachtree Street next to the historic Fox Theatre. We were protesting the very "unChristian" behavior of church ushers. A week prior to the demonstration they had thrown from the church vestibule an elderly white man, an activist, and several black students from the Atlanta University Center. *Thrown* them. The white Baptists used the "word of God" to justify segregation in the "house of the Lord."

I remember circling the church with other demonstrators, blacks and whites, as the white worshippers came out of the church, carrying Bibles bound in leather with special verses highlighted in gold. We sang church songs and carried picket signs. Nonviolently. The worshippers taunted us, their faces demonic with hatred. I expected only words from them. I did not know at first what had caused the sharp pain I suddenly felt until I saw a woman moving from me. She had thrust a long hat pin into my right buttock and walked away in her sanctimonious self-righteousness. Resisting the urge to chase her and pound her with my fists (as my grandmother would have done) was my first test in nonviolence.

I passed it, and many others, over the coming months, choosing symbolic incarceration over violent resistance. I was to know arrests many times. My first arrest occurred in 1963 when I was a new instructor at Spelman college and, because of my CORE experiences, somewhat familiar with movement activism.

Spirit was high, genuine, and infectious in the Atlanta University Center. We held rallies in front of Trevor Arnett, the old library, and at Rush Congregational Church, a block away from the library. The Student Nonviolent Coordinat-

ing Committee (SNCC) headquarters were located in a small
frame house on what was then Chestnut Street, but is now
James T. Brawley. It was approximately ten blocks from the
library and fifteen blocks from Spelman's front gate. Activists would work there all day, especially on Saturdays, and
late into the night seven days a week. We would take lunch
breaks at Paschals, which at that time was one of a few decent eating places for blacks in Atlanta. Others were located
on Auburn Avenue, which was a good distance from our
headquarters. In 1968, it would become the street that symbolized the Movement. Both Ebenezer Baptist Church, from
which Dr. Martin Luther King, Jr., delivered his famous
"Drum Major for Justice" sermon, and his tomb are located
on Auburn Avenue.

We organized, strategized, and demonstrated during the
entire school year. By the hundreds, we marched from
Trevor Arnett to Rich's department store on Broad Street to
protest the ubiquitous signs within that identified this place
as "colored" and that place as "white" and to protest discrimination in hiring. Rich's was a symbol of all that was
racially wrong in white Atlanta. It was within walking distance of our community and symbolically close to the statue
of Atlanta's birth from the ashes. Whites in Atlanta had not
forgotten Sherman's march and the pain of defeat in a war
that hurt slaves, they believed, more than whites.

We were engaged in a new war, without the devastation
of land and people which characterized the Civil War, but
our nonviolent troops were, in their own way, as deadly as
Sherman's soldiers. We were determined to change the city
which promoted itself as "A City Too Busy to Hate." I
marched with my hair straightened and stylishly curled.

Not until we picketed Leb's, a Jewish delicatessen located
a block south of what is now the new Fulton County Library

and directly in front of the Rialto Theatre, did the mass arrests begin. The wagons came by the dozens, and the police (all white at that time) twisted our arms, grabbed us by the legs (females knew to wear pants), jabbed us with billy clubs, and threw us into the wagons. Arrests were always dramatic, but this one was even more so because of the presence of Morris Eisenstein, a Jewish professor at the Atlanta University School of Social Work, his wife Fannie, and their two teenage daughters. The Eisenstein family was known to many students in the Atlanta University Center for their genuine support of racial equality. They were the only whites in the center (and there were more than a few on the faculty) whose children were enrolled in public schools in the black community. When they appeared, we knew they were there not as spectators, but as participants. That was the first time, and perhaps the only time, during the Atlanta movement that an entire white family had chosen arrest with demonstrators rather than the protection their color gave them.

At the downtown station, we were separated into groups on the basis of sex and race, fingerprinted, mug shot, and placed behind bars. The women demonstrators were in a cell that was large and long, narrow and cold. The inmates, all women of course, greeted us with cheers, and we literally danced into the cell block, serenading them with our repertoire of freedom songs. It did not take us long to learn that we were serenading powerless and lost women. Many of them were repeat offenders; none was a hardened criminal. Many were alcoholics, some were vagrants, others were prostitutes, still others were shoplifters. A few were wounded and abused women who had fought at the wrong time and with the wrong weapon. We spent the night listening to them talk about their problems. Often they began by saying, "I'm not a bad woman. I've just had a hard time." We were the dreamers, the messengers of hope, the healing hands who could make a difference in the world and therefore a difference in their lives. We were like royalty in a place where there were no thrones.

In the middle of the night, we heard the screams of one of the young high school demonstrators. While the girl slept, an inmate all of forty years old attempted to fondle her and kiss her. Of course we rallied around our sister demonstrator and confronted the inmate. Not violently, however, for in all things and in all situations we were nonviolent and understanding. We believed in the power of redemptive love. We wanted to know why. The woman talked tearfully about her loneliness, her love for her man and for her children. Physical relationships with other women inmates, she explained, was all she had in the cellblock. She didn't mean any harm. No harm at all. We stayed awake the rest of the night counseling, talking, singing, praying, and watching.

Demonstrations were cruel to my hair. They always made me perspire. Sweat. Because the sun was hot. Because my emotions were high. Because I was moving, expending energy, up and down, back and forth, on picket lines. Incarceration was even crueler because, out of fear, I perspired more. When I was released from jail the next morning, my hair really looked awful. It needed to be "fixed." Once back on Chestnut Street, I went around the corner to a beauty shop.

There were many arrests, but I remember one most vividly because it was so different from any other experience I had in Atlanta. I was placed in solitary confinement with a tenth-grade girl from Washington High School. Without my grandmother's phenomenal memory, I don't remember why the girl and I were in solitary confinement. Perhaps, like my grandmother, I had been smart-mouthed and so had the young girl. Perhaps there were so many demonstrators that the two of us had to be placed in the only space left — solitary — and fate chose us. Whatever the reason, I remember being with her in a concrete cell a little larger than a stall in a public toilet, leaving it only to relieve ourselves. A very bright light burned constantly, keeping us awake and hot, and large roaches, with ominously long antennae and long hairy legs, moved about as if it were their home. The cell was near an area that white male prisoners (the jails were segregated) passed on their way to work or the mess hall. The men peeped in at us and called us obscene names. In explicit terms, they told us what they'd like to do to us, with us and, in what Zora Neale Hurston calls the illusion of male irresistibility, what they'd like to do *for* us.

On the second night (I learned later that we had been in solitary for two whole days), we were awakened in the early morning hours and loaded like cattle into police vans protected by a ferocious German Shepherd large enough to be a pony on its way fast to becoming a stallion. He barked at us from behind a screen that seemed too fragile to hold him. The ride took forever. The road was rough, the night was dark, and the dog never stopped barking. Worse, we had no idea of our destination.

When we arrived at the workhouse somewhere in the county, we were relieved. Lights and four walls are always safer than dark roads and ferocious dogs. I remember two things about this experience: I was cold most of the time and I worked in a huge kitchen, along with other women, preparing food for inmates. I also remember the obscenity of white jailers. In their eyes we were sexually talented because we were black and should be sexually available because we were black. I recalled stories my grandmother had told me about black women sleeping with white men, some of them by choice and many by force. I wanted her near me to give the white jailers "a piece of her mind." She could do it, I thought to myself. I was the coward, following orders and sleeping with fear.

Two days later, untouched by the white jailers, I was released along with my fellow demonstrators. The cold I had experienced in the workhouse lingered. I felt chilled. Sick. I wondered if I would ever again be warm. Demonstrations were suspended for a few days while our attorneys worked on legal matters. I was, quite frankly, relieved. This arrest had taken its toll on my body. And on my hair. It must have been the net and on top of that the bluish-green hats I had to wear in the kitchen that wreaked havoc with my hair. In two days, my hair had perspired more than it had in a month. The ends were frayed. The edges and the "kitchens" (our word for the back hairline) were turning back. Losing their straightness. I went to the beauty salon for a touch-up.

The demonstrations resumed, moving like an uncontrollable river throughout the city. Atlanta, cultured by southern standards, was receiving the "bad press" once reserved for well-known bad cities in Mississippi and Alabama. Faculty at the black colleges who were tampering with Atlanta's image risked losing their jobs. At the end of the school year, I was fired at Spelman. The Eisensteins were fired at Atlanta University. Other faculty, among them Vincent Harding, Howard Zinn, and Staughton Lynd, were either fired or, of their own volition, left the Center.

When the Confederation of Freedom Organizations (COFO) announced what some called "a nonviolent invasion" of the state of Mississippi, I signed on without hesitation. Shortly after Spelman's commencement, I drove my little Volkswagen bug (I think it was green in color) from Memphis, where I bid farewell to my family, to Chicago, where I visited my sister, and on to the University of Miami, in Ohio, where I joined hundreds of volunteers for a week-long training program in nonviolence. During the day, we were kept busy in workshops that examined everything from the power of redemptive love to the corrosive nature of anger; the difference between hating an illness and hating people; the importance of understanding that whites, too, were afflicted by the illness: "And so you must pity them and love them."

At night, we testified and sang, our tears flowing easily. If there were any among us who had signed on because of the drama associated with the movement, by the third day of workshops, we were forced to see the face of danger: CORE activists Chaney and Schwerner and SNCC volunteer Goodman, who were working in Philadelphia, Mississippi, had mysteriously disappeared. Everyone feared the worst. Tears flowed easily, even for men. I have heard that not all of the participants remained true to the words of one of our favorite songs: "Ain't gonna let-a nobody turn me round." Some of them left Ohio for the safety of their own communities.

On the night before our descent into the bowels of Mississippi, I wrote letters to everyone — my family, old friends, new friends, passing acquaintances, my favorite elementary school teachers . . . I did not want to forget anyone because I was not sure I would return from Mississippi alive.

Our chartered Trailways Bus pulled into Memphis for what we thought was a rest stop. The driver announced that the bus was going no farther. "But you were paid to take us to Mississippi," we screamed. It didn't matter. Trailways had decided not to cross the line from Tennessee into Mississippi. Even white people who were not particularly sympathetic to the cause feared a bloodbath.

There we were. Stranded. Without a plan. Someone began to sing, loudly and emphatically, "Ain't gonna let Mr. Trailways turn me round. Turn me round. Turn me round." All of us began singing: "I'm gonna' keep on singing. Keep on praying. Marching on to Freedom Land." Nobody was going to prevent us from reaching our destination. We were expected in Mississippi. New "recruits." Needed reinforcements. We *had* to get there. The word was passed among us that we would go by train.

Every group that left the Miami training program was given a small amount of cash for emergencies, and individual volunteers had money of their own. Clearly, this was an emergency, and Memphis was the best place for the proposed solution. It was what was called in my youth a "depot town" because of its large terminal and heavy rail traffic. I knew the terminal intimately.

I was never a leader in the movement. Women weren't. But outside the bus depot in Memphis, I wielded some influence. I knew where the train terminal was located, and I knew who could transport us there. My mother and my uncles. I called them, and they organized a carpool. Between the few taxis that dared get involved and my Memphis friends, in one trip after another, we made it to the train terminal.

I was never prouder of my mother than I was that night. She was rich in beauty. The fear in her eyes when she first saw me surrendered without struggle to pride. Mama had stood many times on the very platform on which the volunteers gathered when she waved goodbye to my sister and me as we boarded the Illinois Central bound for Chicago. This time, my sister was not with me. I was not headed north for fun and joy with my father. With a group of people who were total strangers to Mama and new acquaintances to me, I was headed south to the Mississippi of my mother's birth and my grandmother's painful memories.

"I'm not going to tell you what to do and what not to do," Mama said. "You're a woman now. And you are serious about what you are doing." There were no tears. Visible. She embraced me and said, "Just be careful, baby. Just be careful." I could see her lips saying, "I love you," as the train pulled out of the terminal. I was wearing my hair in a ponytail swooshed straight up from my pimpled forehead.

When we arrived in Jackson, Mississippi, I was surprised that workers at the headquarters were expecting me. A reporter from a radio station in Atlanta had called to interview me. The piece I had written about my experiences in solitary confinement in Atlanta's jails a few months prior had been published in the *Atlantic Monthly*. Atlanta was angry. I had to explain myself, as if I had not done so in the article. When I talked to the reporter I was unclear, dispassionate, distant, cold, tired. I was unaware that the reporter was taping our conversation. He never told me he was, and I was too naive to think to ask. Only later — in fact, at the end of the Mississippi Summer — did I learn that the station had publicized the interview early that morning, and many people in Atlanta had tuned in. How the station knew when I would arrive in Jackson and where I would go upon my arrival remains, to this day, a mystery.

Thirty years later, I wear the scars of that experience: I have a phobia about talking to the press. I never should have done so in Jackson. I was not interested in the interview because I was not interested in what had happened in Atlanta. I was interested in what was going to happen in Mississippi. Change. And I was eager to get my assignment. It was in Valley View, a small rural area about thirty miles or more north of Jackson. Canton was the closest town, but it was a "one-hoss town," we were told, with mean white folks.

The trip from Canton to Valley View was singularly un-impressive. The road was narrow and dusty, sometimes straight and sometimes winding, moving past open fields, a trio of lean cows, now and then a mule, clotheslines propped at a slant, and frame houses that looked uninhabited. In our arrogance, we decided the area was sorely in need of change.

When we reached Valley View, I discovered the sky over-head. Clearer than any I had ever seen. Nothing disturbed our view of its expansive beauty because there was nothing in Valley View except trees reaching gracefully upward from dry, flat land.

As our caravan approached the small church, I could see the welcome committee, men and women from the commu-nity, many of whom had agreed to let us live with them, in spite of the danger. Some of them shook our hands stiffly, many embraced us as if we were old friends returning home, and a few praised the Lord for our arrival. In the midst of this warm celebration, the police arrived. The guns on their hips looked like small cannons to me. They had orders to take us downtown for fingerprinting.

I remember riding in the back seat of a police car with three other women. I remember my fears. Rape. A beating. Death. I remember my rage. They undressed us with vile language. Remembering the "don'ts" from my early days in Memphis and the sermons on redemptive love from the non-violent workshop prevented me from responding to them in any way. I confess, however, I failed at pitying them and loving them seemed utterly ridiculous.

After driving up and down dusty roads, in circles, they

reached the local jail, a brick building only slightly larger than the restroom in the train terminal in Memphis. They fingerprinted us, made photo IDs, and threatened us with violence. But they released us unharmed.

Activists in overalls, the standard uniform of the civil rights movement, drove volunteers to the families with whom we would be living. Along with Madeline Levine and her husband Steve, who were studying slavic languages and Asian studies, respectively, at Radcliffe and Harvard, I was driven to the home of the McKinneys. Reverend and Mrs. McKinney. It was a three-bedroom white frame house set back from the road. Alone.

The McKinneys were people of few words. I felt dwarfed by their courage. They had lived in Valley View all of their lives, and they knew the risks they were taking by opening their home to civil rights activists. Race mixing was all but a federal crime in the eyes of white Mississippians. People like the McKinneys never made national headlines during Mississippi Summer. Cameras focused on activists, mainly on white activists, whom evening news anchors considered the heroes of the movement. The McKinneys were the real heroes. And like real heroes, they wanted and expected no praise for their courage.

After we settled in, they went on with their lives as if this were not the first time they had dared challenge the system. And it probably wasn't. That is what the movement forgot. It probably wasn't.

At five in the morning, we would awake to the aroma of a breakfast that, in my family, would have been dinner: pork chops or fried chicken, grits or rice, homemade biscuits and gravy, sometimes peas, and always milk. Rev. McKinney would eat in silence and leave the house in silence to work in the fields. Mrs. McKinney was the talker in the family. She stayed home cooking, cleaning house, doing laundry, and feeding the chickens. She looked larger than her size when she threw feed to small fragile chickens who dominated the dusty backyard. How she loved those chickens. She talked to them with affection. And to those she had chosen for dinner, or for breakfast, she clucked in the right tones, enticing them to come closer and closer. She grabbed them with a quick hand. More than once I saw her pull to her bosom a chicken she had loved, but would sacrifice for a meal. She struck me as neither happy nor unhappy. Just suspended. A woman of energy and quiet courage whose life was dominated by routine and loneliness. At breakfast and at dinner, we enjoyed her laughter, though I can't remember what she laughed about.

She was in her late fifties or early sixties. Rev. McKinney appeared to be in his late seventies or early eighties. She was tall and stout. He was short and thin. He moved slowly, but with deliberation, exhibiting the tenacity that had made him, I thought to myself, a "firebrand" militant in his younger years. I respected him and Mrs. McKinney as soon as I met them. I admired them when they responded with courage to the Ku Klux Klan. I remember the evening clearly. We heard cars speeding past the house and within minutes we could smell burning wood. Only in movies at the Georgia Theatre had I seen a burning cross. I was frozen in fear. Mrs. McKinney was calm, but angry. Rev. McKinney went into action. He went into a closet in their bedroom and emerged with a long rifle. It looked old enough to have been used in the Civil War. He opened the front door and fired two shots into the lighted darkness. Later that night, calmer and more secure, I could not conceal my laughter. Rev.

McKinney's rifle made the sound of a cork popping from an under-fizzed bottle of champagne. It was his courage that I heard exploding.

Our schedule was as routine as the McKinneys'. Immediately after breakfast, we went to work, teaching in the freedom schools and registering voters throughout the valley. In the evenings we attended meetings. When we returned home to the McKinneys in the evenings, usually before sunset, we were often physically exhausted, emotionally drained, and frustrated. We could not see our own handiwork, and we began to miss the comforts of our former lives.

One volunteer, a frail white man from somewhere up north, had a nervous breakdown as evidenced by his thunderous banging on the McKinney's door before dawn one morning. He was delivering a puppy I had adopted for the group. I don't know now why the cute puppy was not at the McKinney's. My memory fails me, but not about his behavior. He told me that he could not sleep because of the dog's whining. He began to bark and yelp like the dog. Over and over, he barked. I do not remember seeing him during the remainder of the summer.

Another volunteer, a student at Morehouse College, fancied himself in love with me and more than once proposed. Mississippi was getting to all of us. Although I was only three or four years older than many of the student demonstrators, I was, after all, their "teacher," so a romantic alliance with any of them was unthinkable. That didn't matter to this young man. He was feverishly infatuated with me and always in hot pursuit. He was frail and suffered from frequent and severe asthma attacks. And he was petrified of the Klan. I remember the night he went alone to the outhouse a short distance from headquarters. While inside, he heard the sound of screeching tires, always a sign of danger. We laughed, all of us, but only later, about the sight of this young man running fast toward the open back door with his pants down.

We were not without play during the summer. Some of the volunteers entertained themselves with baseball games, swimming in clear ponds, playing cards, debating politics, and engaging in casual sex. I entertained myself by spending funny moments with my roommates, Madeline and Steve; writing letters to family and friends; daydreaming about a new South; and watching birds. Do not laugh: Mississippi is a wonderful place in which to become a bird-watcher.

I remember watching birds in the pasture behind the McKinney's house, but after stepping in cow dung (which was everywhere and sometimes blended into the earth), I went to the pasture to study the slow, awkward movement of the McKinney's cows. Bovine had new meaning for me when I was in Valley View. Cows are such peaceful animals. I saw them up close for the first time. I would later identify with a character in Alice Walker's *Meridian* who could not eat beef because cows have such serene and beautiful eyes.

It was an unusual summer — productive, frightening, educational, and humbling. The people of Valley View were loving, trusting, and courageous. We were there to change their world, and I suppose in many ways we did. But they were left behind not only to enjoy the benefits, but also to suffer the consequences of our short stay. Some of them lost their jobs in nearby Canton, lost their farms, lost their credit, and were harassed in many ways. They were the heroes of the COFO Project, not the here-today-gone-tomorrow activists.

Mississippi Summer ended in late August when most of the activists, blacks and whites, left the South, promising to continue the struggle in their own cities. I went home to Memphis to recuperate before leaving for Washington, D.C.,

to begin teaching at Howard University. Mississippi dust
had claimed every strand of my hair, and the Mississippi sun
had made every strand brittle. On my second day home, I
washed my hair in the deep kitchen sink. I did not need
Mama's straightening comb and curling irons, however. Years
earlier I had begun using perms that straightened my hair
with chemicals rather than with heated metal.

I can see the road stretching out before me and myself
with straight hair driving once again my trusty VW bug. I
was thirsty. I stopped at a drive-in restaurant in a small town
in North Carolina, for a simple hamburger and a vanilla
milkshake. Behind a screen, a white woman told me to leave.
I told her that I did not have to leave. She was required by
law to serve me. This was not the first time I had heard tires
screeching, moving fast and angrily to arrest me, but this was
the first time I was alone. And I had become impatient. Angry. Less tolerant than I had been earlier in the movement.

Two burly white policemen rushed toward me wearing
badges that were grotesquely large and shiny. They twisted
my arms behind my back, handcuffed me, and threw me into
their car. "If you say one smart thing," one of them said, "I'll
slap the black shit out of you."

The coward in me wished I had stayed in my "place." Did
I really need the hamburger and milkshake? Why had I forgotten how very alone I was? This was the kind of senseless
defiance adults warned us against. Defiance that we think
gives us dignity, but claims our lives. I had been impulsive.
Hot-headed. Irrational. I knew I would be raped by both of
them, and then killed. I prayed that I would faint before they
touched me.

I was relieved when we arrived at the county jail, a concrete square building sitting isolated in a clearing. A jail
never looked so good. The police pulled me roughly from the

car, pushed me in the stomach with a club, and slapped my face. I asked for the right to make a phone call. I was denied.

I was placed in a cell with a strange woman whose appearance and penetrating eyes frightened me. She was a dark-skinned black woman. Large. Silent. She stared at me and said nothing. Just stared. I was afraid and physically uncomfortable because my bladder was about to explode. Using the toilet was a problem because it was in full view of the jailer, an old white man, who walked up and down the long hall, up and down, down and up, peering in. What would be worse: to pull up my dress and relieve myself in his presence, or sleep the night in wet clothes?

Concentrating on making my bladder double its size exhausted me. I fell asleep. When I opened my eyes, the woman was staring at me. She began to talk.

"You scared, ain't you?"

"Oh, not of you," I said. "Just the jailer."

"I ain't gone hurt you," she said.

"Oh, I never thought you were," I answered.

She knew I was lying. Her voice was like gravel. Her hands were calloused. Her hair was plaited in small short braids, so thick that Mama's old rubber, large-toothed comb would have been of little help. My hair, permed straight and styled attractively, began to crawl. I had the strange feeling that a hundred small bugs had invaded my hair and begun marching zigzag, in circles, and in straight lines on my scalp. I realized that I was ashamed of my hair. Ashamed that I had altered it. Ashamed because it was too neat and "pretty" for that place and so very different from her hair.

"Why you in here?" she asked. "You kill somebody? Your boyfriend?"

I told her about the movement. She told me about herself. She had murdered her husband because he had beaten her one time too many. In self-defense, she killed him with a large kitchen knife. A "butcher knife," people in the project called it. She was not distraught over her incarceration. She was grateful to be alive.

My efforts to tell her that she had a right to a new trial, that things were different, that people outside could help her, were pointless. She had no reason to believe that her situation could be otherwise. Her world was the world I had begun to believe would forever resist change.

We became friends. She watched for me when I used the toilet. She never waited for me to watch for her. Hours would pass without our talking to each other, and during those hours she entertained herself by jumping from bed to bed with the skill of a stunt woman. Sometimes she sat on the edge of a bed, always a top bunk, staring into space. Her eyes were incredibly white and clear, and always sad.

She had remained sane because she was convinced of her innocence. She had murdered, but she was not a murderer. What else was she to do? He attempted to kill her; she saved her own life. She remained sane also because she had a sense of humor. She did not have my grandmother's talent for telling stories with details, but she was able to paint pictures for me, using vivid language. She told me about a place — either she worked there or lived there — where the chickens almost took over. I can hear her now, saying in her gravel voice, "Chicken shit was everywhere."

I came to see her as a gentle woman and an attractive woman with unblemished skin and a perfectly round face. Her laughter was deep and musical, like a bass singing a capella. She seemed to like the sound of her voice and to take pleasure in her humor. She was hungry for an ear, a shoulder, a smile, a warm voice. I gave her all of that, and more. I was her company. She was my protection. I wondered who had ever loved her and had she ever loved herself? I multiplied her by thousands and realized how tragic was the plight of poor black women in this country.

When I was released four days later, I cried. She did not. I told her that I would work on the outside for her release. She only smiled with her sad eyes. "You be good to yourself" was all she said.

I could never be the same again. Nor could my hair. A metal comb placed on an open flame, heated, and then pulled through my hair suddenly seemed utterly ridiculous. A chemical packed into hair and burning my scalp. That, too, seemed utterly ridiculous. Straightened hair became a weight pulling my head down when I wanted to hold it up. High. I remembered that some of the women in Mississippi (one a student at Spelman who joined a group which would later become "Sweet Honey in the Rock") had worn Afros in Valley View. I was ashamed that I had not followed their example. An Afro would have said more to my cellmate in North Carolina than all of my well-chosen words about the movement.

An activist with straightened hair was a contradiction. A lie. A joke, really. The right to tout the movement gospel of self-esteem carried with it the obligation to accept and love one's self naturally. Our appearance had to speak the truth before our lips stretched to sing the songs. Never again, I decided, would I alter my hair. In its natural state, my hair would be a badge, a symbol of my self-esteem and racial pride. An act of genuine bonding with black women who were incarcerated in jails all across America and those who were in psychological jails, accepting less from everyone because they believed they deserved less than anyone. I decided to wear an Afro.

I had long ago physically grown the deep kitchen sink and the five-and-dime straightening combs. Finally, I had psychologically outgrown the need to hide my natural beauty. I cut my hair, washed it, picked it, and let it dry naturally. I called my mother and grandmother to give them the news. Having taught me in their stories and their quiet courage about pride and struggle, they responded as I knew they would: "We are not surprised."

Choosing Motherhood and Pro-Choice

Inside, it was the size of a cockpit. Cramped. Barely large enough for the two of us. We would climb in and scoot down into the small bucket seats. Belts snapped. Rear view mirror adjusted. Shades on. Joe turned the key in the ignition, and our little red Triumph convertible responded. Zroom. With the top down, we owned the sky, the wind, our world. Just the two of us. No debts. No encumbrances of any kind.

During the week, we enjoyed each other in a modest frame house that sat in the hills of San Jose where the sun made Joe's roses the envy of the neighborhood. And on the weekends we sampled different delectables in California's smorgasbord of excitement and adventure. Our little red Triumph flirted with the highway, hugging it sensuously, when we traveled to San Francisco, our favorite city, where we saw the opera, visited our friends the LaMars, ate in Chinatown, or watched with fascination the ritual dances of free-spirited people. I thought the city was the eighth wonder of the world with its waterfronts and parks and galleries and theatres, and hills so steep that at night street lights met heaven's stars, forming new constellations.

In a different mood, we traveled to Sacramento, carefully toning down the little Triumph's flirtatious personality. We drove in silence out of respect for the snow that had fallen in silence, or the roads which ran dangerously, but directly, to a wonderland of mountains I would never see in the South. The mountains moved me to sweet rememberings of our courtship in D.C. in 1966. There was so much about him I loved. His voice. Mellifluous, a deep bass chiming. His laughter. Throaty. His wit. Dry and humorous. His conversation. Engaging. His mind. At twenty-five he had earned a Ph.D. in chemistry from Brown University. And his hands. Slender and sensuous. He was fascinating and intriguing, entertaining and serious, charming and suave, urbane and yet earthy. Captivating. In August of 1967 I said good-bye to graduate school and the East Coast. Joe and I married and began our life together in San Jose.

I remember sitting on the deck of the ski lodge above Sacramento. From there I watched backs painted in bright colors dangle long wooden legs from swinging chairs. I wanted to ride the chairs to the higher elevations Joe was negotiating with skill and style. We were happy. Just the two of us and our little red convertible. But we wanted to add a dimension to our joy. We wanted a child.

My pregnancy was uneventful, but not without worry. My grandmother had been paralyzed for a year following the birth of her second child. Was that hereditary? My mother's first child, though born healthy, had died at the age of two months while sleeping in his crib. Was that hereditary?

And what about labor pains and delivery pains? Would I be able to endure them? Mama said that they are the "worst pain imaginable," but you forget them as soon as you hear the baby's cry. I was lucky, I thought often to myself. My baby would be born in a hospital where attending nurses and physicians would administer injections for pain. My mother was not as lucky. When I think about what poor black women went through to give life years ago—and my God, don't let me think about slave women—I wonder why our communities are not decorated with shrines bearing their likeness.

Stories of how I was born were among the favorites I would request of the women in my family. Newspapers. They always began the stories with newspapers.

Months before the due date, family members would begin collecting newspapers and old sheets. They would stack the newspapers in a special place in the house. They would tear the sheets into pieces large enough to be pads. They would boil the pads for hours in a large metal bucket that dominated all the eyes on the old stove. Sterilized, the pads would be stored in a dry place, away from dust and unsanitary hands.

The newspapers I still do not understand, and so I ask my aunt, "Newspapers? Why newspapers?"

She does not understand either. She was young when the practice was common. We garner a guess. Perhaps the newspapers were put under the sheet to soak up the blood in order to protect the mattress. Perhaps they were needed for the afterbirth. Perhaps collecting them was a way of making the delivery a communal experience.

"Did you give Miss Reese any newspapers?" neighbors would ask one another.

"Just came by to drop off some newspapers for the delivery," a friend would say, stepping inside just long enough to make her contribution.

Perhaps it was a way of finding out who was considered

important in the community. "Girl, you should have seen Jennie's house when that baby was born. Newspapers were everywhere." After a funeral, you knew how people felt about your family. A few pies, you weren't liked very much. Many pies and rolls and potato salad and mounds of fried chicken, you were in very good standing with your neighbors and friends.

Perhaps that's how it was with newspapers. A test of your standing. A short stack meant, obviously, that you had a great deal of work yet to do to establish yourself in the community. My aunt remembers that newspapers were stacked almost to the ceiling in the room in which Mama and Daddy slept. The room in which I was born.

She remembers the white doctor who arrived as Mama was giving uterine cries that mean the baby is almost there. She tended the boiling water in the kitchen while the doctor, Grandmama, and Daddy worked behind closed doors with Mama.

"Bertha had a real hard time delivering you," my aunt tells me. I feel guilty.

She adds, "But she was shouting halleleujahs when she saw you."

As the months approach, I think not about Mama, but about my sister Faye. In the hospital that had an affiliation of some kind with the University of Chicago, she had everything Mama did not have, and yet her experiences were far more painful. The pain was unbearable, and she screamed continuously, calling Mama's name. The attending nurse hit her on the thighs with scissors and said disdainfully, "You didn't scream for your mama when you got this baby, so don't call for her now." Faye was doubly humiliated because the nurse was white.

Further into the pregnancy, I forgot about the horrors of

delivery and concentrated on the joy of becoming a mother. I carried the baby low and large. I remember that the pressure on my bladder made season's tickets at the opera wasteful. Every fifteen minutes, I was going to the ladies' room for a trickle that relieved the pressure only momentarily. I remember that my stomach became large, the skin tight and glassy smooth sooner than I expected. It was hard like a rock. A mountain rising from the middle of me which the baby was negotiating. Joe and I would lie on our backs and watch the miracle of life moving inside me, sometimes slowly in a circle and other times with quick thrusts. As the months passed, we were able to distinguish between tiny feet and tiny elbows. We were ecstatic, in love, together, and truly blessed.

When my water broke, we remained calm. I grabbed the small suitcase that had been packed for weeks and Joe, the keys to the little red Triumph. It was in August, the eighth to be exact, but we rode with the top up. After a near accident, we drove in scared silence to the hospital where my obstetrician, who should have been named after a tall tree, was waiting for me.

A quick and painless injection at the base of the spine removed all sensation. The body the nurse prepared for surgery belonged to someone else, and yet I could see that it was attached to me. It followed me from the labor room onto the narrow stretcher, into delivery, and onto the surgical bed. Its legs, not mine, were placed in the metal stirrups. I did not like the feeling that having no feeling gave me. I vowed "Never again" until I saw the head in the overhead mirror and heard Joe talking to me through the intercom from outside the delivery room. The baby moved out of me, turned on its own power and fell into the doctor's waiting hands.

"You have a baby boy," the doctor told Joe through the intercom. "And he's white."

Many black babies are born with little color, but the melanin is there. It comes later, at the same time that the silky birth curls develop texture. Neither Joe nor I echoed the laughter. The doctor realized it was a bad joke badly timed. He began praising me and describing our son. "Long. Healthy. With a head of black curls."

Painlessly, I had delivered our first child on August 8, 1968. We named him appropriately: Jonathan, which is a Biblical version of his father's name, Joseph Nathan. And Ifeanji-Chukw, which not only embraced our African ancestry, but also expressed our sympathy for those slaughtered in the Biafran War then raging in Nigeria. It means, "Nothing is beyond the power of God." Our love conceived him, and God's love brought him into life.

Within six months, I conceived again, by choice. Six months later, we were planning to leave California. Rearing children requires a community of people who know your songs and share your memories. In the white world of San Jose, with the exception of our friends the Harrises and the Hudsons, few people knew our songs and many found our memories interesting cultural artifacts. In 1969 we made the trip to Atlanta, where both of us would be teaching in the Atlanta University Center. I flew with the baby. Joe drove, enjoying what would be his last long-distance trip in the little red Triumph which we had outgrown.

Remembering the strange feeling of carrying someone else's legs, I chose to have the second child by natural birth. But I confess, there was more involved in this decision than the wooden legs. Women were becoming interested in natural birth, and medical research was beginning to give evidence of residual and harmful effects of injections to the spine. But mainly, there was my desire to empower myself, to be in charge when the child was born.

"No medications, please," I told the attending nurse in the delivery room. "I'm having natural birth." Had she bothered to ask me how many Lamaze classes I had attended, she would have heard my frightened answer: "None."

I remember the sharp labor pains that almost split me in two and my resolve to deliver with my own power. I was not breathing properly and, as a result, the pain became more severe. I muffled screams in my pillow.

The nurse, who could not have been more surly or less sympathetic, reprimanded me. "You can't do this without some kind of medicine."

They wheeled me into the delivery room. I saw only nurses. "Where is my doctor?" I asked between gasps.

"He's on his way," the nurse said, "and as soon as he comes, he's going to give you something for your pain."

The doctor was even less sympathetic than the nurse. He stood over me, putting gloves on with, I thought, a rough movement. He would years later work with Joe and others in the founding of the Morehouse School of Medicine, but at the time he was a total stranger. I had seen him only in passing at the office he shared as an associate with my physician who, as fate would have it for a woman delivering naturally without knowledge of how to deliver naturally, was not on call.

"I want to give you medication," he said in a matter-of-fact voice.

"I . . . I don't . . . want . . . anything."

"But you need something," he said struggling with his anger.

I managed to get the sentence out without gasping. "No. I want to have a natural delivery."

I remember his words: "What are you trying to prove?"

Had I not been like a turtle on my back, locked into stirrups, and had I not been at his mercy, I would have told him
about his attitude. How dare he suggest that I was trying to
prove anything. Why couldn't I decide how I was going to
have my baby? Who gave him the right? He only *delivered*
babies. He couldn't conceive them or birth them. And, besides, I would have told him, I can do this without your help.
Maybe I should have considered a midwife. But I couldn't
speak because of the pain which moved like a sharp knife
from the tip of my vagina to the top of my head.

"They will get worse," he said. "I'm telling you. They will
get worse."

I was resolute.

"Have it your way," he said, abandoning me. "But I'm
telling you. The pain will get worse."

He was right. My screams reverberated through the delivery wing of the hospital. Calmly, the doctor told me to push.
With his hands folded, he stood over me in seeming disinter-
est of what was happening below.

"Push," he said again. "You're doing this on your own, so
go ahead and push."

The pains became more severe and my screams, louder.
Joe, hearing them and fearing for my life, bolted through the
door of the delivery room. In street clothes no less.

"What are you doing to her?" I heard him say in his deep
bass voice. I could not see him, but I found comfort in his
presence.

I heard the nurse shouting, "Get out of here! Get out of
here!"

"That's my wife," Joe said angrily. "What are you doing
to her?"

The physician's voice was not as mellifluous as Joe's. "You

can't come in here," it said. "Have you lost your mind? You can contaminate your wife and your baby."

Joe's departure. Silence. Pain. Screams. I gave in.

"I've changed my mind," I screamed. "Give me something. Please. Please. Oh God, please give me something."

"It's too late," the doctor said. "Push. Push."

I saw nothing (there was no overhead mirror), but I felt everything. The body moving from my uterus to the tip of my vagina, turning, and, with a popping sound, thrusting itself out of me. I forgot the pain as soon as I heard the baby's birth cry. A girl. Monica, we named her, and Saliyeka, a Malawi name which means, "She is never alone." She was born October 2, 1969.

I would not have been unhappy if I had conceived a third time, and a fourth, and a fifth. In fact, Joe and I had talked, though not seriously I admit, about having six children, at least two of whom we would adopt. I attribute my interest in babies to my happy marriage and to my upbringing in a community where children were valued even by families who could not well afford them. For, as much as we heard our parents' sermons on not bringing a baby into the world out of wedlock, we knew that, once born, the baby would be claimed with pride and cared for with love.

"Rich white girls, when they get pregnant," the women would say, "their parents send them away to New York or some other place to do away with the baby."

"A sin before God," the women said.

They were not surprised, for what else could they expect from white women who didn't know themselves how to be mothers, or chose not to know, buying the maternal talents of black women whose humanity, in other ways, they denied.

"We the ones who take care of their children," the women would say.

They had been taught to hate themselves, and many of them learned the lesson well. White women possessed a beauty denied to black women at birth. Nothing could give them that beauty. Not Nadinola Bleaching Cream or straightening irons. White women were smarter than they and, without question, more powerful, married, as they were, to white men who owned everything, including white women, they would say.

But black women did not consider themselves totally inferior. Indeed, in many ways, they were convinced that they were better than white women. Morally superior. They were clean, hard-working, and independent women who took care of their children, including daughters who "made a mistake" or who "got caught." Unlike white women, they did not easily commit the sin of abortion.

"The Lord works in mysterious ways, His wonders to perform," some of them would say about a child born out of wedlock. That very child could become a great leader. "We don't know what we killing."

I internalized this thinking and took it with me to communities where the ideological terrain was dramatically different from the one the women of my youth knew. Predominantly white and nonsouthern, or black and southern, but professional. In both communities, women were political, philosophical, and analytical about abortions. They had wider options than the women in my old community and, as a result, they did not seek fulfillment or self-definition in motherhood. Intellectually, I was with them. Intellectually, I supported, and strongly, woman's reproductive rights, but emotionally I was in conflict. The women of my youth held on to me. Between the lines of scholarly postion papers on abortion, I would read their nonscholarly, but passionate words: "You never reject what God gives you because you don't know what you killing."

Significantly, it was a young black mother who helped me resolve the conflict. I met her in 1971 when I was beginning a new volunteer project after working for several weeks transporting elderly black women to a surplus food warehouse located eight blocks south of the Atlanta University Center. In the large unclean building, white sheriffs wearing brown uniforms and holsters buckled around large guns stood on pedestals, with cocked shotguns, while black inmates in striped prison uniforms threw the food on a conveyor belt. With other black people, 90 percent of them women, I stood in long lines to receive busted bags of flour and sugar, bent cans of food, and fruit that was too soft to be edible. Ashamed of my inability to give the people dignity and fearful of my rage, and the white men's guns, I chose another project. I volunteered to work with indigent black mothers recently dismissed from Grady Hospital. She was my first assignment.

A phone call from the downtown office gave me information I needed to do my "job." The young mother was twenty-six, unmarried, and recently unemployed. I recognized the name of the street on which she lived. Fortunately, it was only a few blocks from the Atlanta University, a stone's throw from the statue in downtown Atlanta, alongside Rich's department store, which symbolized the new South rising from the ashes.

My job was to assist the young mother in completing papers for various support services and to befriend her in various ways. I was excited. Too excited, I now realize, and too anxious to be a missionary, a do-gooder who comes in and goes out of the lives of people in need. But I was genuine in my desire to assist her.

I remember reliving my days as a new parent all over. I showed Joe the clothes I had bought for the infant girl. Cute and dainty outfits similar to those we had purchased for Monica. My joy over the woman's joy could be infectious. Dangerous. I put the purchases into boxes and gift wrapped them. They would not be my only gift, I decided. I shopped for groceries, knowing well what a young mother needs.

Sadness overcame me when I reached the deteriorated area in which she lived. It was littered with broken glass and rusted cans and signs reading "Condemned" or "Do Not Trespass." Among several buildings, her complex was the only one still in use. I struggled with my packages up the iron steps to her apartment on the second floor. There was no bell. No knocker. I put the packages down, took a deep breath, and knocked softly. She opened the door without a smile.

I extended my hand. "I'm Gloria Gayles," I said. "I'm from A.D.C.?" My voice made a question rather than a statement because I realized from her expression that the woman was surprised to see me. I would have called her, but she had no phone. I had assumed that downtown would tell her to expect me.

She opened the door, but she did not welcome me in. I hesitated and remembered the packages sitting outside. I picked them up and walked in, talking nervously.

"I'm sorry if I disturbed you and I would have called but — "

"I have no phone," she interrupted me. She extended her hand and told me her name. She motioned me to a place on the worn-out sofa.

"They told me about a volunteer, but they didn't tell me when."

"I'm sorry. I wish I had been able to call you." I handed her the gift-wrapped boxes. "I brought a few gifts for you. "I have a daughter and — "

She interrupted me again. "And a job and a husband."

She went straight for my jugular, with reason. I was walking into her pain wearing a volunteer's smile and carrying pretty boxes wrapped in bright ribbons that contrasted sharply to the dimness of her small apartment. It was small and stuffy. Large roaches crawled on the walls unchallenged. She did not open the boxes. I tried to break the awkward silence with my other gift, the groceries.

"I brought a few food items for you. I remember what it was like when my babies were infants. Getting to the store was such a chore."

She could not use the food. There was no refrigerator for the milk, no stove on which to cook the chicken, and no cabinets for the other items.

I broke the silence with honesty. "I'm so sorry," I said, unable to check my tears. "I didn't know. I had no idea. I'm so sorry, and so . . . so ashamed."

"Don't be." We changed roles. She was the comforter, and I the one needing comfort. "I know you meant well. It's not your fault."

No one from the downtown office had told me how intelligent the young mother was. For them, she was a statistic, nothing more than a name, an address, and an infant born out of wedlock.

My tears convinced her of my sincerity. She began talking about her life, revealing high intelligence, impressive communication skills, and strength.

"In part, it's my own doing." She would have made A-plus in my freshman English course at Spelman. "I forgot to think. I gave in to feeling, and I forgot to think."

From where I sat I could see partially into the small bare kitchen and into the small bedroom where the infant girl lay in a cardboard bassinet, a gift Grady gave indigent mothers at dismissal. I did not know which emotion to give in to. Anger, sadness, pain, or guilt. All of them claimed me, making me far less articulate than she. I stammered and stuttered. Most of all, I cried.

She had known better days. After completing two years in a computer training program, she had been employed in data processing and, with a healthy salary, had lived well in a two-bedroom apartment in a nicer section of the city. She was so bright that she had been promoted twice in one year and was negotiating with the company for tuition and released time for college courses. She was in love with a man whom she was planning to marry. By accident, she conceived. Their marriage date was moved up. When she was at the top of her third month, he abandoned her.

"I did not want to keep the baby," she told me.

I did not believe the voice that came from me. "Why didn't you get an abortion?" I asked, wishing that anything, even that, could have saved her.

Between tightened lips of anger and tears of sadness, she told me of the futility of her efforts to abort the baby. Since there were no legal abortion clinics with medical staffs at the time, she had to go the route familiar to poor women, regardless of race. She chose to keep the baby only because she feared a "coat hanger abortion," which the lateness of her pregnancy made even more dangerous.

She was trapped not only by sanctions against abortion, but also by the absence of paid pregnancy leaves. She lost her job, her apartment, and her car. Weeks before she went into labor, she had moved into the apartment in which I found her.

As a volunteer, I was supposed to assist her in filling out the forms which, I was told, had been given to her at the hospital. What an insult to a woman who was obviously very bright. She could read, write, interpret, read between and under lines. And she had learned, in an on-the-job training program, to enhance her computer skills from simple data processing to programming. I had the degrees; she had the skills that would have positioned her advantageously in the twenty-first century.

She asked nothing of me, and there was nothing I could give her. She had the forms, but she would not complete them. She had pride. She would fight her way back to where she had been.

"That's the only reason I didn't commit suicide," she told me. "I want to win."

She would be a phoenix rising from the ashes, soaring higher than before, now wiser. She would find a job and put her life together again. She was only temporarily destitute. Her words were resonant with my mother's belief in the ability of a woman to overcome obstacles — "if she sets her mind to it," Mama would say.

"With my computer skills," she said confidently, "I will find a very good job."

She was taking charge of her life. Before the delivery, she had made arrangements for the infant to stay at a church center that provided free temporary child care while mothers searched for jobs. She was planning to hunt for jobs the following day, taking with her professional-looking copies of her resume which she had prepared in advance. She was already in flight. Again. There was nothing I could offer her except my voice echoing her resilience and my breath adding to the winds that would carry her where she wanted to go.

The infant slept throughout my visit. The young woman never offered to show her to me, and I'm glad she didn't. I might have suffered again from mixed emotions. I doubt, however, that I would have looked at the infant sleeping in the cardboard bassinet in a roach-infested apartment and said, "This child might be the leader who will change the world for women." How do we know whose life we are killing? I was thinking instead of the many children who are born into and remain in destitution because their mothers, unlike this bright woman, are not skilled and fortunate enough to improve their lives. I was thinking, too, of mothers who themselves might be leaders capable of changing the world for all of us.

When I am asked now how I, a black woman, can "hook up" with white feminists on the abortion issue, I make my own private soap box and wax eloquently on the compelling relevance of choice to black women, who are disproportionately represented among the poor in this nation and the most victimized by self-righteous postions on choice. I tell those who castigate me for my politics about the day I visited a young mother who had no choice but to live in one of Atlanta's abandoned neighborhoods with her newly born child. I silence them with four words: "The woman was black."

The Dilemma of Black Rage
and White Friends

I met Fannie in 1963 when we were colleagues in the Atlanta
University Center, participants in civil rights demonstrations
in downtown Atlanta, and neighbors in a "black" community. She is white and Jewish. I have read her letter many
times. Its subject is our friendship, or its survival in the face
of today's sharp and bitter racial polarization.

The survival of interracial friendships is not a new problem for race relations in this nation. In the nineteenth century, blacks and whites were allies and often friends working
together to abolish slavery. When, because of ideological differences created by race, the political alliance ended, so did
most of the friendships.

The same was true of black women and white women in
the late nineteenth and early twentieth centuries. They were
"sisters" when they addressed issues of gender, but they became antagonists when they could not agree on issues of
race. Angela Davis and Paula Giddings, respectively, in
Women, Race and Class and *When and Where I Enter*, document
schisms in black-white relationships among women. Quoting

from a letter Elizabeth Cady Stanton wrote to the *New York Times* in the late nineteenth century, Davis indicts white suffragettes for unbridled racism.

The problem did not solve itself in the wake of the feminist movement of the sixties. Nor did feminists solve it. It stares at us in the most successful of coalitions across racial lines. It is an unblinking stare that holds the most committed white feminist in its gaze. To paraphrase bell hooks, the racism of white women is a given. Let us move on from there. We should be concerned about the current backlash to the feminist movement which is injected like a drug into the psyche of the nation, dulling our sense of right and wrong and giving us hallucinations of women as monsters set on destroying the world. Many black women feel that we should be equally concerned about racism which was injected long ago into the psyche of white women, dulling their sense of justice and creating hallucinations of themselves as interpreters of black women's reality. Racism is every bit as capable of weakening the movement as organized misogyny.

That is not what we were thinking in the early days of the civil rights movement of the sixties, however, because then our primary concern was racial liberation, not women's empowerment. Interracial alliances and friendships evidenced the insanity of the old world and signaled the beginning of the new. Blacks and whites sang passionately, "We shall overcome," meaning "*together*," of course. We were beaten *together*, water-hosed *together*, jailed *together*. The list of those murdered during the movement includes blacks and whites.

By the decade of the seventies, the Black Power Fist and the chant "Power for the People" signaled the end of one era and the beginning of another. Black people announced to the nation, and to their white friends, that we were taking charge of our destiny as a people. Taking charge meant the following:

That we would support and, thereby, strengthen black businesses so that "*our* money" would turn over in our communities, making us self-sufficient and, therefore, capable of creating and sustaining strong black families.

That we would establish and read our own journals and magazines, giving space and, thereby, voice to black scholars whose works were not accepted by white publications.

That we would support black colleges and make them citadels of learning, thereby enhancing the production of African-American leaders and scholars which, for over a century, had shaped the mission of those institutions.

That we would not let others define or design our struggle for liberation and self-determination.

The break in black-white alliances was sharp and painful, but predictable given the lesson from history and given the many mistakes we made during the movement. One mistake was the decision to send out a nationwide call for white volunteers to work in black communities. The error was not the call, but rather the placement of volunteers. No one worked with white people. We left them alone or, as the old folks used to say, "We let them be." In essence, we planned for a wedding, but told only one party to walk down the aisle.

Some of the white activists should have been assigned to white communities where change was needed most. The problem, after all, was not a black problem, but rather a white problem. In large numbers, white volunteers should have set up camp in the wastelands of the white South, cuddling white babies, teaching white children, bonding with white women, and educating white farmers and businesses about losses they were incurring as a result of their own racism.

And why didn't we ever consider this strategy? Because it was too dangerous? Yes. Connectedness to the racial struggle was, to white southerners, the worst type of betrayal, deserving punishment. The deaths of Chaney, Goodman, and Schwerner, as well as the beatings of countless white workers, evidenced this fact.

And no. Danger was not the only reason we never considered this strategy. Most of us saw white southerners as lost people, beyond redemption and hopelessly mired in ignorance. Backwoods ignorance that speaks wrong, dresses wrong, worships wrong, eats wrong. But that was not logical given our belief in the power of redemptive love. If we were working to change whites, why didn't we work among them? If redemptive love worked in demonstrations, why couldn't it have worked in their communities?

Another explanation for the placement is the unique experience of being around black people, especially black people of the soil. They are warm, embracing, accepting, spirited and spiritual, musical, and, given their big-bosomed religion, nonthreatening. They made all of us feel like saviors, messiahs, angels bearing gifts. They took us in, gave us their best beds, and prepared their best meals. They remembered us in their prayers and in naming ceremonies for children born after our departure.

Is it possible that black southerners were a fascinating primitive people, racial and cultural artifacts whom we activists, black and white, could talk about in the life of comfort to which most of us returned? I think so.

I think also working among them connected us to a humanity we could not, for obvious reasons, associate with whites. "Did you see their eyes?" is a refrain in the black community.

"Did you see their eyes?" Mama would ask whenever I complained about moving to the back of the bus.

"Did you see their eyes?" we asked when whites, among

them mothers with children, jeered at little black children walking to school carrying books escorted by men carrying guns.

"Did you see their eyes?" we asked when white policemen laughed as they unleashed dogs on demonstrators in Birmingham.

"Did you see their eyes?" we asked when the water lifted children from their feet and penned adults against poles and cars and other demonstrators.

"Did you see their eyes?" I ask students who open the pictorial documentary *The Black Book* to the horrifying picture of the charred body of a black man lying naked on still smouldering logs. Fathers with sons, dressed in jackets, knickers, and bow ties, smile broadly for the photographer. I see eyes that see nothing except their own power.

I understand, then, why never once did we consider working among people with those eyes, but for the sake of the movement, I wish the strategy for change had included the harder choice. In nineteenth-century African-American history, replete with chapters of racial violence more heinous than any we experienced during the sixties, I read about white people who wore different eyes. Not the eyes of my people, but different from those we associate with white southerners. I am enough of an idealist to believe that a few people wearing those different eyes would have permitted volunteers (white ones only) to tutor their children and, indirectly, to educate them about the need for change. This strategy would have required us to make changes in our freedom school curriculum, or even changes in the name of the school, but I believe it would have won a few converts to change.

If our first mistake was the result of how we saw white southerners, our second mistake was a result of how we saw ourselves: as brothers and sisters in spite of differences in race. We believed — perhaps we had to for the sake of the movement — that race was not an issue for us. After all, we were, by choice, living together and had pledged ourselves to die together, if necessary. Whatever was wrong in black-white relationships in the South had left us alone.

But we were naive to believe that, in one hot summer, we could erase the damage of centuries. Only after the movement, not during, did we admit that, early on, there were mumblings among black workers that whites felt empowered enough (or superior enough) to take over, and mumblings among white workers that blacks were too hypersensitive and hostile.

We were especially naive about the impact that romantic alliances would have on the movement. We were working in Mississippi to register black southerners to vote, to introduce black southerners to avenues of empowerment, and to liberate them from fear of the white man and desire for the white woman. All of us, regardless of race and gender, worked consistently on removing the fear, but we were not together on removing the desire. By their actions, more than a few black men spoke the wrong message to black farmers. They pursued white women at night and in the light of day. It didn't matter that white women did their share of pursuing. At least not to black women who were struggling with the concept of white beauty. Understandably, when romantic alliances between black men and white women became almost as common as cotton, we lost the harmony with which we had once sung "We Shall Overcome."

The pain many black women in the movement experienced because of our invisibility as desired lovers was exacerbated by the male monopoly of decision-making power. As in the larger world, so, too, in our idyllic summer, sexism was real. Men saw us as bodies and as workers; in both roles, we belonged to them.

Given all of these factors, it was only a matter of time before the glorious movement of the sixties would become history and, with it, would fade many friendships between blacks and whites. Because of our commitment, the South would never be the same again. But neither would many of our relationships.

Many African-Americans who participated in the movement have gone from distancing themselves from white friends, to forgetting that they were ever friends, to adding their friends' names to the lengthening list of white people who cannot be trusted. Who deserve our rage. This was the reason Fannie wrote me. What about *our* friendship, she wanted to know.

I am thinking as I write my response about my rage and my people's rage. I know that rage can galvanize us into action for the liberation of our people, or, mixed with despair and tampered with by the system, it can cripple and blind us, rendering us incapable, to quote Audre Lorde, of "dismantling the master's house." When our rage causes us to hate whites, Jews, Asians, and, in some instances, Latinos, we have connected ourselves to the insanity that holds this entire nation hostage. The moment the system makes us hate other groups rather than love ourselves, it has won, and we have lost.

There is more to black rage than how African-Americans feel about white people. There is more to our rage than the stories which are currently considered to be the only good copy on the subject. In them, black rage is reduced to a hatred of white people, especially of Jews, which translates into murderous designs of their lives. This definition of black rage makes the obsolescence of African-Americans a necessity for national safety. It depicts us as simple-minded people incapable (probably because of genetic inferiority) of understanding the dynamics of a system. Worst of all, it minimizes our phenomenal achievements and ignores the thousands of projects in our communities designed, supported, and sustained by us. In a word, it continues the miseducation of white America.

Nothing in the behavior of black people in this nation supports this distorted definition of black rage. During centuries of egregious injustice, we have not resorted to placing bombs in cars and crowded buildings, nor formed vigilante groups that roam the nation in search of white victims. In fact, I do not remember black-on-white crime ever being a problem in this nation. As a group, African-Americans tend to be forgiving and accepting (to a fault, some would argue), for while screaming epithets at white America, we embrace white individuals. I see this among revolutionary black students who choose white professors as mentors and political rappers who give white associates the "high-five" after recording songs with misogynist lyrics that offend me as much as their so-called black nationalist lyrics frighten white people.

I am convinced that national hysteria surrounding black rage, which results in a proliferation of articles promoting fear and further polarization rather than in struggle for change, is a strategy of divide and conquer, a diversionary tactic, a devious ploy, the purpose of which is to avert attention from the real causes of black rage and from the various crises that prevent this country from being healed and humane. It is a well-constructed trap African-Americans would be wise to avoid.

What will I tell my friend Fannie? How will I explain my friendship with her to African-Americans with whom I work on projects that, of necessity, exclude the participation of whites? Let me answer the second question first.

No one should ever feel compelled to explain a friend. Therefore, I will not apologize for my twenty plus years of friendship with Fannie to anyone. What I will explain, if anything, is my commitment to the race since I do not express it by rejecting white friends. How do I love my people? To use the cliche, let me "count the ways."

I support and believe in Africentricity. To reject it is to reject the truth of scholarship and, therefore, to live and think in darkness. The battle waged against Africentricity is, in my opinion, proof of its legitimacy. Why else do mainstream scholars reduce the field to one book whose documentation is weak and make it the possession of one man whose credentials are questionable? Why do they put before the camera spokespersons whose politics are anti-somebody and, therefore, a disservice to Africentricity. I consider that baiting. Plain and simple. I will not be baited.

I believe that the Egyptians were black people who called themselves black people. Hence their name, "Kemet," which, translated, means "the land of the blacks." I believe Greek scholars, among them the venerable Aristotle, took generously from Egyptian scholars, and that the foundation of many branches of knowledge (among them medicine, astronomy, science, mathematics, and philosophy) was first laid by Egyptians, African people. I believe Jesus was black and so, too, Mary, and so, too, many of the people I studied in my Sunday School classes in Memphis. I believe, as scientists have documented (white scientists!) that life began with black people and that all human beings (see *Newsweek*, January 11, 1987) carry the resilient genes of a woman born hundreds of thousands of years ago in Africa.

When scholars of national repute ask, "So what if this *is* true? What significance does it have for a man walking on a street corner in Harlem?" I am aghast! And I weep for anyone who curries favor with others by rejecting identification with their own. All people deserve to know their history, including their ancient history — the good and the bad of it — for in knowing our ancestors, we are better able to give birth to a whole self.

Although I am "mixed," as all African-Americans are (we *do* have "some Indian blood" and white blood in our veins), I choose to identify genetically and culturally with women and men who were stolen from Africa centuries ago. America is my home. I was born here, I live here, and like so many who have gone before me, I will die here, but Africa is my motherland.

By choice, I have chosen to teach at historically black colleges for over twenty years because I believe in the excellence and mission of these institutions and I am inspired by their history, at the center of which is dedication to our people. I believe they must survive, or we will not survive. Teaching there has been my way of contributing to their struggle for survival which, until the millenium comes, is my people's survival as well.

I study and research, with passion, African-American history, literature, and culture, and regardless of the title of the course, I make our contributions central. I work, when time permits, on service projects in our communities. I am not comfortable with what I am doing. It is so very little for a need so very large. I want to do things that will make a difference, but I think we need a movement for that. No such movement exists. If one came into existence tomorrow, I would again become an activist. And if I thought I could start one, I would.

I make an effort to hear the soul of my Ancestors speaking to all of us. Their voices are in the winds, and in the universe itself is their spirit. I struggle, sometimes in strange ways, to become spiritually connected to them. I believe that, without that connection, we will not reap the harvest of freedom and wholeness we have worked so long to realize.

As Ossie Davis wrote in *Purlie Victorious*, I wish to be "no other race and face, but this." Without apology, I am African-American.

My friendship with white people does not alter this wish or limit the number of ways I can count my commitment to the race. There is no one way, no more authentic way, no more-African-than-thou way to express that commitment. There are many ways. For me, hating white people is not one of them. I can embrace other races without giving up either my racial birthright, or my racial loyalty. Indeed, I want to be so large in my humanity that I will never feel compelled to shut anyone from my life on the basis of race, or from the struggles of my people. If I am true to my study of African-American history — and out of respect for my people, I must be — I will have reason to call the names of whites who chose to struggle on the side of justice. They are in the diaries and stories and memories of my people. To remove them would be tantamount to changing the script my Ancestors wanted us to read.

I speak as a remnant of the sixties. My perspective, therefore, is decidedly different from that of most of the new generation of spokespersons who explain and define "black rage." Their experiences with whites have taken place, primarily, in academia, in corporate America, and in other places in the world of work. I am thinking particularly of a special issue on black rage that appeared in *The Village Voice* in the fall of 1992 which featured analyses by experts em-

ployed by Ivy League institutions. They offered theory detached, I thought, from reality. I wondered whom they interviewed, given the fact that they are removed not only from
the masses of black people who are in a state of rage, but
also from the black students at historically black schools who
dissect rage on a table of analysis *after* they have pulled it out
of their souls. My experiences in all those places (and in the
movement as well), my age, and my connectedness to the
black community shape an approach to rage that brings
Martin, Malcolm, Baldwin, Fannie, Rosa, and Angela into a
marvelous harmony.

Of course I am not the same person Fannie met in the
sixties. I no longer make integration the number one item on
my agenda for change. How can it be when the masses of
African-Americans are colonized in ghettoes across this nation? I would not make mockery of our suffering by propos-
ing that our song for the nineties should be "black and white
together." We tried that and, because of America's misinter-
pretation of integration, we lost. We lost because we were
psychologically enslaved as a people.

White America said, "Let a few enter," and we began the
mild rush to their world, abandoning our own. Unintention-
ally, we weakened black businesses, black colleges, black
community schools, black communities, and, indirectly, black
families. Tragically, we believed that anything white was better than everything black. This time, we must try a different
strategy, at the center of which must be black pride and self-
determination. As long as we are immersed in self-hatred and
negotiate from a position of weakness and extreme need, integration will never be a solution to our problems. We must
strengthen our businesses, support our institutions, and return as volunteers to our communities. We must work to
save our own by claiming, believing in, and remaining with

our own. And whites must work to change their own by struggling in their communities and in their families for racial enlightenment and justice.

I believe in racial solidarity and racial separation, not as the end, however, but as the means to the end. I believe racial integration is the only logical goal for all of us. Either we will live together in harmony or this nation will self-destruct, and soon. Africa is our motherland, but it is not in her bosom that millions of us live, suffer, and dream of a different future. And it is not on her soil that we will die.

I believe this is how the masses of black people feel and, consequently, I am not convinced that the wholesale hatred of white people reported by the media is a true rendering of our feelings. Black rage is not to be interpreted as hatred of whites. It simply does not compute when we look at the behavior of African-Americans. Of course there are African-Americans who hate white people! But the masses of my people have never been and are not now preoccupied with hating others. Resisting their control of our lives, yes. But hating them, no.

For me, the most moving expression of our sentiments about white people came from an elderly black woman in a small community in Florida. After sharing her vivid memories of the day whites slaughtered her parents and other members of her family, she was asked: "How do you feel about whites?" She answered: "Some of them is too nice to be white people."

My friends are too nice to be white people.

I remember my friend Naomi, a formidable opponent to anyone who did not believe in racial justice. An irritant who put long briars in your skin if she suspected you of racism.

On the canvass of my memories, she is very much in focus, as loved in death as she was in life. She had different eyes.

I think of Dick Eakin, who, in his late seventies, makes time to call and to write. Who values the friendship he has with Joe and me. When I think about him, I do not think white. Rather, I think large heart, unconditional kindness, and authentic friendship. And I see different eyes.

And of course I think of my friend Fannie, who in her seventies leaves her home at six in the morning to work in a community center in Manhattan that has programs for the homeless, the elderly, and high school students who, in spite of their matriculation in poor inner-city public schools, are determined to go to college. Need, not race, is the criterion for being served at the center. Dedication and skills, not race, are the criteria for serving. Fannie understands my rage and meets it with her own.

That which we are at any given time in our lives, we are because of whom we have known and what we have experienced. Because of my family, my people, my friends, and my experiences, I have drawn a map for the remaining years of my life which will take me, I hope, to places where people together struggle for change.

I am committed to the struggles of my people and sometimes in ways that separate us, necessarily, from all other groups in this nation. I am committed to dethroning male dominance, a necessary act for the liberation of women and men as well, and to opening all doors to those we define as "handicapped." I am devoted to the sanctity of motherhood and to the children whom we must protect from physical, educational, psychological, and spiritual injury. Before there were national organizations for the defense of children, I had received this moral imperative from my grandmother who, as a child, was not protected, by anyone. I am committed to doing what I can to end oppression in any form. Without apology, I name these as my political and moral priorities. I confess, however, and with apology, that my commitment has had the force of a whisper. Only I hear it.

Where do I put my love for friends who happen to be white into my vision of struggle? At a time when everything white is suspect, understandably so, where do they belong? It takes courage and integrity ("character," Mama would say) to own an unpopular truth. And so, I claim my friends, without apology.

As I sit at the computer to respond to Fannie's letter, I have their names and our friendship on a special disk. I have not pushed "delete," and I never will. I am waiting for the day when I can begin a new document about the health, strength, dignity, and self-love of my people who were ex-pected to self-destruct, but didn't because we refused to die. *Simply refused to die.*

When the new document is written (and I pray that it will be), I will read it with passion and in the middle of the text, I will push Shift F5. I will move the cursor up and down the directory until I find the old document that has no name. The computer will ask, "Retrieve into existing document?" I will answer, "yes," for in a real sense nothing we do in the twenty-first century to survive, to become empowered and whole as a people, can be isolated from past struggles for liberation.

Fannie wrote in her letter: "The world is crazy. It is hard to digest the mayhem in South Africa, the Soviet Union, the U.S. — after a lifetime it is hard to think coherently about anything beyond friends and children." She ended the letter by calling my name and reaching out to me in love and fear:

"Gloria Gayles, do not abandon me in this maelstrom." She signed it: "Much love, undiluted. Fannie."

I will write her a brief note. It will read: "Dear Fannie, only fools abandon friendship and love." I will sign it: "Tested love, unaltered. Gloria."

Letting Go

It was late August in 1987. I was helping my daughter Monica pack for college and thinking to myself that only yesterday I was screaming, "I've changed my mind. Give me something," and Joe was rushing into the delivery room to protect me. There is truth in the cliche that "time flies." Faster than the speed of light or sound, I said to myself, and certainly faster than Monica, who seemed to be taking forever to decide what she would *not* take with her.

She moved slowly, but with excitement. I watched as she placed heirloom items into a trunk I feared we would not be able to close: her first hard-toe ballet shoes; several swim trophies; a handful of swim and track first-place ribbons; music books containing her favorite recital pieces; a small plaque her father and I gave her for reading her first novel (Bette Greene's *Philip Hall Likes Me. I Reckon*); and her favorite stuffed animals. She knew what I was thinking. "Don't even say, Mom," she said. "I know it looks like I'm going a long, long way from home." The drive to Spelman College would take no more than thirty minutes by car, if that long, but I encouraged her to pack whatever she wanted. She would be *in* the city, but *away* from home. Away in her own home. As her brother was during his freshman year in the dorm at Morehouse. Joe and I had promised both children that we wouldn't intrude on their new lives and we wouldn't demand that they come home on weekends. We were letting go.

As we packed her trunk, too many pieces of luggage, and several plastic crates, I felt good about my relationship with her and with her brother. I felt good because I had learned from a master mother how to be a mother friend. I had danced the latest steps with both children to their loud music, often joking with them that at eighty I would be able to hear, and, at thirty, they would be deaf. With their father, I had attended their swim meets, piano recitals, dance recitals, basketball games, and football games. Disheveling my Afro affectionately, Jonathan would tease me in the presence of his friends about the free throws he missed because I screamed at the very second he released the ball, "Remember Mrs. Mooley." She was the cow who jumped over the moon in the story they always wanted to hear every Saturday morning, our day for reading at the library. They loved to hear the librarian read, "I can. I can. I know I can. And she did." I had to confess that a few times I had screamed (but not too loudly) about Mrs. Mooley, but I added, "That's *not* why you missed the basket."

I differed from Mama in that I kept a house full of children. In our three-bedroom suburban home, with a full basement, Joe and I had the room Mama did not have in the project. We used it for the children. My friend Arnisha called me "The Pied Piper" and jokingly said, "These children will eat you out of house and home." Everybody's children gravitated to our house where there were snacks, laughter, conversation, and a basketball hoop Joe had set up for Jonathan when he was thirteen. I had been seen more than once playing on the girls' side to help them win against boys who thought they owned the hoop.

When all the packing was finished, I gave Monica a poem called "Trust" which expressed, in simple words, the joy of our bonding. It begins,

> At fifteen,
> my daughter took me gently
> by the hand
> and walked me
> through the privacy
> of her young life.

In it I recalled times she had shared her thoughts and times I had responded to needs she did not articulate. I confessed the deep and abiding love with which, unknown to her, I had "dusted her shoes with magic" and on class election day had "stuffed the ballots with her name / and cut stars into confetti for her parade." At the moment I was letting go, I wanted her to know that our love had created a mutual trust and the door between us would always be open. We embraced, celebrating with tears our forever bonding.

Jonathan also received a poem when he left home for college. "Initiation Into Tenderness" carried in its few stanzas the best advice I could think to give my son about his first love. It spoke of caution and offered permission. It was a mother's prayer for tenderness and gratitude.

> But
> if
> together
> they embrace the night
> I hope his lovewords will be

            incantations the grateful make
            to a generous god

Joyous fun, bonding, advice, poems — I could let them go.
I had enjoyed parenting them, but, approaching forty fast,
with the speed of time which is faster than light or sound, I
was eager to enter a new stage of my life. With a fellowship
from the Mellon Foundation to work on a critical study of
Alice Walker's novels, I would be relieved for a year of all
teaching responsibilities at Spelman. My leave was well-
timed. In my absence, Monica would be able to develop an
identity independent of mine.

Monica's departure for college and my leave from Spelman were not the only major changes that took place in my
life in 1987. Another, and a very painful one, was my separation from Joe. This change was brought on, I am certain,
more than anything by my need for redefinition or perhaps,
on a subconscious level, by my response to what therapists
call the "empty nest syndrome." Whatever the reason, I
found the separation painful, but I reasoned, on one level,
that I needed at this time in my life to try my hand, finally,
at writing. I was convinced that the separation would be
temporary and that it would strengthen our love rather than
weaken it. Two weeks after Monica moved into her dorm
room, I moved into a small one-bedroom apartment which I
called my writer's space.

Words ran from me, sometimes because of the pain of
the separation and other times because of my worry over
Mama's health. Having suffered from high blood pressure
almost all of her life, at seventy-four Mama had heart problems. I was reading in my aunt's conversation coded messages that Mama's health was deteriorating. Stopping short
of begging her for fear that too much concern would cause

her alarm, I tried to persuade Mama to come to stay with me. Each time she said no because she felt her presence would be a deterrent to a needed reunion with Joe. My insistence, or a feeling she had, finally convinced her to give in to my persuasion.

"I will come for a visit," she told me in October, when I called to celebrate her birthday. She was still beautiful. Still young in spirit. "Just for a visit. But not until the weather is warm."

"What about April?" I asked. "It gets warm here in Atlanta early in April."

"*Sometimes* it gets warm in April," she said. She was right. In the mid-seventies an April ice storm crippled Atlanta for ten days.

We agreed on June, the safest month of all in Mama's opinion. She did not know Faye and I had decided we would not let her return to Memphis, where she lived alone in a very modest two-bedroom frame house in a neighborhood that had changed for the worse over the years. I remember how happy we were when, in 1974, Mama married Joe, a kind man, and moved into the house he had shared with his wife, three years deceased. She had lived unmarried for over thirty years following the death of Dan, her second husband. Finally, like Mr. Clarence, and Miss Annie Bee, and Mr. Hurst and his family, Mama moved from the project into a real house with its own backyard and its own front porch. At sixty, she finally knew the security Daddy had never provided and the space Dan had never permitted. These changes, however, did not change the pattern of Mama's life; one in which joy comes only for a brief stay. In the third year of their marriage, Joe died suddenly of a massive heart attack. It was time, Faye and I decided, for us to take care of Mama.

She would live with me when the weather was cold in Chicago, and during the summer, with Faye.

When I opened my eyes, I was looking at the black history calendar hanging on the wall beyond the end of my bed. In my mind I flipped through its pages of amateurish drawings of black leaders and three-sentence summaries of lives that deserved volumes. APRIL, printed in bold black letters, seemed to speak to me. I was running out of time. In five months a new school year would begin, and my semester's leave would come to an end. If I didn't begin to make headway on the book, I would return to work with nothing to show for my time except stacks of note cards, folders of Xeroxed essays somebody else had written, and notes on conversations with Alice Walker pencilled in the margins of four of her novels.

There was no time for breakfast or the morning paper. I threw on a robe, made a cup of instant coffee, and sat down at the computer to work. "Please wait," the machine ordered. I waited. A second later I had a blank screen. At the far top left was the lighted cursor. At the far bottom right was the line, "Doc 1 Pg 1 Ln 7," which revealed how unproductive I had been for months.

I placed my hands in typing position — my right index finger on "j," my left on "f," and both thumbs on the space bar. I wanted a compelling and poignant opening sentence on Alice Walker's artistic visions. The keys began moving. On the blank screen, lighted in amber, I saw the words: "It is time to go home." I knew, then, I could not wait until June to see Mama. I turned off the computer and called my aunt. It was a very brief conversation. "Tell Mama I am leaving for Memphis the first thing tomorrow morning." She tried to protest. I was impatient with her. "Don't tell me when I can't come home, Aunt Mae." Silence. "Drive carefully" was all she said. I hung up the phone, dressed hurriedly, and went in search of the best rates on a rented car.

If I were to share such an experience with Mama, she would explain it as one of those psychic feelings we get but can't explain.

"People get them. All the time," she would say. "You can feel someone thinking about you, pulling you toward them." She believed there is a dimension where the spirits of the living and the dead come together.

"Some people are more psychic than others," she told me more than once when I was younger. "They're born that way." And she added proudly, "We're psychic, you know. Your grandmother was real psychic, and she passed the gift on to all of us."

She, my sister Faye, and I would debate for hours about politics, sex, religion, racism . . . all subjects. We were never her match. She would draw on her brilliance and her passion, her experiences and her ability to shape analogies with precise and colorful words. The intellectual bantering was entertainment for us, games that gave us a chance to spread our mental feathers for one another.

But when it came to that "other dimension," Mama played no games. There was no bantering. She would end a conversation on its way to a debate with a short sentence that all the adults in my family used to remind us of our youth: "Just keep on living."

If we gave her an irreverent shrug, her caveat would put our college degrees in proper perspective: "I don't care how much education you get, if you lock out the spirit, you're empty. Being connected is a blessing, but it can be taken from you."

Atlanta was sleeping when I left at five the next morning,

earlier than I had planned. Except for the lights of a few passing cars and motel neon signs with missing letters, I drove in darkness. And yet, the highway in front of me seemed to be illuminated by a strange light. My mind began to play tricks on me. I felt as if my car were being pulled by this light. I chuckled to myself, "This is one of those strange phenomena Mama would attribute to the other dimension." I thought I could close my eyes and reach Memphis.

"Naw," I said. "There's nothing to all that talk about the other dimension. Pre-dawn darkness is just eerie, that's all. Just eerie."

The world began to yawn and stretch by the time I reached the Alabama state line. Cows walked slowly in pastures to my right and my left, dropping huge pies. Farmers, all of them white, were boarding tractors for early morning work in the fields. Lights came on in distant houses as if they were answering each other. I was headed west toward Birmingham. The sun was rising in the east behind me, throwing strips of rose light across the hood of the car. I pressed down on the accelerator.

I had six or seven hours alone to think and feel—to get connected to the other dimension. I wondered where it was, what it was, if it were real. One side of me knew that I had "it," the psychic thing. Another wanted to reject it out of fear. Anything that gets into your life without your permission and leaves without your permission, doing whatever it wants without your permission, never explaining why or how, is frightening. You're at the mercy of something you can't see or hear, just feel.

I knew I had "it" in 1965 when something pulled me from my bed at four in the morning. The dense darkness in my graduate student's apartment didn't prevent me from finding my way to the phone and dialing the eleven digits of Mama number without error. I was calling her, but I knew she wasn't home. My stepfather Joe's sleepy voice answered the phone.

"What's wrong with Mama?" I asked with surprising calm.

"Who told you?"

The calm left me. "Who told me what?" I all but screamed into the phone. "Where's Mama? What's wrong with Mama?"

He took too long to answer, and I became hysterical. "Where is my mama? What's happened to my mama?"

It was an eternity before he told me that Mama was scheduled at six that morning for a brain scan. For several weeks she had had double vision: the doctors feared a stroke.

"Who told you?" he asked again.

I had no answer.

I hung up the phone and called Mama at the hospital. I knew she was awake and waiting for the phone to ring. When she heard my voice, she took a deep breath, remained silent for a second, and with a smile shaping her words said, "I told them you'd know. I knew you'd know."

I was thinking about that experience when I saw the large sign: "Mississippi, the Magnolia State." I wanted to skip this state that brought back painful memories, but I knew that was impossible. The Tennessee border was hundreds of miles away. I became anxious and exhausted. Highway 78 was a mean road. It turned and crooked through small towns that offered the same things: fireworks, Indian artifacts, statues of colored jockeys and Aunt Jemimas, chenille bedspreads, and two-pump gas stations where red-necked white men spat chewing tobacco. I was held below the speed limit by tractors I dared not pass and mean-looking white drivers I did not trust to let me in if I moved boldly into the passing lane. I began to sing songs from the movement, appropriate on this highway. "Keep your eyes on the prize. Move on."

That was Mama's philosophy. Set a goal for yourself, keep your eye on it, and "you'll get there." In the prime of health, I was now stronger than Mama, but not as wise. She had a way of seeing around sharp corners, over high fences, beneath thick layers of confusion and uncertainty to the very center of truth and practicality. Her "single eye" focused on my sister and me, on our wholeness, on our ability to stand tall in the light of our own suns. Extraneous nonsense that had nothing to do with her "single eye" she just didn't see, wouldn't see.

I remember running home from high school with the good news that a local sorority had chosen me to be a debutante. That was an honor. I wasn't light-skinned (as we used to say). I didn't have long hair or "good hair." And I lived in a housing project. I had been chosen in spite of my liabilities.

"What's it for?" Mama asked, trying to embrace my joy. I recall that she was cooking hot-water cornbread for our full-family Friday dinner. She was pouring boiling water into a mixture of corn, lard, and salt. When the consistency was right, she began rounding the wet meal with her strong hands, never looking up at me.

"My debut," I answered.

"What's it for?" she asked again. I knew we were going to have court.

"Huh?"

"What will it do for you?"

"Mama!" I was exasperated. This was going to be one of those tests to determine practicality and values. "It's an honor. I mean, they chose *me* to be a debutante."

"Well, that's because they're smart. No one is more beautiful and graceful than my girls." She had placed four cornbread patties on a sheet of wax paper. They were perfect circles. She turned up the flame under the cast-iron skillet.

"What will it do for you?"

I did not answer.

"What will you need?"

I swallowed hard. Mama already knew what I would need, but she was forcing me to say it, to hear myself say it.

"It won't cost that much."

"What will you need?" she asked again, making more cornbread patties.

I read the list, fast. "A long white formal dress, a tiara, elbow-length white gloves . . ."

She stopped me with a you-gotta-be-kidding laugh that came from deep inside. "Now what do you need with elbow-length white gloves?" She made fun of the activity and accused me of trying to be Cinderella.

"Mama you're not being fair to me. This is a *debutante* ball. The biggest event in the city. It symbolizes my debut to society."

"It symbolizes my debut to society," she repeated, mimicking me. "Society?" Mama looked up at me for the first time. "Society? Colored people in Memphis don't have a *society*, baby. Don't you know that? We have communities and churches and families, but not a *society*. They're just copying white folks."

"Well, maybe they are," I said, knowing that she was right. "But what's wrong with that?"

"For people who want it, need it, and can afford it — nothing. We don't need it, can't afford it, and you know I don't want it."

"But we can use it, Mama."

"How? How can we use a debutante ball that will cost us money? How?"

"It will look good on my resume and give me connections when I apply to college."

"Connections. Don't ever depend on connections, baby," she said sweetly. "That's like depending on somebody else. Connect to yourself. Study, make good grades, and —"

I cut her off. "But, Mama, those people are very careful about the girls they choose to be debutantes, and they chose me."

"*Those* people. *Those* people." I had shown my hand. It wasn't about feeling pretty in a long white dress after all. It was about wanting to be with a certain class of people. It was all over for me.

Mama placed the meal patties in the skillet carefully because the oil was piping hot. They made sizzling sounds and popping sounds.

"Those people. THOSE people. I don't care who *those* people are — doctors' wives, dentists' wives, preachers' wives, teachers' wives. You know how I feel about people."

I did not answer.

She separated the meal patties with a black-handled spatula and stepped back from the stove. I knew what she would say. "Everybody is somebody and ain't nobody nothing."

I was on my way to popularity and she was blocking me. Mixing meal, lard, and hot water in a kitchen which was like all the other kitchens in the project, she was saying no to my dream. Every girl wanted to be a debutante. Every girl. Why was I supposed to be different? I resented her for being so practical, so . . . so preachy about values, so . . . so very much herself.

"A colored debutante ball! Hmph. As the old folks used to say, 'Some people don't have a pot to pee in or a window to throw it out of' and we're going around spending money on debutante balls."

"You won't let me have this dream, Mama," I screamed.

"You're taking it away from me just because *you* don't like it. That's not fair, Mama. That's not fair."

Her voice softened. "It's a dream somebody else gave you. It doesn't even fit you."

"It does fit me. It does, Mama. I know it does." She reached to embrace me, but I ran from the room shouting, "This time, Mama. You're wrong. You're wrong. Wrong, Wrong, Wrong."

My anger lasted for only a few days because I knew Mama was not wrong. She wasn't being mean; she was being practical. She was trying to teach me values which rejected showy things, phoniness, and the slightest hint of elitism. "Phony things can mess up your values," she would tell us. "If you start trying to be like other people because of who they are, or who you think they are," she explained, "you'll end up not being yourself."

That was the only major conflict Mama and I ever had. Even during the turbulent and tumultuous adolescent years when mothers and daughters are supposed to become antagonists and sever bonds in a sometimes bitter war, Mama, Faye, and I were friends. We did silly and wonderful things together like walking in the rain for the heck of it and walking home from the neighborhood theatre bumping hips against hips, three bodies moving as one.

Eight hours after leaving Atlanta, I pulled into my aunt's driveway. Before I could get out of the car, I heard the screams from inside the house. "She's here, Bertha. She's here." They had been sitting at the kitchen table waiting for me.

"Thank you, Jesus. Thank you. Thank you," Mama kept repeating.

"Girl, you are something else," my aunt said. "Driving all the way here by yourself. Making it here on time."

Mama held me the way a child holds a doll she was wanted

for years and finally gets. "You made it," she said. "All by yourself, you made it."

I acted cute in order to fight back the tears. "A piece of cake, Mama," I said. "No tickets. No cops. No snoozes. Zip. Zip. Zap. Poof. And heeeerrr I am. Tahdah!" I bowed theatrically.

She turned me around. "Let me see those hips." She was satisfied with my weight. "Now when you lose pounds, remember not to lose those hips."

She went to the phone and dialed my sister. "She made it," Mama said. "Yeah. She looks good. Still got that militant hair cut, but she looks good." She handed me the phone.

Faye and I had worked everything out before I left Atlanta. It made sense for me to make the trip to Memphis because I was on leave from Spelman for a full semester, and Faye was working full-time and overtime, in a large inner-city Chicago high school. Mama would stay with me this summer and through Chicago's harsh winters and with Faye next summer.

Mama had been living for four months with Aunt Mae and Uncle Hosea, who, though he was her brother-in-law, welcomed Mama as if she were his own blood. A widow for three years, she had gone there reluctantly during a time when she was too ill to stay alone, but with the intention of returning home when she was stronger. We would not allow that. No one in the family would allow that. Letting an elder live alone was not consonant with the rhythm of black culture. Nor was putting them in a home. There was a common saying in the black community that, unlike white people, we just didn't throw away our old.

I remember how devoted Aunt Mae and Mama were to Grandmama when she became bedridden with arthritis. For two years, they did everything for her. At home. They

were devastated when the doctor told them she would get
worse if she did not receive around-the-clock care in a nursing home. They cried, though not in her presence, when
they checked her into a nursing home that had once been a
Holiday Inn. They released her only partially to the care of
others.

If someone had told her she was in a nursing home, she
would have responded with the same disbelief and rejection
she gave the canvassers who asked her about life in the
ghetto. She had never lived in a ghetto; she had never slept
in a nursing home. She never wore white muslin tied with
one string and open at the back. In my remembering, I see
nylon gowns, in different colors, hanging in Grandmama's
closet and our hands dressing her pretty for the night.

"Ya'll sure do love your mama," the nurses would say.
"Not like these other people who don't even care." Black
nurses attributed the loneliness of other patients, all of them
white, to differences between black culture and white culture. "These some poor people," they would say. "Just put
away here and forgotten."

Mama agreed, and that is why she became the daughter
of every patient on Grandmama's floor, a good Samaritan
going from room to room taking good cheer and sometimes
bringing from home items they had requested. A lady directly across the hall from Grandmama's room screamed
constantly, at times sounding like a frightened little girl who
had hurt herself at play and other times like a mother who
was punishing a child who had misbehaved. Mama would
become the parent who soothed her or the child begging for
forgiveness.

The woman who stayed in the room at the end of the hall,
on Grandmama's side, was a former school teacher from
Birmingham, Alabama, who, with the hospital's permission,

walked the halls dressed in her finest. Mama's visits with her were always interesting because the two of them talked about ideas — that is, until Mama became the pupil who had an assignment to do. The staff downstairs was on alert to watch for her because on two occasions the woman had wandered from the premises. Once a month she had a visit from her daughter.

"Not all mothers and daughters are close," Mama would say. "Some mothers have alienated their daughters." How sad, I thought to myself. "But that shouldn't matter," she would add, "when they get old. You put aside your anger and take care of them. You just don't throw old people away."

We thought Mama overdid her sympathy for an elderly man at the nursing home. Like the woman from Birmingham, he would walk the corridor fully dressed, shuffling so slowly that it took him thirty minutes to reach the other end. He seemed to know when to expect Mama, or at least that's what the nurses said. He managed to be near the elevator when Mama came to see Grandmama. She was like a Swiss watch, dependable and exact in her arrival. Or like the sun.

One day, when he greeted Mama at the elevator, he squeezed her breasts. Mama did not stop him. We were angry because she did not pull back.

"Mama! How could you? How could you?" I asked, ashamed. "You've taken this thing too far. He's an old white man who probably sees you as the black woman he once had on the side. How *could* you?"

She was calm in her response. "It didn't hurt me, but it might have given him some joy."

"Forget his joy! Who does he think he is? Even when they're old, they think they can treat us that way."

"You go on and be as angry as you want," she told me. Told all of us in the family. "But he didn't hurt me. And how do we know what he was thinking. Maybe he had become a child again. Maybe he was remembering the times he nursed at his mother's breast."

"Yeah, that's right. And you're his black mammy." I was incensed!

"You're free to think what you want to think, and I'm free to do what I want to do." She could be stubborn at times. "But if I brought him a bit of joy, I'm satisfied."

She didn't see race; she saw age, and need. I saw need, but I also saw race. How could I *not* see race. When the elderly white patients went back into their childhood, they saw themselves ordering black people because that's what they were taught they had the right to do. After all, I reminded Mama, they grew up during the worst of Jim Crow time, and they were too old to know that the South had changed.

Mama could not disagree with me, certainly not after a white patient tried to accost one of the black nurses.

"You old black baboon," she had screamed. "Bring your black ass over here and sit down. Did you hear me? I'm talking to you, you black baboon."

The nurse was not Mama. I remember the incident because I happened to be home visiting when it occurred. I remember the woman's screams as the nurse tied her to the bed with sheets. "I'll show you what a black baboon can do," the nurse said repeatedly. "I'll show you what a black baboon can do." The hospital administrators did not reprimand the nurse. Elderly people, like children, they said, had to be disciplined.

I remember the stench of urine that reached you before you entered the building; the singing, loud talking, and babbling of patients; the squeaky sound of food carts rolling unappetizing trays of food to different rooms; the locked doors;

the barren rooms; the barren faces; the lonely lives. We
would care for Mama in our home. She did not need nursing
care, but she couldn't live alone. Her little house on Shasta
Avenue was located in a neighborhood that had become un-
safe, like so many other black neighborhoods in the wake of
high unemployment and a national drug problem.

Fiercely proud and independent, she had no intentions of
staying with anyone, but Faye and I had our own intentions.
We *wanted* Mama with us because there was so much she
could teach us and there was so much we wanted to do for
her. In her winter years, she would keep us connected to the
gifts of spring: love, laughter, growth — life.

I went to the phone prepared to answer Faye's questions:
Had Mama lost weight? Was she steady on her feet? How
did she look? I answered her truthfully: "Mama is beautiful."

Only later that night, after Mama had gone to bed, did I
call Faye to tell the larger truth. Mama was thin and un-
steady on her feet. She was not well, but she didn't appear
to be seriously ill. She was witty, full of fun, feisty, smart as
ever. *Herself,* only older and weaker.

Three days later, Mama and I left before dawn for Atlanta.
We took her tape recorder with us and a bag of tapes my
aunt and I had purchased the day before: selected favorites by
B. B. King, Muddy Waters, Billie Holiday, Sarah Vaughan;
sermons; and the latest in commercial religious music. We
were going to sing our way to Atlanta.

"Caldonia. Bang. Caldonia. Bang. What makes your big
head so hard." Mama sang along, moving her hands as if she
were playing piano, while I remembered Uncle Prince. Mama
loved the blues and the talking-sensual sounds of B. B.
King's guitar. She couldn't carry a tune, but she knew all the
lyrics. "I'd rather drink muddy water," she sang, "and sleep
in a hollow log."

We played Billie Holiday several times. Using reverse and fast forward, I found Mama's favorite by Billie, and she sang meaning into the words: "Mama may have. Papa may have. But God bless the chile that's got his own. That's got his own."

We reached Tupelo and started counting the signs announcing "The Birthplace of Elvis Presley." Mama liked Elvis. I didn't.

"I don't care anything about his music," she said, defending herself. "I just like the fact that he was a poor white boy who never forgot his roots."

"A poor white boy who got rich copying us," I responded.

"Yeah, you're right. He and a whole lot of them. But I respect Elvis. He made a fortune and shared it with his family. And he came home. He could have stayed out in Hollywood, but he came home."

She always talked about roots, about values that were anchored in loving yourself and in loving your people. *Roots.* "Little people make big people," she would say, "and big people become small people when they forget where they came from."

The highway and the weather cooperated with us. The temperature was in the mid-seventies, and the traffic was light to moderate. The highway became a moving carpet. We rode it together in love.

Signs announcing the number of miles to Atlanta became more frequent, and larger, reaching at times into the car and propping themselves on the dashboard for our eyes only.

"Hot dog!" Mama said when we reached Carrollton right outside Atlanta. "Hot dog! We're almost there."

Instead of the blues, she sang "Amazing Grace." I liked that about Mama. She was connected to different rhythms of live just as she was connected to different people. She hated no one, even people who had in some way injured her. She could be secular and earthy when she wanted to be, a high stepper I'd take to anyone's dance. And she could be spiritual and religious, still with her soul and filled with the holy ghost. She embraced and affirmed both parts of herself.

She entered Atlanta in a mood I did not like.

"Gloria, I don't think I'll ever make it back home," she said.

"So you know, huh?" I ignored her reference to death. "Good. That's good. Now Faye and I won't have to pretend that you will be staying with us for more than a visit."

"I don't think I'll ever go home," she said again. She began singing a popular white gospel: "One step at a time, sweet Jesus. That's all I'm asking of you."

Mama was happy in Atlanta, and each day she seemed to get stronger. I pampered her as I knew Faye would pamper her, as Aunt Mae had pampered her, and as Mama had pampered all of us. During the day, I did what she wanted me to do. I sat at the computer and wrote on "the book." She would stand over me sometimes and listen to the click-clapping of the computer keys.

"How's it coming?"

"It's coming."

"I'm glad. I'm glad you know how to use the computer." It was a gift from her. "I'm glad you're writing. I just wish Faye would write. She's really gifted. If she ever sits down to write, watch out."

Mama loved to hear the sound of the printer because that was proof of my productivity. Sometimes, to please her, I would call up old essays or course syllabi and print them. I didn't feel guilty about deceiving her. "Now that's what I call getting it done," she would say. And then she would say something about Faye's talents. The old saying that a mother loves one child more than she loves another did not apply to Mama. She had two daughters in her "single eye."

Nights were wonderful. Intimate. Spiritual. Peaceful. I would lie in the bed next to her, sometimes in the crook of her right arm, watching television or listening to the pleasant sound of her memories. Other times I would sit in the chair with my feet propped up on the bed, as she ordered. She would give me new stories for "the book," and while she talked, she rubbed my feet continuously.

There is something about the night that makes space for subjects we do not discuss during the day. It was at night that Mama talked about "the other dimension," about our psychic family, about the Spirit.

"You still don't believe you're psychic, do you?" she asked one night.

"Here we go again," I said, wanting to change the subject.

"Well, if you don't want to be psychic, that's your business. But I know I'm psychic. I feel things."

"And do you hear voices?" I was being irreverent out of fear.

"My own," she said, "talking to me." She was rubbing my feet, laying on her hands, and I could feel her strength finding its way to my arms, hands, legs, heart, soul.

"Keep on living, baby," she said. "You'll have experience after experience that will convince you that the spiritual world is real. We are connected to it."

"Let's just enjoy ourselves in this dimension," I told her. "Okay? In this dimension."

She began recalling experiences that proved her point. "Do you remember after Prince's death that —"

"Mama. Please! I am *not* ready for this conversation. I think we're both tired. That's the problem."

I tucked her in the way I had begun doing after she became unwell. "Tuck. Tuck," I would say, pulling the covers

tenderly over her and softly hitting the side of the bed.
"Tuck. Tuck." I adjusted her head on the pillows, leaned
over her and kissed her on her forehead. She enjoyed being
the little girl tucked in for the night.

As I turned to leave the room, she said, "I'm so blessed."

"Not as much as we are, Mama."

"I've never been rich, but I have been a wealthy woman.
Truly blessed. All a mother can ever want in life is to see her
daughters become women who like themselves and who can
take care of themselves. I thank God for my blessings."

I was about to turn off my bed lamp when I heard her
calling me.

"Gloria. Baby. Are you asleep?"

"Far from it, Mama. I just left you."

"You know I am not going home again. You know that,
don't you?"

I worked hard that night to communicate with the force,
the power, the spirit in that other dimension. "If you are
listening to me, and I know you are, please, please don't take
Mama away from us. Not yet. Please. Not yet."

When Aunt Mae came to visit, Mama was ecstatic. She
and my aunt got up at the crack of dawn for their coffee and
spent the day savoring each moment of their togetherness.
They were intoxicated with a love that knew no boundaries.
In Atlanta, they shared the same bed. In life, the same heart.

Faye came to Atlanta burdened with worries about Mama's health. I was playfully feisty with Mama. Faye was in-
dulgent and gentle. I was one half of Mama's life. Faye was
the other. Mama lived for the whole.

Faye pampered Mama with good home-cooked meals, a
special treat since I could never cook to please her. I made
casseroles and bland dishes she called "white folks' food."
She wanted turnip and collard greens, snapbeans and squash,

pot roasts and cornbread. Faye took every breath that Mama took, watching her closely, unable to conceal from me her concern and worry. If anything happened to Mama, I feared Faye would collapse and cease to function. She was connected to Mama in a special way. "Mama is my strength," Faye would say. "I can't imagine life without her."

Had Mama heard those words, she would have unleashed her anger at Faye. "Is *that* what I've taught you?" she would ask. "To see your strength in someone else? I never taught you that. "Never," she would emphasize. "You must be your own strength. *That's* what I've always told you. Always."

Faye's departure from Atlanta was stiff, awkwardly painful. "I don't want to leave my mamma," she told me the night before, her use of the possessive "my" disturbing to me suggesting, as it did, an ownership that carried with it sole responsibility for whatever happened to Mama. I told her not to cry in front of Mama. "You know how she is about signs," I reminded her.

Both of them deserved an academy award for their performances. Faye was dry-eyed. So was Mama. We talked about Faye's return in October for Mama's birthday. Everyone was coming for the celebration. Loren, her first grandson, who was studying in a doctoral program at Duke University, would be able to zip up the road from North Carolina. Chiquita, who was like Mama's third daughter and my baby sister, would make the seven-hour trip from Memphis, perhaps with her husband and children and Uncle Hosea and maybe even Uncle Jack, Mama's baby brother. And of course, Jonathan and Monica, enrolled in college in Atlanta, would be present for the celebration.

Mama never got up from the rocking chair in which she was sitting. Faye leaned over and kissed her. "I love you, Mama," she said.

"I know, baby. I know."

As soon as we were outside, Faye burst into tears. She told me about the conversation she and Mama had had the day before. They were drinking coffee early that morning while I slept late. Mama looked at Faye with a smile that was too radiant given what Mama was about to say.

"Whatever happens to me, don't let them cut me open. And after my death, do not, please do not, agree to an autopsy."

En route to the airport, Faye cried. "When it's time for Mama to come to Chicago, let her go, Gloria. I can't wait to have my mamma with me. I can't wait. Please, Gloria, don't try to keep her with you. Let her go. Please let her go."

"You don't have to tell me that," I said. "We've already worked this out. I wouldn't do that to you, Faye. You know I wouldn't do that to you."

But when the time came for Mama to leave, I knew I would ask for more time. Just a little more time. I had begun to see the dawn as Mama's gift.

"It's another day, baby," she would tell me, sitting at the table drinking coffee made in an old-fashioned percolator, not the "new-fangled" coffee-makers with their see-through decanters which, Mama said, caught weak and tepid coffee. She liked hers strong. "It's another day, and a *new* day." "New" meant for her whatever you want to do and didn't do yesterday. Always we have new beginnings and therefore hope.

Around Mama, you couldn't help feeling empowerd and whole, and that is what I wanted the children to feel about themselves: empowered and whole. Mama told them they were giants, but not the kind that stomp with colossal feet on someone else's life. You must never abuse, she taught, or accept abuse. "Nobody likes a doormat. Nobody."

She would engage them in philosophical discussions about life, and they listened eagerly. "You know what the world says?" she would ask rhetorically. "The world says 'Catch a sucker and bump his head.' People are like bloodhounds. They can smell weakness." And uncertainty. And cowardice. "Always stand up for what you believe in and don't turn your life over to anyone." She stressed perseverance. "If you start something that's good, come hell or high water, stay with it. Finish it." And above all, she told them, be honest. "All we have in this life is our conscience. If it's at peace, you can endure anything."

Mama believed that suffering builds character and, as a result, she was impatient with whining. When I was in elementary school, I wanted her to do what other mothers in the project did — take *my* side against teachers — but Mama never would. I would complain about something a teacher had done or said, and Mama would respond: "What did *you* do? What did *you* do, Gloria? Have you told me that?" She insisted that I sift through every experience for my own culpability. I learned early never to "pass the buck" or make excuses or whine. "But it's not fair" got nowhere with Mama. "Whoever told you life is always fair?" she would ask. "Just make sure *you're* fair and keep on going. And stop whining. If you collapse because of something this small, what are you going to do when big things happen?" Strong. She wanted us to be strong and sure of our ability to clear all hurdles. Derailment was not in Mama's vision for us.

Or for her grandchildren. It didn't matter to Mama that they were living in a different day and age. They had to learn the same eternal truths about integrity, honesty, and perseverance that she had taught Faye and me. Jonathan at twenty and Monica at nineteen enjoyed being with her because she could speak their language, and her own. When they came to visit, they literally sat at her feet, and she at theirs. And it was the same with Loren. The four of them were like friends together being silly one moment and serious the next. They solved the problems of the world and problems of the heart. They delighted in her humor and wit. They valued her mind. They admired her authenticity. And they appreciated her willingness to give them their space as teenagers. She was an undemanding grandmother as she had been an undemanding mother.

With the start of school and the departure of Faye and Aunt Mae, Mama and I returned to our quiet days and intimate nights. I continued to write, but I became preoccupied with plans for her birthday in October. Words began to run from me.

Mama said, "Don't worry. I'll catch them."

I remember returning from the grocery one day to find Mama more excited than she had been since Faye and Aunt Mae had returned home.

"You didn't tell me you had finished the book. You didn't tell me!"

"I haven't," I said.

"You needn't try to surprise me, baby. The agent called. The agent called and said she would be in contact with you in a few weeks. Hot dog! You finished the book! You finished the book!"

The agent had called about a manuscript of poems I had sent her so many months ago that I had ceased expecting to hear from her. That wasn't "the book" I was working on, the one Mama's memories and presence were helping me write.

"Oh that?" I said nonchalantly. "That's the poetry."

"Whatever," she answered, no less excited. "It's something you wrote, isn't it? And it will be published."

"Let's hope, Mama."

"But you already have the good news. The agent called, didn't she and —"

"Mama, that's not good news. That's professional courtesy."

"Call it whatever you want, baby, but I'm here to tell you that you will hear from that woman again, and the book *will* be published. I won't be around to see it, but . . ."

As always when I was uncomfortable with references to her death, I became theatrical. "Well, lady love of mine, let's not wait for the phone to ring."

A month later, I was back at work and very distraught because the woman I had hired to stay with mama for three days a week had taken another job. As if she were a fortune teller, Mama had told me in Memphis that my plans for her care would fall through. Negative thinking, I had said. "You'll see," she had responded.

She didn't need anyone. "I'm not an invalid, you know," she told me as I fought my tears and my anger at the woman who had disappointed me. "I can cook, wash, straighten up a bit. You don't need to pamper me."

I had no choice. I returned to work and left Mama at home alone. Luckily, my department chairperson had given me the schedule I requested. I had only one class on Tuesdays and Thursdays, and it did not begin until 1:00. I left home at 12:30 on those days. I was back by 3:00.

Mondays, Wednesdays, and Fridays, however, were difficult days. I had three classes, but, thank God, I had a break between 1:00 and 3:00. I always went home to check on Mama. Each time she was watching television, napping, or cooking. She wished for health in her eyes because she wanted to read the books that talked to her while I was away.

On Friday, September 17, I did not go home during my break. Instead, I drove to a vacant lot behind abandoned apartments. Some of them had been dormitories for one of

the Atlanta University Center colleges, and others had been
the cluster of narrow spaces in which, many years ago, as a
volunteer for ADC, I met the young mother recently released from Grady Hospital. I sat in the car, looking into an
abyss of loneliness. The skies were heavy with the darkness
of a tornado that had hit Atlanta somewhere to the west.
There was no air and, though I was close to Interstate 20,
there were no sounds of passing cars. There was no world. I
knew where I was, and yet I could not remember how I got
there.

I was late reaching my three o'clock class, Images of
Women in Literature, in which we were beginning a new
unit on "mother as person." I gave the students an idea of
what the unit meant by telling them about Mama. Images of
her came faster than I could share them with my students,
speaking without my voice and bringing moisture to the eyes
of everyone. I remember ending the class by saying, "If you
could meet my mother, you would love her."

When I returned home, Mama was unusually energetic.
She did not ask why I had not come home in the middle of
the day. Apparently, she had not missed me. She had cooked
a big pot of chicken stew and a pan of cornbread. I learned
later from Aunt Mae that Mama had called her and talked
for over an hour. She never called long-distance in the
middle of the day and even when she called at night, she did
not talk that long.

That night we cuddled together in her bed. Her laughter
was hearty, and her wit had never been sharper.

"How's your writing coming?" she asked me. Before I
could answer, she said, "You're going to hear from that
agent."

We talked about Faye, "who must write," and Aunt Mae
and the grandchildren and Chiquita — about the family. Noth-

ing maudlin. We seemed to be returning to the joy of her first days with me.

"Just think, Mama," I said, jumping from the bed and doing a silly dance. Just think, today is Friday and tomorrow is Saturday. No school! No school! I will be here all day. *All* day."

"That will be good," she said, sitting up on the side of the bed. "Hand me my purse."

She opened it and took out several cards wrapped with a rubber band. "These are my insurance cards." She reached in for a five-by-seven blue notebook wire-ringed at the top. "I wrote down all the names of my medicines."

I was speechless.

"Don't let them perform surgery on me for anything. Don't let them put me on life-support systems. Don't — "

"Mama, why are you doing this? Why are you doing this?"

"Hush," she said, "and listen to me. I know what I am doing. Don't let them perform surgery on me. It won't do any good. When it is my time to go, I am supposed to go. Don't let them put me on life-support systems and don't let them perform an autopsy. The cause of death will be that it's my time to go."

"Mama, I . . ."

"Do what I tell you, Gloria," she said with firmness. "Put all of this in your purse. And don't worry about me. Wherever I am, I will be connected to you and Faye. I'll be fine, and you'll have to let go, baby. All of you. Now give me a kiss and turn off the light."

I did not sleep well that night. I kept thinking about Mama's belief in psychic feelings and the "other dimension." Her heavy breathing in the next room reassured me. She was fine. As long as I could hear her, we were in *this* dimension. Together.

That's where we were when I awoke on Saturday morning. Mama was unusually beautiful. Glowing really. Her skin was firm and her eyes were tiny jewels, glittering. The world outside was a perfect skyblue, sunny and decorated with fluffy white clouds close enough to touch.

I was behind with my paper grading, especially the themes I had assigned in freshman composition. When I began grading the papers, I smiled to myself. I must have been teaching Mama in all of my classes. The papers were portraits of mothers.

I had finished the last paper in the set and was writing, "You should show this to your mother. It is a testimony of your love for her," when I heard what sounded like the gasp one makes when surprised. I hesitated for only a second before running to Mama.

Mama never returned to Memphis. We buried her in Atlanta.

For weeks after her death, I went to the cemetery every day, sometimes twice a day. I knew she was not there. I remember her saying, "Only the body dies. The spirit lives. And that is what we are. Spirit." I knew I was disobeying her. She had told me that we had to let her go, but I couldn't.

My aunt was split in two, hemorrhaging in her soul, but she was stoic for us. Again and again, she would tell us, giving comfort and truth, "Your mother left the way she wanted to leave—at peace, smiling, and ready. And she would add, "If you don't believe what she believed about the eternity of the spirit, just keep on living. You'll see the signs."

A month after Mama's death, the phone rang. The voice on the other end said, "I never make business calls from my home, but I'm making this one. I just finished your manuscript and . . ." There was a pause. "Something has been directing me to it for days. I read it before reading others I received before yours." There was another pause. "It's . . . I just can't tell you what a moving experience it was. Reading your poetry. I love it. And I wanted you to know that I have a publisher."

The words I had wanted to hear, had wanted Mama to hear, did not move me. Instead of responding jubilantly, I said, "I lost my mother a month ago and . . ."

The agent interrupted me. "Now I understand everything," she said. "I know what was happening to me." She called my name. "Gloria. Gloria. I am your mother's medium."

The Day I Bought A Wig

A LESSON IN GRATITUDE

I wear a natural. I have worn a natural for almost three decades. In the sixties, I wore the movement style. Large, long, and so natural it shaped itself. I did not use clippers then. With a cake cutter, the only grooming tool for naturals, I pulled out the long strands and patted them into a neat style. In the seventies, I wore "the bush," or what some people called "the Angela Davis 'Fro." Very large and very bouffant. Regardless of style, my natural made an emphatic statement about racial pride and activism.

Today I use a pick, especially designed for naturals, with long metal teeth rounded at the end for smooth and painless combing. And I no longer pat my hair into a style. Instead, I select a style from the charts and books available at "Sirius," my favorite unisex salon, appropriately named because Phillis, the owner/barber with small black eyes that squint and then sparkle, squint and then sparkle (flash off, flash on), is serious about black hair. She is an artist with buzzing clippers whose signature I wear with vanity.

Improvements in the care of naturals have made me love

my hair not only for what it says, but also for what it does to my face. In other words, I now like the statement *and* the look, which explains why I am particular about the style I now wear. Never too long or too short. Definitely not too short.

When I left Atlanta for Cambridge in August of 1991 to begin six months of research at the Du Bois Institute at Harvard University, I was wearing, what else? A natural! But it looked as if I had been living in the precare days. It was so long, so uneven, and so brittle that it resisted my hands patting in a style. It had suffered for four weeks in a hot Mexican sun while I studied Spanish in Cuernavaca, where, of course, there are no salons for black hair, natural or permed.

I was concerned about my hair, but I put it on a back burner (no pun intended) while I found an apartment, settled in, and became acquainted with the Institute and various research facilities at Harvard, chief among them Widener Library. How important could my hair be in this idyllic world? No lectures to prepare. No student themes to grade. No committee meetings to attend.

I was in love with my life. I had reached a resting place with my grief over Mama's death. I had needed the help of others to get there, and time had been healing. Both Jonathan and Monica had finished college and were doing well in their graduate studies at Winthrop University in South Carolina and the University of Maryland in College Park, respectively. And Joe and I, once separated, were together again. I was in love with my life. My wings had been repaired, and I could feel myself unfurling them. Soaring as if anointed to do so. I quickly established a routine: from my one-bedroom apartment in the Parlin House (actually the Boston YWCA) located in Copley Square, I took the subway to Harvard

Square, exited the station, and walked a few blocks to the library, where I remained until closing. I *had* to keep this routine because I had so very much to do, to write, in such a short period of time.

In one of my many long-distance conversations with my sister, I casually said, "I must do something about my hair!" She was thrilled that sitting in Chicago, she could solve a problem I was facing in Cambridge. Having studied at Harvard during the summer, she knew where I could find an African-American beautician in the Harvard community.

That she knew of someone did not take me completely by surprise. Boston had changed tremendously since I had last visited it. When I had lived here as a graduate student, from 1959 to 1963, African-Americans, regardless of gender, were rare in the Harvard University area, and naturals were, for the most part, unheard of. Today, we are visible, though still in the minority, and most of the women wear naturals. No doubt some of them knew about the shop my sister described. It was across the street from Widener, she told me.

"Widener?" I asked. "That close?"

"Well, I am not sure that it's across the street," she said, wanting to be exact. "But I remember it's within walking distance of the library."

My sister was taken with the owner of the shop. "An absolutely fascinating woman," she said.

The more she talked about the woman and the more I saw myself able to care for my natural without greatly disturbing my research routine, the more relieved I felt. I grew curious about the "absolutely fascinating woman."

"She's from Haiti, and very political," my sister added. Political was the catchword. "Really fascinating. Married two white men. *Two* and talks about white people like they're dogs."

That would neither hurt nor help my hair. The information wasn't really related to the need at hand, but it did make this woman colorful. At least I wouldn't be bored while I was getting my hair cut.

"And she's very spiritual," my sister continued. "When I was there, I was having trouble with my leg and she talked to me about spiritual healing. I mean, Gloria, being in her shop was an experience."

Haitian. Political. Spiritual. An experience. I was sold.

The next day before I went to the library, I looked for the shop. Without difficulty, I located it in the middle of Harvard Square on the second floor of a building I had passed many times en route to the Dolphin for a quick lunch. I did not go in, however, because I was on my study schedule, but I made a mental note of the name. When I reached home later that day, I called. A woman with an accent (Haitian, I guess) answered the phone, took my name, and gave me an appointment. I called Faye.

"I have an appointment at the shop you mentioned."

"Good. I'm glad," she said. "Who's going to do your hair?"

"I'm not sure," I answered. I couldn't remember that Faye had given me the name of any particular beautician, except, of course, the owner.

"I hope it's not Dee Dee," she said. "Don't let *her* touch your hair."

"But you never told me about any woman named Dee Dee. You told me about the owner and . . ."

There was a pause on the other end. "Well, I hope it's not the one who burned my hair."

"*Burned* your hair?"

"Whole locks," my sister said.

I felt more confusion than sympathy for my sister's unfortunate experience. "But you never told me about *anyone* ex-

cept the fascinating Haitian woman who owns the shop." I
was irritated. Faye was giving me vital information *after* the
appointment had been made. "You never told me you didn't
like what was done to your hair."

She became defensive. "Listen, you asked me about a
shop, and I told you about a shop."

"But why didn't you ever say anything about what happened to your hair?"

"What happened to my hair isn't important," she said. "I
get a perm. You don't."

"So why are you telling me now?" I asked, becoming more
confused and concerned.

"I don't know," my sister said. "I was just asking who's
supposed to do your hair. Is it the lady who works at the
chair near the . . ." She stopped.

"I haven't *been* to the shop, Faye. I *called* for the appointment. I don't know where anyone works or what anyone
looks like."

Silence.

"Did you see anybody working on a natural when you
were there?" I asked.

"Not when I was there," she answered. "But I know they
cut naturals because I saw clippers. At the other woman's
table. That's why I asked you who was cutting your hair."

"But Faye, do you realize you talked about one woman.
One fascinating Haitian woman, and you said she could really do hair."

"She can. I saw what she did for another woman, but she
wasn't the one who did my hair."

"But she was the one you talked about."

"I guess we miscommunicated," my sister said, obviously
concerned that we might have a real argument. "I talked
about her because she's fascinating, and I know you'll like

her, and I recommended the shop because it's close to the library. I thought I told you about the other woman. The one who burned my hair."

Well, I didn't have to worry about that since no one would be putting heat or chemicals on my hair. With me, it would be clip-clip, snip-snip, pick-pick, and off would go the apron which had caught the hair. There was no need for worry. The appointment stood as it was.

Anyone who knows anything about a natural knows that you should wash it before you get it trimmed. That way, you can get a good cut and, after the cut, you have clean hair. You don't dare wash your hair *after* a cut, or you'll need to return immediately for another cut. So, on Friday evening, I washed my hair in preparation for my first cut in Cambridge.

On Monday morning, I left my apartment at nine o'clock in order to be on time for my eleven o'clock appointment. I was early. That was fine because I needed to see whether the bookstore had Paule Marshall's new novel, *Daughters*. If it were in, I would buy it and read it on the train going home.

I browsed in the bookstore and ended up spending more money than I could afford, buying a handful of books, among them *Daughters*, of course, and Bharati Mukherjee's *Jasmine* and Sandra Cisneros's *House on Mango Street*, which I had been wanting to read. With the books in a thin paper bag that was splitting in the folds by the time I left the store, I walked to the beauty shop, arriving at exactly eleven o'clock.

The door was closed. Actually locked. I knocked, not too hard, and a smooth-skinned black woman opened the door without the smile I had been led from my sister to expect. No one else was in the shop. I identified myself, and she directed me to the middle chair. The shop was small and very clean. It was a red shop. That was what I thought to myself as I sat in the chair: "A red shop." Deep passionate red was everywhere. I thought of brothels.

My sister was right. The woman was fascinating. Different. She had been married to two white men, a fact she reported five minutes after I sat down in the chair. Her interracial marriages were none of my concern and really not that big of a deal in my opinion, but they were the subject of our conversation, or the subject of her diatribe.

I made her remember my sister. "When she came in, she was having trouble with her leg," I told her. "She looks a little like me."

The woman looked closely at me. "Oh I see it," she said, though I wondered. "I remember her. Did she do what I told her? Did she go to a healer?"

She did not wait for me to answer. "Cause, girl, these western doctors don't know nothing. They push and pull, and jab and poke, and when you leave, you sore but not healed."

I agreed with her. She was about to cut my hair.

"Me, I go to acupuncture," she continued, moving toward a table to her left on which clippers, washed free of the hair of yesterday's customers, were lying. It was clear I was the first customer of the day. "Thirty minutes. That's all. Thirty minutes and I leave feeling good." She threw back her long pony tail, obviously not her own hair, but very attractive on her. "Once a month I go. I tell all the women who come in here to go to acupuncture."

I understood why my sister's leg had been a subject of conversation at the shop. It fit neatly into the woman's everyday discussion of healing. Even if my sister had not been present and even if she had not injured her leg, the woman would have held forth with stories of the time when she walked out healed after acupuncture.

As she chose the clippers she was going to use, I decided it was time for me to tell her how I wanted my hair cut.

"I don't want much off," I explained, probably not as forcefully as I should have. "I don't wear short Afros well. Just even it up and round it out. And, please, don't cut out my ears."

"I know what you want," she answered. "Just evened up."

She put the apron around me and swirled the chair so that I no longer faced the large mirror. The phone rang.

"But you were expected here this morning," she said to the person on the other line. "We opened at ten. You have customers. What's your problem?"

I remember thinking to myself that the person on the phone was probably the woman who was supposed to cut my hair. The thought should have given me cause for concern, but it didn't. This woman was fascinating, political, spiritual. An experience. She had the clippers in her hand, and I needed a haircut. I had to return to the library.

"Well, I for sure can't do the next one," I heard her say. "Got a long-haired perm next." She listened. I don't remember her saying goodbye, but she must have. She was returning to my hair.

She chose the clippers, turned them on, and touched my hair on the left side, directly above my ear. Without looking in the mirror, I knew immediately that she had cut to the very scalp. I screamed.

"My god, what have you done?"

I turned around to the mirror. A naked avenue, and a wide one at that, ran from the front of my face to midway the back of my head. The tears came before I knew it.

"Oh my god! Oh no. No." I bent over in pain.

"Please," she said nervously. "Please. Please don't do that. You'll mess up my rhythm."

Her rhythm? What rhythm? She had *ruined* my hair with one touch of the clippers. .

"I can't believe this," I said, the tears rushing from me. "I can't believe you cut my hair to the scalp."

"Don't. Don't do this," she said again. "You will mess up my rhythm and . . . I have to try to finish this. Don't. My rhythm."

I was at her mercy. I could not leave the shop with a wide avenue one one side of my head and a bush on the other, so I agreed to let her make the damage at least symmetrical. The more she tried to get the right side to look like the left side, the more she cut.

She was out of control and quite afraid. It was clear to me at this point that this fascinating, political, and spiritual woman who was an experience had never cut a natural. Even she had to admit the damage.

"Too short," she said, shaking her head. "It's too short."

I must have been reared to be a peaceful woman because this situation called for war. And war was what was on my mind when she said something about "next time." Next time I go to a barber, make certain that I tell her I don't want my hair cut to the scalp. Insane. The woman was insane.

"Just brush it every day," she advised me, brushing my naked scalp so hard I thought the bristles were drawing blood. "Just brush it and . . . see, if you brush it, these —

"Those are gaps in my hair," I said angrily. "Gashes. Not only did you cut my hair to the scalp. You didn't cut it smooth. You didn't cut it even. There are gaps in my hair."

"Just brush it," she continued, repeating the phrase to the rhythm of her brushing. "Just brush it." Brush. "Just brush it." Brush. "That's what you have to do now. If you brush it . . ."

I was crying too hard to answer. I looked awful. I was

bald on both sides of my head and all over except the very top. There I had a little hair only because I had said, "Stop. That's enough. You can't fix it. You can't fix it." I looked in the mirror at the new damage. She had given me a Pee-Wee Herman style. I wept into my hands.

"You know the hair on your head is like the hair on your face," she said, in the same tone of authority with which she had told me about acupuncture. An all-knowing woman who knew nothing. That's what she was.

"By tonight you will have a beard. You know, like on the face, and those gaps will hardly be noticeable." A beard on my head. The woman was insane.

The bells on the door indicating that someone was entering rang lightly. Unable to stop my tears, I rushed into the bathroom which was decorated in brighter reds than those in the shop. I looked into the mirror. Pee-Wee Herman. I put my hands over my mouth to muffle the scream.

Years ago, I learned, probably from my mother, that if something is done and can't be fixed, you move on. You learn to cope with it. I dried my eyes, left the bathroom and left the shop, never to return.

I had planned to spend the rest of the day at the library, but I went immediately to the train station. I wanted to go home where I could cry uncontrollably and bite my screams into a pillow. I was so conscious of my hair that I was sure everyone on the train was looking at me with pity. A black woman wearing a Pee-Wee Herman haircut, and a bad version at that.

The train was slower that day reaching the Back Bay Station.

The elevator was slower that day coming from the top floor to the first. More residents gathered in the lobby that day. It seemed smaller that day than ever in my four weeks of living in the building. The elevator stopped at every floor that day before reaching the floor where my apartment was visible when the doors opened.

As soon as I entered my apartment, I fell across the bed and wept. I did not look at myself in the mirror. I had seen enough of that face with the hair cut to last me a lifetime. I cried the heaving kind of cry that makes your nose run and chokes you on tears. That kind of cry.

If I could get through this, I would never again, I promised myself, wear a natural. I would go the safe route: I would get a perm. After three decades, it was time for me to have a new look. I never had been a blacker-than-thou-natural-wearing African woman who commented on what other women did to their hair. Every female in my family wore straightened or permed hair, including my daughter, and while I admitted to biases when it came to her, I couldn't imagine her being more beautiful with a natural.

Besides, I told myself, the natural no longer means what it meant in the sixties and the seventies. I know women with naturals who don't know the first thing about political statements, emphatic or otherwise. In fact, some of the most revolutionary sisters I know own stock in Clairol and Revlon. It just wasn't the same anymore with the natural. Maybe I would look newer in a perm. Naturals are the same-ole, same-ole, but perms? You can style them: swirl to the right, swirl to the left, page-boy, flipover . . . The styles were endless, and you could change them to suit the occasion. The new me who would return home after this adventure would be a me with a new look, a permed look. Maybe my husband would like the look. And my daughter? We could go to the salon together. That would be a nice mother-daughter outing every two weeks. My son? He was once into dreads; I knew he would think I had lost my mind. But it isn't their decision.

It was mine in the beginning, and it was mine now. Yes, I would perm my hair.

But what was I going to do in the meantime? There wasn't enough hair to perm! What was I going to do now? I certainly couldn't go to the first banquet of the program looking like a black female version of Pee-Wee Herman.

That was the conversation I was having with myself when my sister called at her usual time. Her voice was cheery.

"So, how did you like her? Did she give you a good cut?" I started crying again.

"Gloria," she was screaming into the phone. "Gloria. Gloria. Talk to me. Say something. What's wrong?"

It was that heaving cry again. My nose was running, and I began coughing my tears.

"I'm bald, Faye. I'm bald. The lady made me bald."

"Wait. Just get yourself together," she said. "It can't be that bad. You're just overreacting."

"Don't tell me I'm overreacting." I was furious with her. "I have a mirror. I can see myself. I know how I look. How dare you make light of my pain!"

It *was* that bad, I knew my sister was saying to herself. I had never talked to her like that. Never. She was speechless for a few seconds.

"I'm so sorry," she said, her voice breaking. "I'm so sorry. It's all my fault."

I mumbled something about it being nobody's fault.

"Yes it is."

"No it isn't."

"Yes it is. I should never have recommended her," my sister said. "I never saw her cut a natural. I forgot. I always forget you don't have a perm. I never should have recommended her."

Well, she did have a point there.

"I feel so bad, Gloria," she said again. "It's all my fault."

"No it isn't."

"Yes, it is."

No, it wasn't her fault that the lady cut my hair *knowing* that she was only filling in for the no-show barber, *knowing* that she had never cut a natural before in her life.

But we went back and forth with "It's my fault" and "No, it's not your fault," until I screamed, "WHAT CAN I DO?"

My situation was so bad that it didn't take either of us long to come up with the same answer: "Buy a wig."

That was an easy solution given what wigs have come to mean. They are not substitutes for hair, but rather accessories which, like jewelry and scarves, compliment outfits and change moods.

Yes, I thought to myself, that's what I will do. I will buy a wig and wear it until my hair grows out, and then I will decide what route I will take from that point on.

The next morning, as soon as I awoke, I went straight to the yellow pages. Wedding. Weight. Welding. Wheels. Whirlpool. Whiskey. Wicker Products. There it was: Wigs and Hairpieces. The list was not very long, and I could tell from the locations and the names (French) that most of them were white shops.

Choking on my wounded pride, I called shop after shop, asking, "Do you have wigs for black women?" All of them said yes, of course, because there is no one hairstyle for black women. We wear straight wigs, Chinese-cut wigs, Cher wigs, even blonde wigs. So they were not lying. They *did* have wigs for black women. But if the shops were obviously white, I scratched them off my list.

Finally I came to a listing for a wig shop located on Mass Avenue near the mother church of Christian Science. After calling it, I dressed, caught the train at Back Bay Station, and got off at the very next stop, Mass Ave. How different it was from the Mass Ave. I had known in the early sixties. Then it was a predominantly (a euphemism for all) white area. As I walked down the avenue past Symphony Hall, I saw a concentration of African-Americans I had associated only with Roxbury.

I located the wig shop without difficulty. When I entered I was greeted by a smiling white man who said immediately, "We have some excellent buys on jewelry." Overpriced tinsel jewelry, he should have said. Gold chains that were too shiny. Earrings long enough to reach the breasts and gold knuckle bars thick enough to break a jaw. The American dollar puts white men in the most unlikely of places, or the best of places. I did not want to tell this white man I was there to buy a wig. At *his* store. A store with black patrons only. A store with only one cash register that only he could open. I wanted to walk out. That has been my policy for years. If a white owner hires blacks as salespersons but will not permit them to handle money — it's leaving time for me. But I stayed, hating myself for doing so.

Without answering him, I walked to the back of the store into a world of white Styrofoam faces without eyes, but with plenty of hair. It was the type of shop I had seen in the black sections of Atlanta that angered me because they exploited black women's self-hatred. Most in Atlanta were owned by Asians who have no need for wigs. Irony of all ironies. What in heaven's name was I, an activist, doing in a shop like this? I had a strange feeling, as if I were inhabiting someone else's body, or drifting in a nightmare.

I felt better about my decision to buy a wig when the saleswoman, a lovely and articulate African-American in her early twenties (a student at Northeastern, she told me), said she understood my problem. I did not think she was trying to make a sale. Her pity was genuine. No self-respecting African-American woman should look like Pee-Wee Herman about the head.

She worked patiently with me. I must have tried on every wig in the store until, out of desperation, I finally decided on one. The young woman said it looked good on me — "very natural looking, doesn't look a wig."

"But there's too much hair," I told her.

"Yes, you might want it cut down a little," she answered. She gave me the name of a shop down the street where someone would "style it" for me. Style. That was it. I just needed a style.

I walked out of the store past the cheap jewelry, fake leather bags, vials of perfume, and the white man guarding his money. I was wearing my wig.

When I walked into the beauty salon, I knew this was the place for me — not only for this emergency, but also for the future when I would be getting permed styles. It was a large shop with attractive decor. Young beautiful African-Americans were sitting under metal bonnets or in armed salon chairs while other beautiful African-Americans, women and men, worked deftly with hot irons or plastic styling combs. This was going to be my world in the future.

"Can I help you?" a fashionably dressed African-American woman in her early twenties asked, her perfectly manicured nails catching my eye. She was opening a large black appointment book. I cleared my throat.

"I want someone to style my wig," I said. My words reverberated throughout the shop. At least I thought they did. Everyone, it seemed, suddenly turned from what they were doing to look at "my wig."

It didn't look real. I could tell that from expressions on the faces of everyone, especially a young woman who was sitting at her station without a customer. I thought I saw pity in her eyes. Yes. That's the one I want to style my wig. She must have read my mind because she volunteered to do the job.

I began talking immediately. Nonstop. I told her about my experience. She said she would do what she could, but synthetic hair was not easy to style.

Synthetic hair? I was wearing synthetic hair?

I sat in the chair, and she began combing and cutting. The wig was so loose it almost came off. I had to hold it, using both hands, while she cut. Clip-clip, snip-snip. The wig was looking worse, not better.

"I really don't think I should cut anymore," she said. "I am getting down close to the mat."

Mat? I was wearing a mat?

"Look, Miss," she had decided to be honest with me. "You don't want to wear this wig. It doesn't look good, and tomorrow it will look even worse."

"But you haven't seen what is under this wig," I told her. Throwing pride to the wind out of sheer desperation and frustration, I took off the wig and exposed my nakedness. She was too much of a professional to laugh.

"Yes, I see what you mean," she said, touching my head where the gaps were. "But we have a barber who could make this look a little better. Why don't you let him see what he can do?"

Any help I could get, I would take.

She gave me an appointment with Bruce, the best barber in the shop, who would be able to take me in thirty minutes. Fine. I would go down the street to get a sandwich and would return in thirty minutes. I left wearing my altered wig.

I didn't have to walk far. Four doors down from the salon was a Chinese restaurant—perfect for me because I love Chinese cuisine. Inside, there were only two other customers. I sat down in a booth near the front, in a dark area. While I was trying to force myself to swallow the worst sweet and sour chicken I have ever eaten, my head began pounding. Rockets inside were firing up and about to explode.

"It's only your imagination," I told myself. "Just don't think about it. Keep eating. It will go away."

The pounding continued, and I began to feel flushed. Very hot. It's the sweater, I thought to myself. A sweater and a covered head were simply too much in a hot restaurant.

I took off the sweater and laid it on the seat next to the wall. That would make me feel better. The pounding got worse. I couldn't take it any longer. I jumped up from the booth and rushed into the ladies' room. Once inside, and certain the door was locked, I snatched the wig off my head. What relief. What relief. I reached into my purse and found my pick. I tried to use it, but there was not enough hair for me to comb. So I patted my hair. Just patted it. I returned to my booth and my food, now cold.

As soon as I sat down, the woman who had directed me to the table and given me a menu descended on me, talking fast and with agitation.

"Can't eat. Not your food."

I didn't understand.

"Can't eat. Not your food." She was shouting at me now and waving her hands threateningly.

It suddenly dawned on me that she had been in the back of the restaurant when I went to the ladies room. She thought I was a freeloader off the street. I had entered wearing (an appropriate word) curly hair and a rust sweater. I sat before her without either.

I'm an African-American, I thought to myself, accused of a crime which, in my experience, meant the likelihood of police arriving with guns drawn. That was the last thing I needed. A mug shot in a Pee-Wee Herman haircut. In order to protect myself, before she actually called the police, I pulled the wig out of my purse and plopped it on my head. The woman looked at me in disbelief and turned away without saying another world. Probably to laugh.

THAT WAS IT! I would NOT wear a wig.

I paid for the largely uneaten food and returned to the beauty salon, where Bruce was waiting for me at the second chair on the left. As he put the apron around my neck, he said, "When we are finished, we are going to kill whoever did this to your hair." It was worse than I had imagined. I left the shop more bald than before with my Pee-Wee Herman tuft shorter, but no less noticeable.

That night I made peace with the disaster. I would suffer through the months ahead while my hair was growing and after that . . . After that? I didn't know. Either I would find a good barber who could cut a mean natural. Surely there were barbers in Roxbury. They wouldn't be as talented as Phillis (no one can be), but they would know what not to do. Or, I would perm my hair. One thing I knew for sure: I would never, never, never again wear a wig.

The next morning, early, I received a call from Leah, the only African-American woman I know who speaks with a Kennedy-Boston accent. Her voice is a tinkly piano played with love. As administrative assistant to the associate director of the Du Bois Institute at Harvard, she would be the person with whom Fellows would interact closely for major and minor needs.

"Gloria, this is Leah," she said in her singing voice. "How are (broad A) you?"

Of course I was fine.

She asked if I had been able to print my document at the computer center to which she had directed me. Always, she followed up on details.

Everything was fine.

"Well, listen," she said, her voice touching different keys, "I am calling to remind you about the opening luncheon for all the Fellows. A photographer will be present to take a group photo, so, Gloria, don't get lost in Widener and forget about the luncheon."

Photo. A group photo. I hung up the phone and went immediately to the mirror in my small bathroom. I practiced how to turn my head, searching for the best angle at which to reveal the African-American *woman* no longer visible in the mirror image before me. There were no good angles. It was as if I were looking at myself in a circus mirror that elongates heads, broadens noses, makes the middle fatter, and the feet eensy-bitsy small. Every time I looked at myself, regardless of the angle or the pose, I looked frightfully awful. A caricature.

Well, maybe under the circumstances, I should wear a wig. I had a crisis: a group picture which would be shared with God-knows-who and might fall into the hands of my grandchildren and great-grandchildren! For me, reared in a family that loves albums, a picture was very important.

I tried on my wig, but it had been cut down to the mat and, as the young woman had predicted, it looked worse than it had yesterday.

I went to the yellow pages again and decided on the one shop I had rejected because I knew it was white. It was located on Boylston Street across from or near the Ritz Carlton. That should have told me something, but I wasn't listening. I pushed the button in an elevator so small I felt I would suffocate during the second's trip from the first floor to the second. The elevator opened into an elegant shop decorated with plush sofas, art work, and plaques commending the owner for excellent work.

In a line of bonnet-chairs sat white women who, strangely enough, did not look surprised to see me. Perhaps they thought I was a woman coming to sweep up their hair from a floor that shone as brightly as the chandeliers. Large chandeliers in a beauty salon?

I could not turn around and leave. The elevator opened inside the shop. I was visible. I guess I could have left, but . . . desperation. And vanity.

My race identified me.

"You called about the wig for a black woman?" a blond woman in her seventies asked, smiling. A slightly balding man in his early forties was talking animatedly to a young woman as he teased her hair. Up he combed the bleached hair and down he combed, with short movements, designing small hills that, after the spray, would harden. The women would leave the shop looking ridiculous in their plucked eyebrows and stacked hair.

I thought to myself, "What in heaven's name am I doing here? I have lost my mind."

"It's really a very attractive wig," the woman said, motioning for me to follow her. "Come with me. The wig area is very private. It's in the back."

This was one of those times I had heard about when you move without knowing that you are moving. You shut down the mind and push a button that turns you into a robot. That's what I was, a robot. A mindless robot.

I followed her. I did not run, nor did I walk too fast. I just followed, walking in someone else's body. As I walked past the women wearing bleached hair, I observed in my peripheral vision well-manicured hands accented with large diamonds, glittering more than the chandeliers. They were, without question, wealthy women, probably guests at the Ritz Carlton. There *are* two Americas, I thought to myself.

The wig room which the woman and I entered was only a closet. Inside was a comfortable chair which faced a large mirror. To the left of the chair, wigs adorning Styrofoam faces were displayed on a shelf also stacked with boxes containing wigs. The wig that was waiting for me was on the counter in front of the mirror.

I tried it on. A new Gloria was in the mirror. I didn't know her, and I wasn't sure I liked her. I confess, however, that the more I turned my head at different angles, the more I accepted the face.

"Yes," I said to myself. "Yes. You can get used to this. Yes. This is more like it. Yes. This is the wig for the picture."

I liked it because it was not a permed wig. It was a natural-looking Afro wig. Yes, this one had my name on it.

The woman began fluffing the hair with a small pick.

"This is very attractive on you," she said. "I can make it tighter if you want."

"No," I said, "it's just fine." I had not forgotten the tight wig that fired rockets in my head.

"Now when you wash it," she said, "all you do is dip it in Woolite. You see, this is synthetic hair."

I became concerned. Synthetic wigs don't look good on the second day, the beautician on Mass Ave. had told me.

"How much are natural hair wigs?" I asked, not able to bring myself to say "human hair." The very thought of wearing someone else's hair was repulsive.

"They begin at $500.00," she answered. "But I don't have any human hair wigs that would be suitable for you."

What I really wanted to know was the price of the wig I was wearing.

"Don't you like this one?" she asked, using the pick with dexterity.

"It's okay. I've just never worn a wig before. And the only reason I am here is that a beautician cut off all of my hair." Wanting to let her know that I was not about to be a wig-wearing woman, that I had racial pride, I added, "I don't wear wigs. In fact, I don't do anything to my hair. I wear it natural; that's why I like this wig. It's natural. I'll just wear it until my hair grows back."

"I think this is a good choice," she said, taking the wig carefully off my head. "It's one of our best synthetic wigs, and it's reasonably priced. Only $200.00."

I wanted to scream, "Did you say *two hundred* dollars?" I was not desperate or vain enough to pay *that* kind of money for a wig. I said nothing, remaining cool and plotting the best way to tell her I would not purchase the wig.

"You're lucky, you know," she said, putting the wig in a plastic bag, the kind that says whatever is inside was purchased at a very exclusive shop. She was packaging the item too soon. I began the sentence that would give her the bad news.

"This is a very lovely wig, but — "

"You need a wig," she interrupted me, "because someone cut off your hair. Most of our customers are completely bald." She drew the string on the bag. "From chemotherapy."

My stomach fell to my ankles, and I thought the rest of me was falling as well. I thought of two Sarahs I had known. One had died of cancer in her forties, and the other, in her twenties. I thought of my husband's friend, a gifted physician, who handled his baldness from chemotherapy with dignity. They had wanted more than anything to live, with or without hair.

I felt small. Sinful. Unclean.

Nausea consumed me.

"It's a lovely wig," I said, fighting the sickness and the tears, "but it's just not for me."

"What do you want?" she asked angrily.

My compassion for people undergoing chemotherapy was greater than my vanity, but hers was not greater than her interest in the dollar.

"You have taken up my time," she said with anger. "Are you going to buy this wig or not?"

Not. Certainly not. No. No. No. I felt faint.

"I'm feeling very sick. I . . ."

She opened the door with force and walked out of the wig room in anger. I followed, but not robotically. I was an African-American woman with a mind, with memories, with pride, with emotions so strong that I wanted to run through the shop screaming, "Forgive me. Oh God, please forgive."

I walked past the row of white women without seeing them. I took the steps rather than the elevator. I ran down them. When I reached outside, tears rushed from me with a sound I had not heard when I cried in the shop in Harvard Square. A sound of pain and deep, deep guilt.

I recalled my mother's words about vanity and about ingratitude. Both, she taught me, could be the ruin of a person. She was right about everything. Because of vanity, I had turned my back on my values, my priorities, my commitment to make a visual statement about my politics, and my determination to feel good about myself under and in all circumstances. Because of ingratitude, I had failed to see my hair and my life as blessings.

When I entered the Parlin House, I did not rush to the elevator to avoid the eyes of women at the desk or the security guard at the door. I took my time — as old folks in the church used to say, "my own blessed time." I greeted every-

one with warm hellos and even engaged them in brief conversations. I sang arias of gratitude.

I pushed the button for the twelfth floor. The elevator
stopped several times at other floors. People entered. I did
not crouch in the corner. I sang the arias. The elevator finally
opened onto the twelfth floor. I exited and walked to my
apartment door. Inside I went immediately to the mirror in
my bathroom.

I was grateful for the reflection and liked it.

"Yes," I said, talking out loud to myself. "Yes, I can live
with this. I can live with this."

In Need of Healing
and Reconnections

You Are Invited to Meet and Experience

MADAME FATOU SEK
AN NDEPP PRIESTESS FROM SENEGAL

at

4:00 p.m.

in

The Living Learning Center

I remember preparing the flier on the computer in my office and taking it for duplication to the basement of Rockefeller Hall in April 1989. I coded my number into the huge machine that stood as high as my waist and loaded paper the colors of the rainbow. Her name — Madame Fatou Sek — emblazoned in red and green and blue and yellow fell face up in the tray. Ten. Twenty. Thirty. Fifty. Sixty. Enough copies to post in the most conspicuous places in the center.

I was participating in a spiritual ritual, I felt, ceremoniously sweeping the path before her with a short-handled broom, bending and bowing in reverence. I was excited, but concerned. Luminaries of national and international distinction were not new to Spelman College. Indeed, their visits helped the institution prepare women of African descent for leadership in all fields. But Madame Fatou Sek was different. She had no college degrees. She had written no books. She would not come bearing gifts that an academic community values.

Unfortunately, in America, becoming educated means worshipping that which is rational and minimizing that which is spiritual. It means believing that the world of ideas is the only important world, or at least the only world to which upwardly mobile people should be connected. And who more than people of African descent want to make gains in American society, even if doing so means dismissing the importance of a dark woman from the Motherland who has a way of seeing and being we cannot explain.

Those of us at Spelman College who were ceremoniously preparing for Madame Sek's visit were also concerned that many of our students, products of a media-saturated culture, might be desensitized to the spiritual world. From the media, all of us learn the pleasure of the now, the glitter of the material, the power of men with money and position, and the beauty of youth. We were concerned that successful media manipulation might prevent our students from responding properly (spiritually, that is) to an elderly African woman who represented the opposite of what they had been taught to value. We had work to do.

Our strategy was very simple. We would tell our students about our experiences with women from our past whose spiritual power was uncontested. I could do that easily, I thought, because of my experience of growing up in a segregated housing project in the South in the late forties. My generation never sang songs like "I am a material girl living in a material world," and we were not bombarded with the media images that render elderly women invisible, or expendable, or both.

What I remember most vividly from my youth is my respect for women, especially my elders. To me, they were powerful beings, forces that belonged, I thought, to another world, but chose to live in this one because we needed them. As blacks, we struggled for personhood and freedom in the physical world, but that was not the only world in which we lived. Women guided us to the other world, the spiritual world, where neither race nor gender was of consequence, and there they nurtured us and made us whole. We called the women wise; they were, in fact, spiritual.

My mother was one of those women. She was, and is, spiritual. In one breath, she taught my sister and me about the dangers of white men in cars who cruised the streets of the project stalking vulnerable black women, and in another breath she taught us about the power of the inner self which is vulnerable to nothing except lack of sufficient will to be. I remember her as a woman who made decisions rooted in logic, but also decisions for which there were no logical explanations — only a feeling she had, a dream that woke her in the night, a premonition that came to her during the day, an encounter with a stranger whose eyes held messages, or a sign from nature.

When I was a young girl, and even into my teenage years, I considered my mother an enigma, two different persons in one body. She was both intellectual and spiritual. She sent my sister and me to college, but she made us humble ourselves in the presence of forces unrecognized in academia. She believed in medical science, but told engaging stories about strange illnesses which no one could explain. One of these stories I was forced to accept as real because I was a witness.

I remember it vividly because Mama was ill. She had awakened one day with double vision, an incapacitating and strange ailment. Visits to the best of doctors brought no cure. "You will just have to live with it," they had told her. But a woman whom mother met in the hospital believed otherwise. When Mama was dismissed, her vision still double, the woman began working a miracle. Though a perfect stranger, she called Mama every day, at the same hour, for several weeks. She would tell Mama about the power of the spirit in stories, in songs, and in prayers. Mama began to expect the calls, to arrange her schedule around them, and to prepare to make her own contribution to the ritual. When the phone did not ring at the expected time, Mama became concerned until she realized, suddenly, that the double vision was gone. She could see clearly. The woman never called again. That was spiritual.

I also remember conversations I had with Mama about "the other dimension" on our last trip together from Memphis to Atlanta.

"And what do you make of the fact that Mama never saw Prince until *after* he had died?" she asked me. I pretended to be concentrating too much on my driving to answer her.

"All those times she was laid up," Mama continued, "she never said 'Prince came to see me today. Didn't you see him? He just left.' He didn't visit her until after his death. How do you explain that?"

"I can't," I had answered, "but then I don't try."

She would not turn it loose. "And remember when

Mama's mama came to her in a dream to tell her something about a large hole and heavy rains? Remember, she had that dream *after* Prince died."

I knew Mama was telling the truth. The doctor had advised the family to keep Prince's death from Grandmama while she was in the hospital. It would kill her, he thought. We didn't want to, but we had no choice. Doctor's orders. On the day of Prince's burial it rained so hard that the grave was filled with water by the time we arrived at the cemetery. It was strange that Grandmama would get that information from her mother in a dream. That was spiritual.

I remember Mama telling us, again and again, that everyone has the gift of prophecy; we could become connected to it by claiming it, she would say. That was spiritual.

But I remember most of all her litany about women as special beings who, unlike men, do not fear the unknown. They reach for it. It embraces them; it empowers them. That was spiritual.

I shared these and other experiences with my students, and with choruses of "Amen," they told their own stories. They had known women like Mama all their lives. Their mothers, their grandmothers and great-grandmothers, women in their communities and in their churches read signs, listened to the winds, studied the heavens, related stories about strange incidents, laid on healing hands, and humbled themselves before unseen powers. Their strong sense of self as empowered black women came, the students told me, from the spiritual power of women they had known in their youth.

We did not need the fliers I had prepared. On its own spiritual power, word about Madame Sek's visit spread throughout the campus, touching administrators, faculty, and staff who were anxious to meet her. Students were quickly convinced of her significance when they heard that she had been invited to Reynolds' Cottage, the president's home, and that President Johnnetta Cole (according to a rumor) believed in spiritual readings. We were ready for the visit of the Priestess from Senegal.

She was in Atlanta at the invitation of the Office of International Health of the Morehouse School of Medicine, Spelman's neighbor. The contact person was Dr. Charles Finch, an internationally known Egyptologist, whom Madame Sek had "adopted" in 1986 and with whom she would be living during her stay in Atlanta. He had come to know her personally through his study of Ndepp, the ancient Wolof spiritual and religious ritual. Madame Sek, Dr. Finch explained, is called Ndepp Kat, which, translated, means the High Priestess of Ndepp. Her powers attract the attention of Senegalese, French, and other psychiatrists who seek to understand the secret of her success with mental and emotional illnesses they can neither diagnose nor cure.

In conversations with Dr. Finch and with his equally knowledgeable wife Ellen, I learned that Madame Sek did not herself choose to be a priestess. She was chosen by Coumba Lamba, the Rab of the Ocean, who is also the patron Rab of the city of Rufisque in Senegal, where Madame Sek makes her home. The Rab came to her in dreams and in signs when she was in her early twenties, instructing her in the mysteries of Ndepp and giving her the spiritual power which people from around the world had sought for over six decades.

When I met her, I marveled at how good Coumba Lamba had been to her. At eighty-three, Madame (a Francophone title of respect) had the energy of a much younger woman. She brought with her two of her three daughters — Oulimata, who was fifty-six but looked no older than thirty, and Nene, who was forty-five, but looked no older than twenty-five. A miracle, the students said.

She also brought with her a young man who would translate what Madame Sek said in Wolof, the native language of Senegal, into English. He, too, was a miracle. Many years ago, in a Ndepp ritual, she had cured him of a speech impediment which made it impossible for him to function in society. He now spoke seven languages!

When the four of them entered the small auditorium at Spelman College, I was immediately struck by the velvet-smooth blackness of their skin. The sun had been good to them. I was also struck by the colors they wore: bright yellow, orange, green, peach, and blue. I knew the colors made a statement, perhaps about different seasons, different emotions, and different energies. But I was impressed, most of all, by the sense of peace and calm which emanated from them collectively.

Madame Sek smiled, almost continuously, and she looked at faces as if she were looking beyond the body into the soul. Speaking Wolof, she prayed for us collectively, and yet there were moments during her prayer when we felt that some of her words were meant for us individually. When she touched us individually, she held the hands of some students and faculty longer than others, touching not only their hands, but also their arms and their heads. There was more to her touching than the laying on of hands African-Americans talk about and often sing about in old church songs. There was something . . . Different. Special. Spiritual.

Impressed with Fatou Sek's powers, one by one, we signed up for private sessions. Had I been one of the unlucky persons denied an audience (there were more requests than she could accommodate), I think I would have lost my mind.

Selfishly (desperate people who are in pain can be selfish), I believed Madame Sek had come to Spelman just for me. I needed to make a connection with my mother.

I was sure the priestess from Senegal was real, and yet I needed reassurance. Without apology for my boldness, I called those who had preceded me in private sessions. I did not want to know what the shells had revealed about them. That was private. I just wanted to know, how did they feel? They shared, selectively. Fatou Sek moved the shells for Tammarah, an administrator who wears gold like the sun, and they spoke a secret only she and her husband knew. Tammarah become a convert.

Fatou Sek moved the shells for a Spelman student whose hair was braided into ribbons of beauty, and they revealed a small scar on the bottom of her right foot. Only she and her parents know about the time she had fallen on her bicycle, at the age of four, and cut her foot. The student became a convert.

And there was Clinton, the Morehouse student who had received the tightest embrace from Fatou Sek in the general session. It was at her request that he had gone for a private session at dawn the morning after the general session. He had had a moving experience with her spiritual powers. The three women held him in their arms as if he were an infant. They wept with him. They touched his eyes, his head, his hands, and his arms. Madame Sek, speaking in a rhythm that soothed even as it commanded respect, instructed him, as the Rab instructed her, on what he should do to be healed. His grandmother had died that morning.

At seven in the morning, I drove thirty minutes to the home of Charles and Ellen Finch, where Madame Sek was waiting for me. She instructed me to sit next to her on a small two-cushion sofa. I obeyed, eagerly. I held her hand tightly and stroked it repeatedly. I think she understood. I think she knew why I was there.

She placed four cowrie shells in my right hand and, speaking through the interpreter, told me to place the shells in a handmade straw tray. She shook the tray and touched the shells — four times — and then she smiled. The reading began with immediate proof of her power. Speaking through the interpreter, she informed me that she had expected my pregnant friend. "Incredible!" I thought to myself. My friend Fleda, former director of the Living Learning Center at Spelman, had planned to ride with me, hoping that, even without an appointment, she might be able to see Fatou Sek. A bad morning had prevented her from making the trip which only she and I knew about. Fleda was six months pregnant.

Fatou Sek shook the tray again, and the cowrie shells moved again. "The old woman sees many pages," the interpreter said. She tilted the tray in my direction and again she saw "many pages." I realized the shells had revealed a book of poetry I was working on and hoping would be published.

With each reading of the cowrie shells, Fatou Sek demonstrated her incredible spiritual powers. I was certain she could help me make the connection I was seeking.

"Tell Madame Fatou Sek I want — "

The interpreter interrupted me. "You cannot tell the old woman what to look for," he said. "She speaks only what she sees in the shells." I was impatient with the shells. I wanted them to tell her about Mama's death eight months ago, about my need for healing, for reconnection.

I had succeeded in concealing my grief from colleagues and friends so well that they marveled at how quickly I had returned to Spelman and become my "bouncy" and "spastic" self, and while the children knew my grief was profound, they thought I was handling it well. I never "broke down" in their presence.

Only with a counselor did I permit myself to cry. Once a week I would ring the front bell at the Catholic Church in which Jim's office was located and feel relief when he answered on the second ring. We would walk together to a room of muted colors and warmth that contained, of course, the proverbial couch. In the first session, he handed me a box of tissues and told me to cry. "Go ahead and cry as much as you need to. As long as you'd like." For thirty minutes, the only sound in the small room was my heaving cry and the silence of his understanding. When I checked my tears, he said, "And now let me tell you about my pain." As if we were already kindred souls, he talked to me about his mother's death and his wrenching grief. He, too, had sought counseling.

Once a week I bared my soul. To him. If asked to attend an activity on the night of my session, I would say, "I'm really sorry I can't make it; that's my therapy night." I liked the sound of it: "my" night; "my therapy night." I felt compelled to tell people what I was doing as if the act of claiming my therapy would help me heal. Also, I wanted to challenge their suspicions about counseling which are, I think, a problem with African-American culture.

The sessions were painful, but liberating. I would cry ("as much as you need to," he told me), talk, and listen as Jim guided me to the inside where I saw fears my conscious mind had not accepted. Once inside, I learned that I was obsessed with my mortality. In fact, paranoid about dying. As a result, I had a sense of terrible urgency about life. I was impatient with everything: a short line at the bank, a slow-moving salesperson, a recording on a phone answering machine, and even a traffic light. To avoid stopping, I would turn right on red, and right again, circling blocks in order to continue moving.

I was also obsessed with a need to have every issue in my life resolved and every question answered. I wanted to step out of myself and in one quick glance see my past, my present, and my future — separate and then together. I now understood what women and men in my community back home meant when they said they were "weary to the bones." I was weary. Very weary.

I was never fearful of losing my mind (which is the only reason you seek counseling, some people believe). In fact, I never stopped functioning in any of my roles, and I was more than productive and creative in some of them. Nor did I think I was going through "the change," which some people believe causes confusion in women. I had none of the big symptoms: hot flashes, perspiration, crying spells for the hell of it, and toss-n-turn nights. I was often awakened in the middle of the night, but each time by the sound of Mama taking her last breath in my arms. "Her last breath," I told Jim, crying. "Her *last* breath." I was suffering from consummate grief.

I learned that I was also suffering from guilt which, like anger, is often one of the stages of grief. We can do everything for our loved ones while they are living, but after their death we remember only what we did not do. I remember being too rushed to prepare a big breakfast for Mama one morning. "But there's more, isn't there, Gloria?" Jim asked. "I want you to go inside. Go deep inside and tell me what you really feel guilt about? Once you name it, you can ask your mother's forgiveness. That's what you want, isn't it? You want her to forgive you for something you have not named." He gave me the box of tissues, and I wept as I had during the first session. "Get in touch with your real feelings," he continued to say in a comforting voice. "Get in touch with your real feelings." I could not deny them any longer. I was experiencing guilt because we had buried Mama in Atlanta. She never went back home to Memphis. The more questions Jim asked and the more I answered them from the inside, the more I understood why I felt guilty about a decision I shared with my sister and my aunt. I remembered the conversation and the very day, two weeks after the burial, when a friend asked why we had not returned Mama home. She said something about the spirit of the dead not being at peace when this happens and that happens. "Of course, you know you can never leave Atlanta," she told me.

"What do you mean?" I asked.

"Well, think about it," she answered. "If you ever move from Atlanta, that would mean your mother would be buried in a city where no one else in the family is buried and where no one in the family lives."

Only now do I see how insensitive the entire conversation was, but at the time, I was vulnerable to anything and everything that had to do with Mama's death, and with my good-bye.

"That is why you let it into your subconscious," Jim said. "Now I want you to hear your mother's voice telling you about her core beliefs. About death and dying."

I could hear myself speaking in Mama's voice and saying, as she often had, how foolish it is for the living to spend thousands of dollars on funerals and burials for the dead.

"Why did she feel that way?" he asked.

I spoke again with her voice. "Because we are spirit, not flesh." The sound of the word — "spirit" — was liberating.

"What does that tell you?" Jim asked, knowing that he had made a breakthrough.

I remembered Mama telling me that she did not expect to go home again, telling me not to worry, to let go.

I smiled as I explained that no matter where we had buried Mama, no matter where we lived and where, one day, we ourselves would be buried, Mama was connected to us in spirit.

I knew all of this when I sent to see Fatou Sek, but I wanted reassurance. That was what I was trying to tell the interpreter when he interrupted me with his words: "You cannot tell the old woman what to look for." I wished for my friend Jim, who encouraged me to talk and who responded only to what I said, and did not say. Though impressed with the old woman's powers, I was already growing impatient with the reading. I wanted the shells to tell her that eight months ago I lost my mother.

I must have influenced them because when the shells moved again, Fatou Sek spoke about Mama's death, my grief, and my need for healing. I no longer needed the interpreter's skills. I was in another place where the language was not Wolof, but the Spirit. The two worlds came together in the shells: mine and the other dimension in which Mama believed. I felt her peace, and mine.

I was pleased with the reading and ready to leave. But one leaves a spiritual reading, I learned, only when the shells say it is time. They moved again, and as the old woman spoke, I knew that the shells had seen my separation from Joe. In a love poem written early in our relationship, I described us as "a giant tree covered with shining lights and ornaments." I wanted no loose connections to darken us. I wanted healing and love. The shells saw a reconnection.

The reading lasted for less than an hour, but it covered a lifetime. It was not a seance; no tables were lifted in the air, and no wind-blown sounds entered the room. But I had seen the other dimension speaking through the cowrie shells, through Madame Fatou Sek. I had made a connection. The healing had already begun.

For My Children's Remembering

It always happened during the summer. The children knew that. They also knew never to ask me when a southern heat owned the night and made even empty beds sweat. That would have been the logical time to "give in," but it was never about logic. It was about remembering my own childhood and making it magical for my own children. Only cool summer nights, I was convinced, were made for magic.

The steps were always the same. I would sit on the floor next to the bathtub while they played with their favorite animals or their imaginary friend who dressed in white suds and spoke in a little bitty voice. When they were so clean their brown bodies glistened like polished oak, they raced to their beds where Winnie the Pooh or Babar the Elephant lay waiting to cover the nakedness that felt good to them, and to me.

Dressed cuddly, they returned to the bathroom to stroke their teeth and sing the song I had composed just for them: "Mister Yellow, Mister Yellow. Won't you come out. Oh, Mister Yellow, you gotta come out."

And then the inspection. Tiny fingers stretched tiny lips to

reveal tiny teeth we named "you-can't-find-any-cavities-here
teeth."

"Story time!" The children would grab their books, usually too many, and race to the family room to the long leather
sofa that had been reupholstered several times. We rarely
used the small bedroom they shared because reading stories
involved all four of us, and it required moving-around-in
space. We would read the stories and then turn them into
dramas the children would act out to the background sounds
their father and I provided. Reading bedtime stories and
touching were inseparable.

On a cool night which promised magic, it would happen.
I would give in, having decided to do so before the children
asked. I would read the last story, announce that it was time
for bed, and then the game would begin. On a cool night
which promised magic.

"Mommie, tell us about the girl named Harriet," one of
the children would request. "Harriet," they knew was the
imaginary girl whose experiences in Memphis, Tennessee,
were exactly the same as their mother's. Harriet *is* their
mother.

I would, of course, say no. That was one of the rules of
the game. We had to pretend that I didn't really want them
to stay up later, but that they had succeeded in changing
my mind.

"Not tonight," I would say in mock firmness. "It's already
past your bedtime."

The rules called for them to beg for stories about Harriet
by covering me with kisses and hugs.

"Please. Please. Please, Mommie," they would whine in
unison. "Just a little bit. Please. Please. Pretty please."

I would give in.

"Okay, just a little bit. Just two minutes and that's all."

The children would quickly arrange themselves on the floor. The sofa would become the stage from which I would tell the stories about my childhood that the children had already heard many times.

"Once upon a time," I would begin.

"There lived a girl named Harriet," the children would say.

"How old is Harriet this time?" I would ask.

They were never in agreement, and they never chose the age I wanted, which didn't matter because my remembering went in and out of years. The story was pretty much the same whether "Harriet" was seven or seventeen.

"Let's say she is twelve this time," I would tell them. The questions guiding me through my remembering would begin.

"Is she pretty?"

"Well, yes and no," I would answer. "Let me describe her for you, and you can decide whether or not she's pretty." Images of me as a young girl were always vivid.

"She is tall for her age, and she is small. The children tease her because she is small. They call her Skinny Harriet and sometimes Boney Maroney or Toothpick Tillie."

Making happy or sad faces throughout the story was the children's contribution, and they loved it. They made a sad face.

"Does she cry?" one of them asked.

"At first, yes, but that was before her grandmother, her mother, and her aunt teach her how to like herself just the way she is."

"Because she is special," one of the children would remember from my earlier remembering. "And there is only one Harriet like her in the whole wide world."

"Right," I would say and continue. "Besides, the other children are jealous of her."

Faces with question marks.

"Why are they jealous?"

"Because Harriet is happy. You see, when you are happy, you are pretty on the inside, and when you are pretty on the inside, you are also pretty on the outside."

I could hear the three women in my family talking to me, their voices a cacophony of love. In a world where being neither black nor female was an asset, I had incredible self-esteem. I owe it all to my socialization in a family of women who groomed my spirit and my mind. When I listen very closely to my remembering, I hear more references to my being "a girl" than to my being a "Negro." No one talked then about women's empowerment, but that was precisely what I learned. Empowerment. According to their teaching, that meant loving myself and grooming both my spirit and my mind.

The children rarely began their questions with where "Harriet" lived. Children see people before they see places. Only after I had described Harriet would they ask, "What kind of house does Harriet live in?" They knew the answer.

"She does not live in a house. She lives in a housing project."

"What's a housing project, Mommie?"

This was always a difficult question to answer. Children apply word descriptions to places they have seen either in life or in books. Jonathan and Monica had never seen a housing project, not like the one in which "Harriet" was reared. I could take them to one of the projects in Atlanta and say, "This is a housing project," but they wouldn't see the project I remember.

How could I explain that housing projects were stretches of red-brick units facing clean boulevards and beckoning to passersby with petunias, buttercups, and violets.

The flowers said, "This is our home. We love it." The flowers said, "We are a proud people." The flowers said also, "Do not trespass." These flowers were no ragged patches of wild blossoms scattered here and there throughout the community. They were gardens, designed and nurtured beauty representing the people's dignity and their hope.

The "project," my home, was a class-mixed community, a concept the children would not understand. Professionals, semi-professionals, skilled laborers, and unskilled laborers lived in my community. And regardless of class, the people worked hard, saved well, and, in time, moved into private homes, proud of their achievement, but remaining connected to friends in the old neighborhood. Whenever a family moved, their neighbors were jubilant, not jealous. The promise of upward mobility belonged to all of us.

I do not explain all of this to the children. Instead, I tell them about the many look-alike units and the large park in which community children played. I also tell them about my love for the Mississippi River. They remember my past remembering.

"It is long and wide," one of them says.

"And it is real, real deep," the other adds.

They demand that I tell them again about Harriet's skill in making flat rocks skip one, two, three across the muddy bosom of the river. I show them how she angled her hand, and for their delight I throw an imaginary rock across an imaginary river. The children count, "One, two, three, four . . ." I do not tell them that the real Harriet was rarely without pain when she skipped rocks. I do not tell them that I could skip rocks only from an area overgrown with weeds. Downstream. Away from the riverboats. Isolated. And without a park. The park near the river was a wonderland of flowers and white benches painted each spring. Where it ended and the river began, no one could measure. It received kisses from the Mississippi. It was a beautiful park open only to whites. I remember as a young girl wanting desperately to sit on one of the benches and pretend that I was giving orders to boat captains on the Mississippi through a walkie-talkie. I remember my mother's fear that, in my defiance, I would one day walk into Confederate Park and claim the whitest bench as my very own.

I loved the Mississippi River. It was grand, spectacular, powerful, and in charge of itself. It seemed to be lying on its back communing with the sky. Nothing stood between the river and the sky. I envied the freedom with which they spoke to each other.

How could I explain my love-hate relationship with the Mississippi? That I could love it passionately at one moment and, in the next, hate it intensely? That I loved its majesty and hated its cooperation with people of violence? For hundreds, perhaps thousands, of my people, it is a watery grave.

But it was the love of my youth, the source of my most exciting fantasies and dreams. Until I began my remembering with my children, many decades after my youth, only the Mississippi and I knew about our love affair.

The children become restless. I have not moved quickly enough to the remembering they like best. And so I call for the question that will move me where they want me to go.

"Did we decide what day it is?" I ask. "You know we have to name the day."

"Monday," Monica says. "It's Monday, Mommie."

"No, it's Saturday," Jonathan predictably insists since Saturday is his favorite day.

If it is Monday or any other day of the week, and summer, my remembering will bring into sharp focus the segregated schools Harriet attends. If it is Sunday, I will tell them about preparations Harriet is making for church. My mother is in the center of my remembering. On Sundays, she would awake my sister and me with the aroma of fried sausage, scrambled eggs, grits, and biscuits she had made from "scratch" while we slept. Our destination was Sunday School at a Baptist church within walking distance of our home. We would be dressed in the colorful outfits my grandmother had made on an old pedal machine that stood prominently in the kitchen to the right of the back door.

I see again my Grandmother laying newspaper on the kitchen table. Again, she is cutting the pattern for a dress she has seen on one of her trips to Main Street. She is laying the pattern on colorful fabric. She is cutting. She is pushing the pedal rhythmically. She is hand stitching. She is calling my sister and me for fittings. She is smiling.

I tell the children again about Sunday School, Easter pageants, and Christmas plays; about the little old ladies who were in charge of the "sunshine band" for young children; about my aunt, their great-aunt, whose voice was all by itself a choir of angels; and about my mother, their grandmother, who could not carry a tune, but who always sang the words with passion.

They like Sunday remembering because I sing old songs for them: "Yes, Jesus loves me. Yes, Jesus loves me. Yes, Jesus loves me, for the Bible tells me."

But today is not Sunday. It is Saturday. Harriet is waking up on Saturday.

"What do you think Harriet is doing?" I ask. "She is just waking up." I yawn and stretch for them. They imitate me.

"Cartoons," Jonathan says after his yawn. "She's watching cartoons." That is what middle-class children do on Saturdays, I tell myself. My children included. They awake at

the crack of dawn, and at the crack of dawn media is prepared for them. One cartoon after another flickers on the
screen.

"No, Harriet is not watching cartoons," I tell them.

"How come?" Jonathan asks, disappointed.

"Not 'how come,'" I correct him. "What should you say?"

"Why? *Why,*" he says with emphasis on the correct word,
"can't Harriet be watching television?"

"Because her mommie and daddy didn't buy her a television," Jonathan says.

"No, that's not the reason," says Monica.

"Well, how come. I mean *why* can't Harriet be watching
television?" Jonathan asks again.

Sad faces.

"Well, she has a television," I tell them.

"Is it a color television?" Jonathan asks.

"No," I answer.

"How come?" they ask in unison and correct themselves
in unison, "I mean *why?*"

"Because color televisions cost a whole lot of money," one
of them says.

Sad faces again. Monica says, "Harriet's family is poor."

"You are forgetting," I tell them. "Remember? Remember
we said that Harriet's family is rich?"

"Rich in love." They are proud that they come in on cue
to repeat the phrase handed down from my mother.

"Harriet isn't watching cartoons," I explain, "because cartoons weren't all that important then."

"Well, what is she going to do?" In their world, what else
can a young girl do on Saturday except begin the day by
watching cartoons?

I tell them about spring cleaning days. Washing windows,
scrubbing floors, cleaning the oven, and putting curtains on

the stretcher. Each time, they say "stretcher" makes them think about very sick people. Well, they have a point. But stretchers stretched curtains. They were wooden frames filled with small nails that could be adjusted to different sizes. We would wash curtains, soak them in starch, and stretch them, dripping wet, from nail to nail, leaving them to dry outside, propped against the wall underneath the kitchen windows. We would have all of this work completed no later than nine in the morning so that the curtains could get the full morning sun. Our parents valued work and cleanliness.

Jonathan and Monica are much too young to understand such heavy chores. They are responsible only for minor tasks. When they ask whether or not Harriet liked doing all that work, I answer honestly that Harriet was anxious to get outside where she could play games, talk to boys, or go to the Saturday matinee with her friends. But I add that Harriet will learn when she is older what the chores meant to her. In spite of all the hours of play the chores stole from me, I value them. They made my mother, my sister, and me workers together and, in so doing, they gave me a sense of worth. They taught me the meaning of cooperative effort, the joy of accomplishment, and the importance of planning which is all about priorities and about sacrifice as well. My mother, and other adults with her, planned Saturdays, especially spring-cleaning Saturdays, with skill.

The children remember my remembering of these special Saturdays, mainly because my remembering usually includes stories about a horse.

"It could not gallop from your nose to your toes if his life depended on it," I tell them.

"And when Harriet puts the curtains on the stretcher," one of them asks, "is that when the horse comes clippety-cloppety?"

This gives them an opportunity to stand up and imitate the horse. They move around the room, saying "Giddy up," and "Clippety. Cloppety." I let them enjoy themselves for a few seconds, and then I say in a deep voice, "Whoa, horse. Whoa."

In the summer, an Italian marketman came down our driveway every Saturday morning, early morning, with a wagonload of greens, onions, yams, corn, and other vegetables sold at higher prices at the market down the street and across the boulevard named Mississippi. The wagon was old, and so was the horse. And so, too, the marketman. I remember that he had snow-white hair which contrasted sharply to the dirty clothes he always wore. Since our unit was midway through the court, he stopped his wagon almost directly in front of our door. Women from units on both sides of the street came from their kitchens with money in their hands. We had no fear of robberies.

The marketman was grouchy. I remember that. When I was older and processed race differently, I was incensed that he was grouchy. He, an outsider coming into our community to sell his wares! How dare he be grouchy! And why did the women purchase his wares? Why didn't they kick him out of the neighborhood. All they had to do was lean a little too hard on the wagon. It would have collapsed. Or they could have tapped the old horse on his nose. He would have rolled over and died. How did they turn the produce he sold with contempt into dinners that were family feasts, rituals that really brought us together joyous in our own world?

At this point in my remembering, I search for answers. My mother and other women were visible targets of racial and sexual rage and violence. Yet after each hard day in that cruel world, they returned home undiminished. They never gave in to the corrosion of hatred.

What made it possible for them to love in the face of such violence and hatred?

What inspired them to plant flowers, to sing, and to plan days, even nights, for themselves and their families? What prevented them from becoming like the women we rarely talked to; the women who were splintered, scarred, damaged, destroyed. What was their armor? Their secret potion? Their magic?

The answer shapes the way I am rearing my children. The women remained whole because they were certain of their own goodness and equally certain that goodness, in time, wins over evil. It is not by accident that black women poets call these women "sturdy oaks." Like trees in fierce storms, they knew how deep in the soil of goodness their roots were planted and, like giant trees, they reached beyond themselves to embrace others. But the how of their knowing, the source of their certainty, remains a mystery to me.

In other rememberings, I have wrapped the women in their own colors and presented them as gifts to the children, who knew some of the women by name. But I can tell they are anxious to hear about the horse. I indulge them and myself.

"And just when the lady who lived at the top of the hill reached for the biggest bunch of greens you could ever find anywhere, guess what the horse did?"

They begin giggling, scooting a bit on their wee-little behinds, and covering their mouths with their wee-little hands.

"Everytime," I continue. "Every single time that old horse would . . ." I make the remembering exciting. "Every single time that old horse would . . ."

They begin screaming. "Tell us, Mommie. Tell us. Tell us."

I put my index finger to my lips, "Shh." No one can hear

what I was about to say except the four of us. I look around to make certain that we are alone. I speak barely above a whisper.

"Everytime. Every single time that old horse would . . ." I only mouth the word.

They scream. "What did the horse do, Mommie? What did the horse do?"

"He," I pause, "urinated."

The laughter rolls them over on their backs and on their stomachs. They love the laughter.

The children know about race. We have taught them about discrimination, but not so much that they will search for it as children search for goblins and monsters they have heard about. They know about race from their school, a rather unorthodox nursery with children from different economic classes (thanks to a sliding tuition scale no one was denied for want of funds) and different racial/ethnic backgrounds. The teachers, two very creative and talented women, one black and the other white, have taught the little ones to love themselves and to love others different from themselves.

How different their world is from my own. I grew up in an all-black world. My teachers were black and so, too, my classmates and my playmates. I know the stories, legion in the South, about black children and white children playing together well before Carpetbaggers, or outside agitators, interfered. In my world, that simply did not happen. White boys and white girls were people we saw downtown and avoided brushing up against for fear they would whine to their parents that we hit them. They were the little white people we saw drinking from water fountains that were polished to a shine or entering toilets we knew had paper in abundance and hot water. They were the decorated queens and kings we saw on floats moving down Main Street in the white parades. They were the privileged people whose names were written in cursive in the used textbooks we received. They were the children who attended schools on the other side of the city closed to black children. Our parents taught us that white children were neither demons nor saints. They were children just like us, we were told, but they were sad children because they missed out on knowing us.

Years later, when white children got a chance to know black children in the South, we missed out in more ways than we could ever have imagined. The first order of business for those who were forced to integrate schools in the South was to transfer the most gifted black teachers and principals from our schools to schools on the other side of the city. The second order of business was to encourage parents of the brightest black students to sign their children up for the majority-minority program. The third order of business was to send to black schools the most inexperienced teachers, white and black, who had little promise of creativity. The result is evident in our nation. Black neighborhood schools of academic excellence (in spite of limitations) and high self-esteem (in spite of racism) are fast disappearing. It was never intended that they would survive.

And what about the culture which created them and which they nourished? In my remembering, I am hanging on to that culture and passing it on to my children. That is the purpose of the performance that goes on past bedtime. The children think it lets them stay awake longer. I am praying it will help them stay alive, culturally and spiritually.

They remember from my remembering. I quiz them. "What does Harriet do on Saturday night? And don't tell me she watches television."

They wave their little hands. "I know. I know."

It is like school now; they are eager pupils learning from their ancestors who speak through me.

"She goes. Sometimes Harriet goes to the lady on the end and the lady gives her some cake and ice cream."

Monica is proud that she remembers the lady who invited girls in the neighborhood into her one-bedroom apartment where, without fail, she served us pound cake and lectures on purity. We went for the dessert, not the lectures, having heard them from our mothers, and sometimes our fathers.

"And she goes to the man who tells ghost stories," Jonathan remembers. "Tell us a ghost story, Mommie. Please. Please. Pretty please."

Of course I don't give in to this request. Pretty please or not. No ghost stories for my children. Not real ones anyhow. But the request makes me remember with fondness the childless couple who lived in the upstairs apartment that faced Mississippi Boulevard. They loved children! He loved to tell us ghost stories. We knew he was telling true stories; he worked as an undertaker's assistant. He was not a rare commodity in our neighborhood. Back then, we talked to, sought advice from, and played with black men who were the fathers, uncles, brothers, or cousins of our friends. The men, too, strange as it is considered these days, lectured the boys on being "mannish" and the girls on being "fast." They wanted all the children, regardless of gender, to be good kids, which meant achieving in school. They expected that of us. Just like the women, they expected that of us.

The children know that it doesn't matter how old Harriet is or on what day Harriet has awakened; we will end the game with song and dance.

"What songs does Harriet hear in her neighborhood?" I ask.

تظفؤئءغ؟ژضذإًٌُْ

They are on their feet ready to perform. How sad that they will hear these songs only in a before-bedtime game. How sad that hundreds of thousands of black children don't know the songs ever existed. Today there are boom-blasters blasting music that leaves nothing to the imagination in more ways than one. After all, the sexually explicit songs come with music videos. What you hear is also what you see. So much for lying on a sofa in a red-brick unit creating your own scene from a sweet song.

The love songs I listened to as a young girl in Memphis are not the songs that have disappeared. Those are still around, reproduced now with full orchestras and in stereo arrangements that make even a mediocre singer sound good. Those songs are still around because they make money. The songs of my remembering that I pass on to my children never made it to the turntable. They were the music of a creative people still in possession of their imagination, and their soul.

"When it is very, very hot," I ask the children, "what do Harriet and her friends buy to cool them off?"

The answer, of course, is snowballs. My children listen for the dull electronic ringing of bells that the ice cream man makes. He drives a van covered with pictures of ice cream cones and popsicles and milkshakes. I listened for the snowball man who pushed a cart that had no pictures. A cake of ice, a scraper, four or five bottles of colored liquid, and he was in business.

We heard him coming because he sang for us. I will never forget the tune itself, though some of the worlds I know I have forgotten. The children sing those I have passed on to them. I dance the snowball man's funny steps as they sing: "Snowball man. Snowball man. Let me talk about it, tell you 'bout it. Tell you what it do. It cools your fever. It curls your hair. It makes you feel like a millionaire. Oh snowballlll man. Oh snowballlll man.

"And when it is cold," I ask them, "what does Harriet eat as a late-night snack?"

The answer of course is hot tamales. In my remembering, I see the hot tamale man, for some reason always small in stature, pushing a two-wheeled wagon hot to the touch. He sang before he reached our unit; he sang while he wrapped the tamales, hot with fire and pepper, in plastic paper he had cut unevenly. He sang as he moved on to other units. His was a slow, dragging song.

"Let me be the hot tamale man," Jonathan begs.

He stands up in the middle of the room and pretends that he is pushing a cart.

"Hey hot tamale man. Hey. Hey hot tamale man. Hey. I got your reddddd hottttt tamaleeees. I got your reddddd hottttt tamaleeees."

I help him out with the rest of the lyrics: "Hot tamales for one thin dime. Would give 'em free, but they sho ain't mine."

We sing together: "Got your reddddd hottttt tamaleeees."

My mother's favorite vendor was the lye hominy man. I never heard him. By the time I was born, black women in the South no longer bought lye, at least not from vendors. In my mother's remembering which is vivid to me, she would demonstrate how the lye hominy man poured lye into the empty cups the women provided. His song was always sad, Mama said. Plaintive tones that echoed through the valley of the neighborhood. "Lye hominy man. Lye hominy man. It's your po lye hominy man."

It is the old world I remember and cherish. It was never meant to remain. Time is a magician. In its poof of smoke, worlds vanish before our eyes, and new worlds appear, to vanish in other poofs of smoke for newer worlds. It is the Old World I remember and cherish.

Now that my children are adults themselves, they could very easily challenge my remembering. They could accuse me of romanticizing my past. The older we get, the more we do precisely that.

If they wished, they could lay my stories and songs next to pages from thick volumes assigned in their college classes. They could say the truth is in those volumes, not in my remembering, because the volumes were written by reputable scholars with credentials.

"Scholars with credentials, but without rememberings," I would say.

I do not believe they will ever do that. I do not believe they will go only to books for the Old World of our culture. They learned in the bedtime game on cool summer nights that culture comes from the soul of a people. What scholar can research the soul?

I also hope they learned to believe, as I do, that some things reappear when the poofs of smoke clear. They might appear in different forms, but they come back.

That is what I am now praying for on cool summer nights with my rememberings. I know the songs will not be sung again, the places have been changed beyond recognition, and most of the people of my remembering now live in the Village of Eternity. But I am praying that new songs, new places, and new people will be blessed with the old spirit.

Appreciation for beauty, cleanliness, and simplicity; refusal to be diminished by adversity of any kind; and an unshakeable faith in the power of goodness and love to make the world right. That is the spirit I invite into my remembering.

I do not believe the children will forget my Old World. It

has shaped them as it shaped me. It has caught root in their imagination, in their souls. I know it has. I know it has.

As my children walk reluctantly, and sleepily, to their beds, they ask me to tell them tomorrow night about the stray cat Harriet keeps in her bedroom closet. I tuck them in, kiss them, and turn out the light. Before I reach the den, I hear the soft voices they think I can't hear: "Snowballll man. Snowballll man. Let me talk about it, tell you 'bout it . . ."